I0400977

حكي كل يوم

١

Haki Kill Yoom

Situational Levantine Arabic

Rita Housseiny
Alaa Abou El Nour
Matthew Aldrich

lingualism

ISBN: 978-1-949650-06-8

Written by Rita Housseiny, Alaa Abou El Nour, and Matthew Aldrich
Edited by Nadine-Lama Choucaire and Matthew Aldrich
Illustrated by Heba Khater
Audio by Nadine-Lama Choucaire, Dayana Choucaire, and Mohammed Ellaz
Cover art: photo: © iStockphoto/Onnes; illustration: Heba Khater

website: www.lingualism.com
email: contact@lingualism.com

Table of Contents

Table of Contents .... *i*
Introduction .... *ii*
How to Use This Book .... *iv*
Taking a Taxi 1
Asking for Directions 17
Taking a Bus 31
At the Airport 45
At a Restaurant 58
At a Bakery 73
Making Small Talk 90
Visiting Someone's Home 104
Making Appointments 119
At a Language Institute 133
At the Doctor's 148
At the Pharmacy 163
At the Gym 179
At a Barbershop 198
At a Beauty Salon 213

Introduction

Haki Kill Yoom: Situational Levantine Arabic was written to help intermediate learners succeed at critical moments during everyday communicative tasks.

This is the first of two books in a series. Each book has been divided into 15 chapters, which are not meant to be studied in order and do not increase in the level of difficulty. Instead, you should find the chapter to navigate your way through a particular transactional or social situation that is relevant to your needs.

Learning natural, idiomatic phrasing and vocabulary is essential to both listening and speaking, not only for living in Lebanon or another Levantine Arabic speaking country, but also for communicating in Arabic with immigrants in your own country.

Each chapter has several dialogues, vocabulary lists, bonus expressions, footnotes, and cultural information. (See How to Use This Book on page iv to learn more about the organization and features of the chapters.)

Levantine Arabic is the umbrella term for a number of closely related and mutually intelligible dialects in the Levant (Lebanon, Syria, Jordan, and Palestine). Beiruti Lebanese, specifically, is the variety featured in Haki Kill Yoom. That said, you should find it easy to communicate with people throughout the region using what you learn from this book. Of course, there may be subtle differences in pronunciation, vocabulary, and even grammar, but these you can note, as needed, when dealing with speakers from other parts of the Levant to hone your style to match theirs, if that is your goal.

I would like to thank Rita Housseiny for adapting the original dialogues (written by Alaa Abou El Nour) to reflect authentic, everyday Levantine Arabic and for adding original dialogues and cultural notes to include high-frequency vocabulary and phrases likely to be heard and used in specific situations. I would also like to thank Nadine-Lama Choucaire for her help proofreading and

Table of Contents

Introduction

Haki Kill Yoom: Situational Levantine Arabic was written to help intermediate learners succeed at critical moments during everyday communicative tasks.

This is the first of two books in a series. Each book has been divided into 15 chapters, which are not meant to be studied in order and do not increase in the level of difficulty. Instead, you should find the chapter to navigate your way through a particular transactional or social situation that is relevant to your needs.

Learning natural, idiomatic phrasing and vocabulary is essential to both listening and speaking, not only for living in Lebanon or another Levantine Arabic speaking country, but also for communicating in Arabic with immigrants in your own country.

Each chapter has several dialogues, vocabulary lists, bonus expressions, footnotes, and cultural information. (See How to Use This Book on page iv to learn more about the organization and features of the chapters.)

Levantine Arabic is the umbrella term for a number of closely related and mutually intelligible dialects in the Levant (Lebanon, Syria, Jordan, and Palestine). Beiruti Lebanese, specifically, is the variety featured in Haki Kill Yoom. That said, you should find it easy to communicate with people throughout the region using what you learn from this book. Of course, there may be subtle differences in pronunciation, vocabulary, and even grammar, but these you can note, as needed, when dealing with speakers from other parts of the Levant to hone your style to match theirs, if that is your goal.

I would like to thank Rita Housseiny for adapting the original dialogues (written by Alaa Abou El Nour) to reflect authentic, everyday Levantine Arabic and for adding original dialogues and cultural notes to include high-frequency vocabulary and phrases likely to be heard and used in specific situations. I would also like to thank Nadine-Lama Choucaire for her help proofreading and editing the dialogues and vocabulary lists. Special thanks also to Heba Khater for providing illustrations and to Nadine-Lama Choucaire, Dayana Choucaire, and Mohammed Ellaz for recording the accompanying audio.

Matthew Aldrich

Audio

Visit www.lingualism.com/audio, where you can find the free accompanying audio to download or stream (at variable playback rates).

Anki Flashcards

Enhance your learning with our Anki digital flashcards, available for separate purchase on our website. This comprehensive deck features all the vocabulary and expressions from this book, complete with audio, to help you memorize and master the material more effectively.

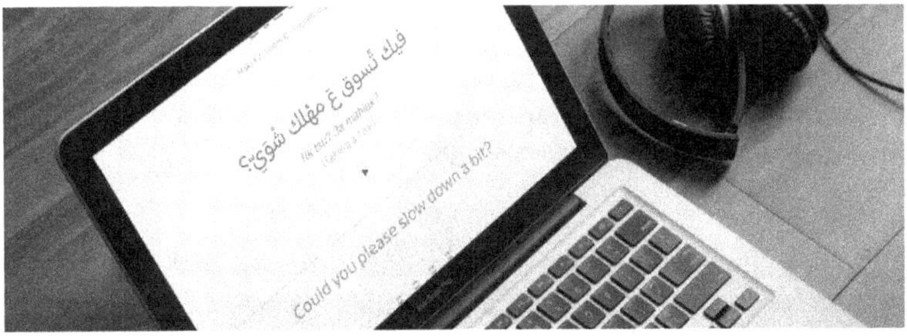

How to Use This Book

This is not a coursebook with chapters that build on each other and need to be studied in order. Use the **Table of Contents** at the front of the book (also located on the back cover of the paperback edition, for your convenience) to find the topic that interests you for your immediate or future communicative goals. Of course, you're not going to go out into the real world and have conversations with people that follow the dialogues line by line. The purpose of the dialogues is to teach you different words and phrases that you can use and that you may hear. Synonyms, alternative expressions, and supplementary vocabulary are provided to help you form your own sentences to express yourself and to be prepared for the variety of possible things you may hear people say to you.

Introductory Paragraph

On the first page of each chapter, you will see an illustration above the chapter's title in English and Levantine Arabic. An introduction to the topic follows and often presents key vocabulary.

Mini-Dialogues

Next, we have several short dialogues. Each dialogue has a title that shows you the goal of the specific "subtask"–for example, paying the bill, offering your seat to someone, reporting a theft.

Symbols

Notice that the lines of dialogue are preceded by symbols.

○ You–the foreigner, the customer. (Things you might need to say.)

◇ A local–merchant, barber, waiter, landlord, friend, etc. etc. (Things you might hear other people say.)

The symbols are there to help you decide whether you need to memorize the phrases so you can actively use them yourself, or if you just need to be able to passively understand them when you hear them.

Arabic Script

Each dialogue appears three times on the page. The first is written in Arabic script with tashkeel (diacritics). At first glance, it may seem that many letters are missing diacritics. A final consonant is assumed to take sukuun, as Levantine Arabic does not have case endings as MSA does.

We write كْتاب *ktēb* **book** (and not كِتاب). Non-final consonants without diacritics are understood to take the short vowel fatha (◌َ): مكْتب *máktab* **desk** (and not مَكْتَب). This was done intentionally to keep the texts from being cluttered with redundancies and streamline fluent reading. You can find a detailed online guide on Levantine Arabic pronunciation and Lingualism's system of orthography in the Resources section of this book's product page on our website.

Phonemic Transcription

Each dialogue also appears as phonemic transcription. This can be helpful for learners who are not yet comfortable enough with the Arabic alphabet. Some of the phonemic characters may seem unfamiliar and confusing, but by investing just a short time learning the sounds each character represents, you will find the system intuitive and easy to read. The phonemic transcription shows some pronunciation information, such as word stress, that the Arabic script does not. So even learners who prefer Arabic script can benefit by referring to the phonemic transcription. Words borrowed from English (and pronounced, more or less, as in English) are shown between [square brackets]. French words are, also shown in square brackets and preceded by a superscript ^{F}. Follow the link above for a guide to Lingualism's phonemic transcription system.

English Translation

Between the dialogues of Arabic script and phonemic transcription, English translations appear to help you understand the dialogues and quickly find words and phrases you want to learn. Some style was sacrificed in the translations to keep them direct and true to the original Levantine Arabic. This allows you to easily match up phrases and words by comparing the translations to the Arabic.

Footnotes

Underlined words and phrases are followed by superscript numbers that reference footnotes. When an entire line of dialogue is referenced, it is not underlined:

- Synonyms are preceded by equal signs (=). These show you words and expressions which can replace those in the dialogue without significantly changing the meaning.

- Alternative expressions show examples of other things you might want to say or might hear instead. These are followed by English translations.

Culture and Information Notes

The real focus of the book is, of course, the language itself. Other information–on culture and services in Lebanon–is provided as a bonus. Hopefully, you will find some information useful and interesting, but keep in mind that the comments on culture are generalizations–there are always exceptions. Likewise, the information on services (companies, procedures, transportation options, etc.) is subject to change. You should always double-check such information from other sources, especially Lebanese friends and acquaintances.

The Extended Dialogue

The mini-dialogues in each chapter are followed by a longer dialogue that combines several of the subtasks into a full communicative exchange.

Vocabulary

Vocabulary lists in three columns (English, phonemic transcription, and Arabic script) follow the dialogues. These are not glossaries containing all of the words from the dialogues, but rather lists of keywords related to the topic and those likely to be needed in various circumstances–that is, they are there to save you time searching in dictionaries for words you might need.

Expressions

Expressions are divided into two sections, preceded by the same symbols used in the dialogues. First are expressions you may need to use, and second are statements and questions you may hear others say.

Audio

All of the dialogues have been recorded by native-speaker voice artists. You can download or stream the audio free of charge from our website.

Taking a Taxi بِالتّاكْسي

There are a number of ways to get a تاكْسي *táksi* **taxi** in Lebanon. You can call a taxi company or book a cab on their website. Some well-known taxi companies are Allo Taxi, Elegance, and Byblos Taxi. In larger cities, there are areas where taxis gather, and you can hail one from the side of the street. Taxis in Lebanon don't have عدّادات *3addēdēt* **fare meters**, so always agree on the fare first.

Taxis can also operate as what the Lebanese call سِرْڤيس *[Fservice]* **a shared taxi**. This "service" system has been around for decades. When you hail a taxi, say تاكْسي عَ __ *táksi 3a* __ **Taxi to __** if you don't want the driver to pick up others and سِرْڤيس عَ __ *[Fservice] 3a* __ **Service to __** if you prefer to pay less but don't mind the trip taking longer as the driver picks up other passengers along the way.

Most taxi drivers are men in Lebanon; and, keeping in mind cultural expectations, it is okay for men to sit in the front next to the driver, but it is not appropriate for women to.

AGREEING ON THE DESTINATION AND A PRICE IN ADVANCE (1)

o ساحْةْ[1] الشُّهدا ريِّس؟[2]

◇ أيْه تْفضّل.

o بِدْفع عشِرْتلاف[3] ليرة أوْكي؟

◇ ماشي إسْتاذ، ما رح نِخْتِلِف.[4]

o Martyrs' Square, sir?

◇ Yes. Please, get in.

o I'll pay 10,000 L.L., all right?

◇ Okay, sir. We won't argue.

o *sēħt*[1] *iššúhada, ráyyis*[2]*?*

◇ *ē, tfáddal.*

o *bídfa3 3aširtalēf*[3] *līra, okē?*

◇ *mēši, istēz. ma raħ nixtílif.*[4]

[1] ساحة *sēħa* **square, plaza**. When the first element in an idaafa construction (compound noun), the ending ـة is pronounced *-it,* and sometimes just *-t* in natural, spoken language. In this book, it is written ـةْ (with sukuun). ساحِة الشُّهدا *sēħit iššúhada* → ساحْةْ الشُّهدا *sēħt iššúhada.*

[2] ريِّس *ráyyis* **sir, boss** is a polite but casual form of address for a man. A more formal variant is إسْتاذ *istēz.*

[3] Notice in the audio that the *r* is swallowed in this word, which ends up sounding more like *3aštalēf.* Such reduced pronunciations are typical of relaxed, natural-speed speech; they may seem daunting at first, but you are encouraged to train your ear by comparing what you hear on the audio to the Arabic script and phonemic transcriptions.

[4] لأ، ما بِتْوَفّي معي. *la?, ma bitwáffi má3i.* **No, that wouldn't make sense (be profitable) for me.**

②

Agreeing on the destination and a price in advance (2)

o فيك تْقِلّي[1] قدّيْ بيكلِّفْني إذا بدّي روح عَ جْبيْل؟

◇ أوْكيْ مدام. خلّيني جِبْلِك[2] تِسْعيرة مْن الشِّرْكِة.

(The driver speaks into his walkie talkie.)

◇ مركزية مركزية، فيك تعْطيني تِسْعيرة عَ جْبيْل مِن مطار بَيْروت؟

(He turns back to the customer.)

◇ أوْكيْ مدام، خمْسين ألْف ليرة.

o أوْكيْ عظيم.

o Could you tell me how much it would cost me to get to Jbeil?

◇ Okay, ma'am, let me get a quote for you from the company.

(The driver speaks into his walkie talkie.)

◇ Central Station, Central Station. Can you give me a quote to Jbeil from Beirut Airport?...

(He turns back to the customer.)

◇ Okay, ma'am. It'll be 50,000 L.L.

o Okay, perfect.

o *fīk t?ílli[1] ?addē bikallífni íza báddi rūḫ 3a jbēl?*

◇ *okē, [Fmadame]. xallīni jíblik[2] tis3īra mn iššírki.*

(The driver speaks into his walkie talkie.)

◇ *markazíyyi markazíyyi, fīk ta3ṭīni tis3īra 3a jbēl min maṭār bayrūt?*

(He turns back to the customer.)

◇ *okē, [Fmadame], xamsīn alf līra.*

o *okē, 3aẓīm.*

[1] The long vowel in تْقول *t?ūl* **you say/tell** shortens to *i* when an indirect object suffix is added: تْقول *t?ūl* + ـلي *-li* **to me** → تْقِلّي *t?ílli* **you tell me**

[2] جيب *jīb* **I bring/get** + ـلِك *-lik* **to you** → جِبْلِك *jíblik* **I get for you**

③

Paying the fare

o بنْزل هوْن حدّ وودِن بيكري[1] لَوْ سمحِت.

◇ تْفضّلي مدام.

o هَوْدي خمْسة[2] وخمْسين ألْف ليرة[3]. خلّي الباقي لإلك.

◇ مرْسي كْتير مدام. الله يْوَفّقِك.

o I'll get out here by Wooden Bakery[1], please.

◇ There you are, ma'am.

o Okay, here's 55,000 L.L.[3] Keep the change.

◇ Thank you so much ma'am. God bless you.

o *bínzal hōn ɦadd [Wooden Bakery][1], law samáɦit.*

◇ *tfáḍḍali, [Fmadame].*

o *háwdi xámsa[2] w xamsīn alf līra[3]. xálli -lbēʔi la-ílak.*

◇ *[Fmerci] ktīr, [Fmadame]. álla ywáffʔik.*

[1] Wooden Bakery is a popular Lebanese chain with dozens of locations. www.woodenbakery.com

[2] خمْسِة *xámsi* **five** becomes خمْسة *xámsa* in compound numbers (25, 35, 45, etc.). The same pronunciation change occurs with the numbers ستّة *sítti* **six** and تمْانْية *tamēnyi* **eight**.

[3] The ليرة *līra* **Lebanese pound** is abbreviated L.L. (Livre Libanaise) and is pegged to the U.S. dollar at approximately 1,500 L.L. to the dollar:

It is advisable to book a taxi before landing at the Beirut-Rafic Hariri International Airport, as opposed to booking one outside the airport. See the note on p. 46 for more details.

A taxi is significantly more expensive than a service (but slightly more expensive than a bus). In this dialogue, the fare is the equivalent of $36 because the passenger is taking a longer trip, from the airport to Byblos, for example.

4

TELLING THE TAXI DRIVER TO TAKE A CERTAIN ROUTE

o عاليونسْكو؟
◇ أوْكيْ تْفضّلي. مْناخُد البحْرية أَوْ الأُتوسْتْراد؟
o لأ خلّينا عالأُتوستراد أحْسن. سْمِعِت إنّو في حادِث عالبحْرية وأنا مِسْتعْجِلة[1].
◇ أوْكيْ، وَلا يْهِمّك.

o UNESCO?
◇ Okay, get in. Shall we go along the seaside road or take the freeway?
o No, let's stick to the freeway. I heard there was an accident on the seaside road earlier today, and I'm in a hurry.
◇ Okay, don't worry.

o *3a-l[UNEşCO]?*
◇ *okē tfáḍḍali. mnēxud ilbaɧríyyi aw ilʔ[ᶠautostrade]?*
o *laʔ, xallīna 3a-lʔ[ᶠautostrade] áɧsan. smí3it ínnu fī ɧēdis 3a-lbaɧríyyi w ána mistá3jali*[1].
◇ *okē, wála yhímmik.*

[1] مِسْتعْجِلة *mistá3jali* is a feminine adjective. The masculine form doesn't have the ending ـة: مِسْتعْجِل *mistá3jal.* Keep in mind that the dialogues may have male or female speakers and that you will need to make changes, especially to adjective and verb forms, when speaking, depending on your gender and that of the person you are speaking to or about.

You can find words and expressions for giving directions in the vocabulary section at the end of this chapter and the next chapter (p. 27).

⑤

ASKING YOUR RIDESHARE DRIVER TO MAKE A STOP ON THE WAY

o مونْسْيور طوْني؟

◇ أيْه مظْبوط. إسْتاذ مايْك؟

o أيْه. عَ بْرْمانا پْليز.

◇ تِكْرم عَيْنك إسْتاذ.

o إذا فيك، فينا نوقف حدّ پاتيسْري عالطّريق وناخُد حِلو؟

◇ ما في مشْكل إسْتاذ. في كذا پاتيسْري مْناح عالطّريق. وَلا يْهِمّك.

o Mr. Tony?

◇ Yes, correct. Mr. Mike?

o Yes... to Broumana, please.

◇ Yes, sir.

o If you could, I'd love to stop by a pastry shop on the way and pick up some sweets.

◇ No problem, sir. There are a few good ones on the way. No worries.

o *[ᶠmonsieur] ţōni?*

◇ *ē, maẓbūţ. istēz [Mike]?*

o *ē. 3a brumāna, [please].*

◇ *tíkram 3áynak, istēz.*

o *íza fīk, fīna nūʔaf ḩadd [ᶠpâtisserie] 3a-ţţarīʔ w nēxud ḩílu?*

◇ *ma fī máškal, istēz. fī káza [ᶠpâtisserie] mnēḩ 3a-ţţarīʔ. wála yhímmak.*

Although rideshares, such as Uber, are available in Lebanon, they are still not as popular as taxis, services, and buses.

When you hail a taxi or a service, always make sure that the license plate is red, which is the designated license plate for taxis, services, and buses. Otherwise, the vehicle is not legally authorized to pick up customers; and, although they often do, it's better to err on the side of caution.

6

Paying your rideshare driver

o أوْكيْ بِنْزل هوْن حدّ الصَّيْدلية.

◇ أوْكيْ مدام.

o قدّيْ بدّك مِنّي؟

◇ سبِعْتّلاف مدام.

o هَيْدي عشْرة. فيك تْرِدِّلّي بسّ ألْف؟

◇ أوْكيْ مدام. يِسْلمو. حمْدِالله عالسّلامِة.[1] انْتبْهي إنْتي ونازْلِة منْ السِّيّارة، في جورة كْتير كْبيرِة هوْن.

o Okay, I'll get out next to the pharmacy.

◇ All right, ma'am.

o How much do I owe you?

◇ It's 7,000 L.L., ma'am.

o Here's 10,000 L.L. Can you just give me 1,000 L.L. back?

◇ Okay, ma'am. Thank you. Thank God you arrived safely. Be careful when you get out of the car; there's a pothole there.

o *okē, bínzal hōn ḫadd iṣṣaydalíyyi.*

◇ *okē, [^F madame].*

o *ʔaddē báddak mínni?*

◇ *sabi3talēf, [^F madame].*

o *háydi 3ášra. fīk triddílli bass alf?*

◇ *okē, [^F madame]. yíslamu. ḫamdílla 3a-ssalēmi.*[1] *ntíbhi ínti w nēzli mn issiyyāra, fī jūra ktīr kbīri hōn.*

[1] حمْدِالله عالسّلامِة *ḫamdílla 3a-ssalēmi* is a formulaic wish to someone who has completed a journey (or recovered from an illness). The response is الله يْسلْمك *álla ysállmak.*

7

Renting a Taxi for an Extended Time

○ مرْحبا مْعلِّم. بدّي روح عالجامْعة الأميرْكية بِبيْروت، بسّ بدّي وَقِّف كم مطْرح عالطّريق. فاضي؟

◇ أوْكي ْ ريِّس. بسّ ويْن بدّك تْوَقِّف؟[1]

○ مِنْروح عالكسْليك بِالأوّل، بدّي جيب كم غرض بِسِرْعة، ومْنِرْجع مِنْروح مِنْوَصِّلْن عالجامْعة.

◇ بسّ رح تاخُد كْتير وَقِت، خْصوصي بِعجْقِةْ السّيْر بِهالوَقِت.

○ كْراميْتك محْفوظة ريِّس. خمْسين دوْلار مْنيحة؟

◇ أوْكي ْ إسْتاذ، مِتِل ما بْتؤْمُر.

○ Hey, sir! I wanted to go to the American University in Beirut but have a few stops on the way. Are you free?

◇ All right, sir, but where are these destinations?

○ We'll first go to Kaslik to pick up a few things quickly, and then head to AUB to drop them off.

◇ But it'll take us so long, especially with the traffic at this time of day.

○ I'll make it worth your while, sir. Don't worry. Is $50 good?

◇ All right, sir. As you wish.

○ *márħaba, m3állim. báddi rūħ 3a-ljēm3a -lʔamērkíyyi bi-bayrūt, bass báddi wáʔʔif kam máṭraħ 3a-ṭṭarīʔ. fāḍi?*

◇ *okē ráyyis. bass wēn báddak twáʔʔif?*[1]

○ *minrūħ 3a-lkaslīk bi-lʔáwwal, báddi jīb kam ɣáraḍ bi-sír3a, w mnírja3 minrūħ minwáṣṣilun 3a-ljēm3a.*

◇ *bass raħ tēxud ktīr wáʔit, xṣūṣi bi-3ájʔit issēr bi-ha-lwáʔit.*

○ *kramíytak maħfūẓa, ráyyis. xamsīn dólar mnīħa?*

◇ *okē istēz, mítil ma btíʔmur.*

[1] لأ والله. ما معي إلّا رِبع ساعة. *laʔ, wálla. ma má3i ílla ríbi3 sē3a.* **No, I swear. I only have fifteen minutes.**

Extended Dialogue

(stops a taxi)

○ سرْڤيس عَ سوق العتيق إسْتاذ؟

◇ لأ مِش سرْڤيس. منّي رايِح صوْب السّوق، كْتير في عجْقةْ سيرْ. وبْشِكّ ركّاب غَيْرِك رح يِطْلعوا سرْڤيس بِهالوَقِت. فِيي آخْدِك تاكْسي.

○ لأ مرْسي.[1]

(stops another)

○ مرْحبا مْعلِّم. سرْڤيس عَ سوق العتيق؟

◇ سوْري تِسْلميلي، بسّ مِنّي رايِح صوْب هونيك أبداً.

(stops a taxi with passengers already in it)

○ سوق العتيق؟

◇ أيْه تْفضّلي. سِتّلاف.

○ سِتّلاف عَ سرْڤيس؟ معك تْلاتِة بِالسِّيّارة، قاعْدين فوْق بعْضُن مِتْل السّرْدين. بِدْفع أرْبعْتلاف.

◇ لأ ما بِتْوَفّي. باي.

(stops yet another taxi)

○ سرْڤيس عَ سوق العتيق إسْتاذ؟ صِرْلي[2] ساعة عم جرِّب وَقِّف سرْڤيس.

◇ أيْه أوْكيْ تْفضّلي. للصّراحة منّي رايِح صوْب السّوق، بسّ ما فِيي خلّي بِنِت زْغيرِة صبية مِتْلِك توقف بِهالهِبّ. بِتْموتي!

○ مرْسي كْتير كِلّك ذوْق.

◇ وَلا يْهِمّك بِنْتي. بِتْكوني هونيك بعْد نِتْفِة[3].

○ مرْسي كْتير.

(They approach the souk.)

○ قدّيْ لازِم إدْفع إسْتاذ؟

◇ سرْڤيس عالسّوق أرْبعْتلاف بسّ.

o شو مِذْوِق! كِنْت دفعِت شو ما كان بسّ عَ لُطْفك.

◇ ما في مِشْكْلِة أبداً!

o فيك تْنزِّلْني حدّ القدّوم عْموْل معْروف؟

◇ اه! أوعي ما تاكْلي كوكْتيْل الِفْواكِه تبعُن. كْتير مشْهورين فيه.

o مرْسي كْتير. رح دوقو. إنْتَ مِن أحْسن النّاس اللي تْعرّفْت عْلَيْنُ هوْن.

◇ حمْدِالله عالسّلامِة دُمْوازيْل. انْشالله تِنْبُسْطي عِنّا بِالمدينِة.

o هَيْدي عشِرْتلاف. تْروك الباقي.

◇ يا بِنْتي، كْتير هالقدّ. ما فِيي إقْبلُن.

o لأ پْليز. بِنْبُسِط كْتير إذا بْتاخِدُن.

◇ طيِّب بِنْتي. مرْسي كْتير. الله يْعوِّضْن عْلَيْكي أضْعاف.

(stops a taxi)

o Service to the old souk, sir?

◇ No, not service. I'm not going that way; there's too much traffic now. And I doubt any other passengers will be going that way at this time of day. I can take you as a taxi.

o No, thanks.

(stops another taxi)

o Hello, sir. Service to the old souk?

◇ I'm sorry, darling, but it's not on my way at all.

(stops a taxi with passengers already in it)

o Old souk?

◇ Yes, get in. It's 6,000 L.L.

o 6,000 L.L. for a service?! You have three people in the car already, crammed like sardines. I'll only pay 4,000.

◇ No can do. Goodbye.

(stops yet another taxi)

- ○ Service to the old souk, sir? I've been trying to stop a service for the last hour.
- ◇ Yes, okay , get in. To be honest, I'm not going that way, but I won't leave a pretty young girl like you standing in this heat. You'd die.
- ○ Thank you so much, sir. I really appreciate it.
- ◇ Don't you worry, my child. I'll get you there in a bit.
- ○ Thank you!

(They approach the souk.)

- ○ How much should I pay, sir?
- ◇ Service is only 4,000 L.L. to the old souk.
- ○ That's so kind. I would have paid anything just for your kindness.
- ◇ It's no problem at all!
- ○ Could you drop me off by Al Kaddoum over there?
- ◇ Oh! Be sure to try out their fruit cocktails. They're famous for those.
- ○ Thank you very much. I will do. You're one of the kindest people I have met here.
- ◇ Thank God you arrived safely, miss. I hope you enjoy your stay in our city.
- ○ Here's 10,000 L.L. Keep the change.
- ◇ My child, that's too much. I can't accept it.
- ○ No, please do. It would make me so happy.
- ◇ Okay, my child. Thank you so much. May God make it up to you in doubles!

(stops a taxi)

- ○ *[[F]service] 3a sūʔ il3atīʔ, istēz?*
- ◇ *laʔ, miš [[F]service]. mánni rāyiɧ şōb issūʔ, ktīr fī 3ájʔit sēr. w bšikk rikkēb ɣáyrik raɧ yíţla3u [[F]service] bi-ha-lwáʔit. fíyi ēxdik táksi.*
- ○ *laʔ [[F]merci].*[1]

(stops another taxi)

- ○ *márɧaba, m3állim. [[F]service] 3a sūʔ il3atīʔ?*
- ◇ *[sorry] tislamīli, bass mánni rāyiɧ şōb hunīk ábadan.*

(stops a taxi with passengers already in it)

○ *sūʔ il3atīʔ?*

◇ *ē, tfáḍḍali. sittalēf.*

○ *sittalēf 3a [ᶠservice]? má3ak tlēti bi-ssiyyāra, ʔē3dīn fōʔ bá3ḍun mítl -ssardīn. bídfa3 arba3talēf.*

◇ *laʔ ma bitwáffi. [bye].*

(stops yet another taxi)

○ *[ᶠservice] 3a sūʔ il3atīʔ istēz? ṣárli[2] sē3a 3am járrib wáʔʔif [ᶠservice].*

◇ *ē, okē tfáḍḍali. la-ṣṣarāḫa mánni rāyiḫ ṣōb issūʔ, bass ma fíyi xálli bínit zɣīri ṣabíyyi mítlik tūʔaf bi-ha-lhíbb. bitmūti!*

○ *[ᶠmerci] ktīr kíllak zōʔ.*

◇ *wála yhímmik bínti. bitkūni hunīk ba3d nítfi[3].*

○ *[ᶠmerci] ktīr.*

(They approach the souk.)

○ *ʔaddē lēzim ídfa3 istēz?*

◇ *[ᶠservice] 3a-ssūʔ arba3talēf bass.*

○ *šū mízwiʔ! kínt dafá3it šū ma kēn bass 3a lúṭfak.*

◇ *ma fī míškli ábadan!*

○ *fīk tnazzílni ḫadd ilʔaddūm, 3mōl ma3rūf?*

◇ *āh! ū3i ma tēkli kōktēl lifwēki tába3un. ktīr mašhūrīn fī.*

○ *[ᶠmerci] ktīr. raḫ dūʔu. ínta min áḫsan innēs -lli t3arráft 3láyun hōn.*

◇ *ḫamdílla 3a-ssalēmi, [ᶠdemoiselle]. nšálla tinbúsṭi 3ínna bi-lmadīni.*

○ *háydi 3aširtalēf. trōk ilbēʔi.*

◇ *ya bínti, ktīr ha-lʔádd. ma fíyi íʔbalun.*

○ *laʔ [please]. binbúsiṭ ktīr íza btēxidun.*

◇ *ṭáyyib bínti. [ᶠmerci] ktīr. álla y3awwíḍun 3láyki aḍ3āf.*

[1] طيِّب، أوْكي. ما في مشْكل. *ṭáyyib, okē. ma fī máškal.* **Well, okay. That's fine.**

[2] صار *ṣār* + ـلي *-li* → صرْلي *ṣárli*

[3] = شْوَيّ *šwayy*

Vocabulary

taxi	*táksi*	تاكْسي
(rideshare) app	*[application]* *taṭbīʔ*	أبْليكيْشُن تطْبيق
driver	*[Fchauffeur]*	شوْفور
meter	*3addēd*	عدّاد
fare	*újra*	أُجْرة
change (money back)	*-lbēʔi*	الباقي
change (small change, change for a larger bill)	*frāṭa*	فْراطة
the next corner	*-lmáfraʔ iljēyi*	المفْرق الجاي
street	*šēri3 (šawēri3)*	شارِع (شَوارِع)
narrow street, side street, alley	*zārūb/zārūbi (zwērīb)*	زاروب/زاروبِة (زْواريب)
license plate number	*nímra* *nímrit siyyāra*	نِمْرة نِمْرِةْ سِيّارة
police report	*máḫḍar (maḫāḍir)*	محْضر (محاضِر)
police station	*máxfar*	مخْفر
traffic, congestion	*3ájʔit sēr*	عجْقِةْ سيْر
traffic sign	*išāra*	إشارة
police checkpoint	*ḫājiz*	حاجِز
license	*rúxṣa*	رُخْصة

credit	*raṣīd*	رصيد
rating, evaluation	*taʔyīm*	تقْييم
square, plaza	*sēḫa*	ساحة
bridge	*jísir (jsūra)*	جِسِر (جْسورة)
tunnel	*náfaʔ (anfēʔ)*	نفق (أنْفاق)
highway	*[ᶠautostrade]*	أوْتوْسْتْراد
roundabout, traffic circle	*[ᶠrond point]*	روْنْد پْوانْت
corniche, waterfront road	*kornīš*	كوْرْنيش
taxi door	*bēb ittáksi*	باب التّاكْسى
window	*šibbēk (šbēbīk)*	شِبّاك (شْبابيك)
front seat	*-lkírsi -lʔidmēni*	الكِرْسي القِدْماني
back seat	*-lkírsi -lwarāni*	الكِرْسي الوَراني
trunk (UK: boot)	*ṣandūʔ (siyyāra)*	صنْدوق (سِيّارة)
hood (UK: bonnet)	*ɣáṭa -l[ᶠmoteur]*	غطا الموْتور
tire (UK: tyre)	*dūlēb (dwēlīb)*	دولاب (دْواليب)
(car) horn	*zammūr*	زمّور
seat belt	*ḫizēm ilʔamēn [ᶠceinture]*	حِزام الأمان سيْنْتور
windshield wipers	*massēḫēt*	مسّاحات
mirrors	*mrēyēt*	مْرايات
gas tank (UK: petrol tank)	*tánkit benzīn*	تنْكِة بنْزين

Expressions

I want to go to __.	*báddi rūɧ __.*	بدّي روح __.
Do you know where __ is?	*3ārif wēn __?*	عارِف ويْن __؟
If you don't mind, I would like to open the window.	*íza ma 3índak míškli, ɧābib íftaɧ iššibbēk.*	إذا ما عِنْدك مِشْكْلِه، حابِب إفْتح الشِّبّاك.
Excuse me, I will stop here for a minute to get something.	*law samáɧit, báddi wáʔʔif hōn šwayy ta-ēxud šī.*	لَوْ سمحِت، بدّي وقِّف هوْن شْوَيّ تآخُد شي.
If there is a shortcut, I'd be grateful.	*íza fī ţarīʔ áʔşar, bkūn mamnūnak.*	إذا في طريق أقْصر، بْكون ممْنونك.
You're taking us for a long ride when the trip is actually short!	*ēxidna 3a ţarīʔ ţawīli, ma3 ínnu -lmasēfi mánna ha-lʔádd b3īdi.*	آخِدْنا عَ طريق طَويلِة، مع إنّو المسافِة منّا هالقدّ بْعيدِة.
Can we take the Jal-El-Dib bridge?	*fīna nēxud jísir jal iddīb?*	فينا ناخُد جِسِر جل الدّيب؟
Please, drive faster because I'm in a hurry.	*[please], sūʔ ásra3 šwayy li-ánnu mistá3jil.* *stá3jil šwayy li-ánnu mistá3jil.*	پْليز سوق أسْرع شْوَيّ، لِأنّي مِسْتعْجِل. سْتعْجِل شْوَيّ لأنّي مِسْتعْجِل.
Could you please slow down a bit?	*fīk tsūʔ 3a máhlak?*	فيك تْسوق عَ مهْلك شْوَيّ؟
Go straight.	*rūɧ díɣri.*	روح دِغْري.
Turn right.	*rūɧ yamīn.*	روح يمَين.

Turn left.	*rūḫ šmēl.*	روح شْمال.
Here is fine. (Stop here.)	*hūn mnīḫ.*	هون مْنيح.
The next street on the right.	*tēni šēri3 3a-lyamīn.*	تاني شارِع عاليَمين.
The corner after the next one.	*-lmáfraʔ ittēni. miš háyda -lmáfraʔ, -lli bá3du.*	المفْرق التّاني. مِش هَيْدا المفْرق، اللي بعْدو.
How much is the fare, please?	*ʔaddē báddak mínni?*	قدّيْ بدّك مِنّي؟
Do you have change?	*má3ak frāṭa?*	معك فْراطة؟
	◇	
Do you want me to open the trunk for you?	*báddak iftáḫlak iṣṣandūʔ?*	بدّك إفْتحْلك الصّنْدوق؟
Is it okay if I stop quickly and fill up the tank?	*ma3lē íza waʔʔáfit šwayy ta-3ábbi benzīn?*	معْليْه إذا وَقّفِت شْوَيّ تعبّي بنْزين؟
Where will you get out?	*wēn nēzil ḫáḍirtak?*	ويْن نازِل حضِرْتك؟
Wait, I'll pull over in a comfortable spot.	*láḫẓa, raḫ waʔʔíflak bi-lwás3a.*	لحْظة رح وقِّفْلك بِالوَسْعة.
Listen, I'll drop you off at the end of the bridge, and you will just need to cross the road.	*smē3, raḫ názzlak 3a ēxir iljísir, w bass biṣīr báddak tíʔṭa3 iṭṭarīʔ.*	سْماع، رح نزّْلك عَ آخِر الجِسِر، وبسّ بيصير بدّك تِقْطع الطّريق.
I'm sorry, I really don't have any change.	*[sorry][1] bass ma má3i frāṭa.*	سوْري[1] بسّ ما معي فْراطة.

[1] = ما توْاخِذْني *ma twēxízni*

Asking for Directions عالطّريق

Except for a few sporadic spots, Lebanon does not have an official, unified system for street addresses. As a result, people use landmark names to give directions. When in doubt, just ask. Most people will be helpful when you ask for directions, especially when they hear an accent and realize you're a foreigner. Because direction-giving is such a subjective exercise, it's always best to ask more than one person along the way to you successfully reach your destination.

Because there's no official address system, when you ask someone for directions, people will sometimes ask you وينْ قالولك بِالظّبِط؟ *wēn ʔēlūlak bi-ẓẓábiṭ*? **Where did they tell you it was exactly?** This usually means that the person you're asking doesn't exactly know the place you're referring to but is still trying to help by asking for any landmark you've been told about, and they still might be able to guide you. That said, this is another reason that you should be asking more than one person... just in case. For all of the reasons mentioned above, when you're being given an address by someone, it is always best to get detailed instructions and landmarks. That way, you can help those trying to guide you along the way.

ASKING FOR DIRECTIONS (1)

o لَوْ سمحْتي، أقْرب مَوْقف تاكْسِيات وِيْن؟

◇ بِتْضلّك رايِح دِغْري تِتوصل[1] عالسّاحة، قْطاع الطّريق، وبِتْلاقي سِيّارات التّاكْسي واقْفين.

o كْتير بْعيدِة مِن هوْن؟

◇ لأ، بسّ عشْر دْقايِق مشي.[2]

o Excuse me, where is the nearest taxi stop?

◇ You'll go straight until you reach the square, cross it and you'll find a bunch of taxis waiting.

o Is it very far from here?

◇ No, it's just a ten-minute walk.

o *law samáħti, áʔrab máwʔaf taksiyēt wēn?*

◇ *bitḍállak rāyiħ díɣri ṯa-tūṣal[1] 3a-ssēħa, ʔṭā3 iṭṭarīʔ, w bitlēʔi siyyārāt ittáksi wēʔfīn.*

o *ktīr b3īdi min hōn?*

◇ *laʔ, bass 3ašr dʔāyiʔ máši.[2]*

[1] تـ ta- = لـ *la-* (+ imperfect verb) **in order to, so that**; تتوصل *ta-tūṣal* **so that you arrive**

[2] لأ أبداً. كْتير قريب. *laʔ, ábadan. ktīr ʔarīb.* **No, not at all. It's very close.**

2

Asking for directions (2)

○ عفْواً، كيف بوصل عَ شارِع الحمْرا؟

◇ إذا بِتْقرْبي لقِدّام شْوَيّ وبْتِفْرْقي عالشْمال وبْترِْجعي بِترْوحي دِغْري بْتوصلي عَ شارِع الحمْرا.[1]

○ Excuse me, how can I get to Al-Hamra Street?

◇ If you go straight, then make a left, then go straight again, you'll find yourself on Al-Hamra street.

○ *3áfwan, kīf būṣal 3a šēri3 ilħámra?*

◇ *íza bitʔárrbi la-ʔiddēm šwayy w btífrʔi 3a-ššmēl w btírja3i bitrūħi díɣri btūṣali 3a šēri3 ilħámra.*[1]

1 وبْتاخْدي المفْرق يَلّي عَ إيدِك الشْمال، كمْلي دِغْري، بْيِطْلع بِوِجّك. *w btēxdi -lmáfraʔ yálli 3a īdik iššmēl, kámmli díɣri, byíṭla3 bi-wíjjik.* **Take the turn on your left, keep going straight, and it'll be right in front of you.**

3

Asking for directions (3)

○ وين مطْعم بابِل؟

◇ بآخِر الشّارِع بْتِفْرُق شْمال وبِتْضلّك رايح دِغْري، وبِتْلاقي المطْعم عَ تاني مَيْلِة[1] مْن الشّارِع.

○ مرْسي كْتير.[2]

○ Where is the restaurant Babel, please?

◇ At the end of this street, you'll turn left and keep walking straight, you'll find the restaurant on the opposite side of the street.

○ Thanks so much!

○ *wēn máṭ3am bēbil?*

◇ *bi-ēxir iššēri3 btífruʔ šmēl w bitḍállak rāyiḫ díɣri, w bitlēʔi -lmáṭ3am 3a tēni máyli[1] mn iššēri3.*

○ *[^F^merci] ktīr.[2]*

[1] = تاني جِهة *tēni jíha*

[2] = يِسْلمو *yíslamu*

Asking for Directions (4)

○ مرْحبا، أوْتيْل فينيسْيا بْعيد مِن هوْن؟

◇ لأ أبداً. بْتاخُد تالِت شارِع[1] عاليَمين[2]، وبْترْجع بْتاخُد أوّل شارِع عالشْمال.

○ عظيم، ومِن بعْد هيْك؟

◇ بِتْلاقيه عَ إيدك اليَمين. في نَوافير ميّ قِدّامِ[3] الأوْتيْل.

○ Hello. Is Phoenicia hotel far from here?

◇ Not at all. You'll take the third street on the right and then the first one on the left.

○ Great. And after that?

◇ You'll find it on the right. There are water fountains in front of the hotel.

○ *márɧaba, [ᶠhôtel] fīnīsya b3īd min hōn?*

◇ *la? ábadan. btēxud tēlit šēri3*[1] *3a-lyamīn*[2]*, w btírja3 btēxud áwwal šēri3 3a-ššmēl.*

○ *3aẓīm, w min ba3d hēk?*

◇ *bitlē?ī 3a īdak ilyamīn. fī nawēfīr mayy ?iddēm*[3] *il?[ᶠhôtel].*

[1] = مفْرق *máfra?* **corner**

[2] عالشْمال *3a-ššmēl* **on the left**

[3] = بِوِجْه *bi-wíjh*

5

Asking for directions (5)

o كيف فِيي أوصل عَ جامِع مْحمّد الأمين؟

◇ رْجعي شْوَيّ لَوَرا لحدّ ما تْشوفي المتْحف الوَطني، رْجعي روحي عالشْمال وضلّي ماشْية لآخِر الشّارِع[1]. رْجعي سْألي حدا هونيك.

o مرْسي، كلِّك ذوْق.[2]

o How can I get to Mohammad Al-Amin mosque?

◇ Go back a bit until you see the National Museum, then go left and keep walking until the end of the street. Then ask someone else over there.

o Thanks a lot.

o *kīf fíyi ūṣal 3a jēmi3 mħámmad ilʔamīn?*

◇ *rjá3i šwayy la-wára la-ħádd ma tšūfi -lmátħaf ilwáṭani, rjá3i rūħi 3a-ššmēl w ḍálli mēšyi la-ēxir iššēri3[1]. rjá3i sʔáli ħáda hunīk.*

o *[Fmerci], kíllik zōʔ.[2]*

[1] على طول *3ála ṭūl* **straight ahead**

[2] = يِسْلمو *yíslamu*

6

Asking for Directions (6)

o في صالوْن شعِر هوْن اِسْمو جيهان؟

◇ويْن قالولك بِالظّبْط؟

o رايْحة زور بيْت حدا هونيك وقلّي إنّو بِآخِر شارِع المير مجيد اِرْسْلان، فوْق صالوْن جيهان.

◇ اه أوْكي. هُوِّ تالِت شارِع عاليَمين، بسّ أحْسن تْوَقّْفي هوْن محلّ ما في مطْرح وتِتْمشّي لهونيك[1].

o طيِّب يِسْلمو.

o Is there a "Jihan" hair salon around here?

◇ Where exactly were you told it was?

o I'm visiting someone's house over there, and he told me it's at the end of Mir Majid Erslan Street, above "Jihan" hair salon.

◇ Ah, okay. That street is the third one on your right, but you'd better park where there's space here and walk.

o Okay, thank you very much!

o *fī [Fsalon] šá3ir hōn ísmu jīhān?*

◇ *wēn ʔālūlik bi-ẓẓábṭ?*

o *rāyħa zūr bēt ħáda hunīk w ʔálli ínnu bi-ēxir šēri3 ilmīr majīd irslēn, fōʔ [Fsalon] jīhān.*

◇ *āh okē. húwwi tēlit šēri3 3a-lyamīn, bass áħsan twáʔʔfi hōn maħáll ma fī máṭraħ w titmášši la-hunīk[1].*

o *ṭáyyib yíslamu.*

[1] أحْسن تْروحي مشي عَ إجْرَيْكي *áħsan trūħi máši 3a ijráyki* **you'd better walk**

Extended Dialogue

o إذا بِتْريد، بدّي أوصل[1] عَ أسْواق بَيْروت.

◇ هُوِّ بْعيد شْوَيّ إذا بدِّك تمِْشي. بدِّك شي عِشْرين دْقيقة تتوصلي.[2]

o معْليْه، فيي إمْشي.

◇ أوْكيْ، بْتاخْدي تاني شارِع عالشّمال، بْترِْجعي بْتاخْدي تاني شارِع عاليَمين، وبِتْضلِّك تمِْشي[3] تتوصلي عَ ساحةْ الشُّهدا. وهونيك رْجعي سْألي حدا تاني.

o أوْكيْ، يِسْلمو.

◇ بسّ لحْظة ويْن بِالضّبِط[4] رايْحة بِأسْواق بَيْروت؟ المشْروع كْبير.

o رايْحة عالفيرجْين ميْجاستوْر.

◇ بسّ انْتبِْهي لِأنّو بيسكِّر السّاعة عشْرة.

o اه، إذا هيْك لازِم آخُد تاكْسي أَوْ إطْلُب أوبر تأوصل.

◇ خِدي تاكْسي. أظْبط شي مِن هوْن.

o أوْكيْ، قدّيْ لازِم أعْطيه؟

◇ فيكي تعْطيه خمْسْتلاف ليرة، بسّ مِش أكْتر مِن هيْك.

o أوْكيْ، آخِر سُؤال، پْليز.

◇ أكيد!

o في شي مطْرح فيي إتْعشّ فيه؟ لِأنّو رايْحة دِغْري عالمطار مِن بعْد ما فِلّ مْن الڤيرجْين[5]. طيّارْتي السّاعة وِحْدِة بعْد نُصّ ليْل.

◇ أيْه أسْواق بَيْروت كِلّا مطاعِم وقهاوي. بسّ بِفْتِكِر أحْسن تِطِلْبي أكِل قبِل ما تْفوتي عالڤيرجْين. هيْك بسّ تِخْلصي بيكون جهِز الأكِل.

o أيْه معك حقّ! مرسي كْتير.

◇ أهْلا وسهْلا. انْتبِْهي عالطّريق.

o إذا فيك تِشْرح للتّاكْسي[6] أقْصر طريق، هيْك ما بْياخُد الطّريق الطّويل وما عاد لحِّق المحلّ.

◇ أكيد! يَلّا ثانْيِة تَوَقِّفْلِك تاكْسي.

o Excuse me, I wanted to get to Beirut Souks.

◇ It's a bit far if you're going on foot. It will take you about 20 minutes.

o Well, it's okay. I can walk.

◇ Okay, you will take the next street on the left, then the second street on the right, and keep walking straight until you reach Martyr's Square. And from there, ask again.

o All right, thanks a lot!

◇ Hold on, where exactly are you going in Beirut Souks? It's a big complex.

o I'm going to the Virgin Megastore.

◇ But, keep in mind that it closes at 10 p.m.

o Oh my goodness! Then, I'd better take an uber or a taxi to make it.

◇ Take a taxi. That's best from here.

o Okay, how much shall I give him?

◇ You can give him 5,000 L.L. but no more than that.

o All right. One last question, please.

◇ Sure!

o Is there any place over there I can have dinner at? Because I'll leave Virgin and head straight to the airport. I have a flight at 1:00 am.

◇ Yes, Beirut Souks is full of restaurants and cafés, but I think you'd better order something and then go into Virgin. By the time you're done, the order will be ready.

o Yes, you're right! Thanks a lot!

◇ You're welcome. Be safe!

○ If you could just please explain to the taxi the shortest way so that he won't take a long way and I miss getting to the store on time.

◇ Sure! Just a second and I'll stop a taxi for you.

○ *íza bitrīd, báddi ūṣal![1] 3a aswēʔ bayrūt.*

◇ *húwwi b3īd šwayy íza báddik tímši. báddik šī 3išrīn dʔīʔa ta-tūṣali.*[2]

○ *ma3lē, fíyi ímši.*

◇ *okē, btēxdi tēni šēri3 3a-ššmēl, btirjá3i btēxdi tēni šēri3 3a-lyamīn, w bitḍállik tímši[3] ta-tūṣali 3a sēɦt iššúhada. w hunīk rjá3i sʔáli ɦáda tēni.*

○ *okē, yíslamu.*

◇ *bass láɦẓa, wēn bi-ḍḍábiṭ[4] rāyɦa bi-aswēʔ bayrūt? -lmašrū3 kbīr.*

○ *rāyɦa 3a-l[Virgin Megastore].*

◇ *bass ntíbhi li-ánnu bisákkir issē3a 3ášra.*

○ *āh, íza hēk lēzim ēxud táksi aw íṭlub [Uber] ta-ūṣal.*

◇ *xídi táksi. áẓbaṭ šī min hōn.*

○ *okē, ʔaddē lēzim a3ṭī?*

◇ *fīki ta3ṭī xamstalēf līra, bass miš áktar min hēk.*

○ *okē, ēxir suʔāl, [please].*

◇ *akīd!*

○ *fī šī máṭraɦ fíyi it3áššа fīʔ li-ánnu rāyɦa díɣri 3a-lmaṭār min ba3d ma fill mn il[Virgin][5]. ṭayyārti -ssē3a wíɦdi ba3d nuṣṣ lēl.*

◇ *ē, aswēʔ bayrūt kílla maṭā3im w ʔahāwi. bass bíftikir áɦsan tiṭílbi ákil ʔábil ma tfūti 3a-l[Virgin]. hēk bass tíxlaṣi bikūn jíhiz ilʔákil.*

○ *ē, má3ak ɦaʔʔ! [[F]merci] ktīr.*

◇ *áhla w sáhla. ntíbhi 3a-ṭṭarīʔ.*

○ *íza fīk tíšraɦ la-táksi[6] áʔṣar ṭarīʔ, hēk ma byēxud iṭṭarīʔ iṭṭawīl w ma 3ēd láɦɦiʔ ilmaɦáll.*

◇ *akīd! yálla sēnyi ta-waʔʔíflik táksi.*

[1] = روح *rūɦ* **(I) go**

[2] .كْتير قريب، فشْخة *ktīr ʔarīb, fášxa.* **It's very close. Just few steps.**

[3] بِتْضلِّك رايْحة دِغْري *bitḍállik rāyɦa díɣri* **keep going straight**

[4] بِالضّبِط *bi-ḍḍábiṭ* = بِالظّبِط *bi-ẓẓábiṭ*

[5] مِن بعْد ما خلِّص *min ba3d ma xálliṣ* **after I'm done**

[6] إذا فيك تْدِلّ التّاكسي *íza fīk tdíll ittáksi* **if you could direct the taxi...**

Vocabulary

to go	*rāḥ (yrūḥ)* *míši (yímši)*	راح (يْروح) مِشي (يمِشي)
to turn	*fáraʔ (yífruʔ)* *kásar (yíksir)*	فرق (يِفْرُق) كسر (يِكْسِر)
right	*yamīn*	يمَين
left	*šmēl*	شْمال
straight ahead	*díɣri*	دِغْري
to park	*wáʔʔaf (ywáʔʔif)*	وَقّف (يْوَقِّف)
street	*šēri3 (šawēri3)*	شارِع (شَوارِع)
pedestrian sidewalk	*manáṣṣa*	منصّة
square, plaza	*sēḥa*	ساحة
bridge	*jísir (jsūra)*	جِسِر (جْسورة)
tunnel	*náfaʔ (anfēʔ)*	نفق (أنْفاق)
bend, turn	*ḥányi*	حنْيِة
across from it; across the street	*bi-wíjju*	بِوِجّو
behind	*wára*	وَرا
next to	*ḥadd*	حدّ
on foot, walking	*máši*	مشي

Landmarks

bakery	*fúrun (afrān, frān)*	فُرُن (أفْران، فْران)
barber	*ḥallāʔ*	حلّاق

butcher's	*laħħām*	لحّام
carpenter's	*najjār*	نجّار
church	*knīsi (kanēyis)*	كْنيسِة (كنايِس)
confectioner's	*maħáll ħílu* *[^{F}pâtisserie]*	محلّ حِلو پاتيسْري
electrician's	*káhrabji*	كهْربْجي
fish shop	*sammēk*	سمّاك
fruit & vegetable market	*sūʔ xúḍra*	سوق خُضْرة
fruit & vegetable shop	*maħáll xúḍra*	محلّ خُضْرة
gas station	*mħáṭṭit benzīn*	مْحطّة بنْزين
hairdresser	*[^{F}coiffeur]*	كْوافير
mechanic's	*[^{F}mécanicien]*	ميكانيسْيان
monastery, convent	*dēr*	ديْر
(street) market	*sūʔ (aswēʔ)*	سوق (أسْواق)
(big) mosque	*jēmi3 (jawēmi3)*	جامِع (جَوامِع)
(small) mosque	*másjid (masējid)*	مسْجِد (مساجِد)
pharmacy	*ṣaydalíyyi* *farmašíyyi*	صَيْدلية فرْمشية
poultry shop	*maħáll frērīj*	محلّ فْراريج
restaurant	*máṭ3am (maṭā3im)*	مطْعم (مطاعِم)
salon	*[^{F}salon]*	صالوْن
station	*mħáṭṭa*	مْحطّة

supermarket	*[supermarket]*	سوپِرْمارْكِت
tailor's	*xiyyāṭ*	خِيّاط
workshop	*wárši*	وَرْشِة

Expressions

Excuse me, where is __?	*law samáḫit, wēn __?*	لَوْ سمحِت، وِيْن __؟
Where is the beginning of __ street?	*min wēn ilfáwti 3a šēri3 __?* *wēn bibálliš šēri3 __?*	مِن وِيْن الفَوْتِة عَ شارِع __؟ وِيْن بيبلِّش شارِع __؟
How can I get to __?	*kīf fíyi ūṣal 3a __?* *kīf brūḫ 3a __?* *min wēn báddi rūḫ 3a __?*	كيف فِيي أوصل عَ __؟ كيف بْروح عَ __؟ مِن وِيْن بدّي روح عَ __؟
What is the shortest way to __?	*šū áʔṣar/áʔrab ṭarīʔ ta-ūṣal 3a__?*	شو أقْصر/أقْرب طريق تأوصل عَ__؟
Is there a __ around here?	*fī šī __ ʔarīb min hōn?*	في شي __ قريب مِن هوْن؟
What [trans-portation] can I take to reach __?	*šū lēzim ēxud min hōn ta-ūṣal 3a__?*	شو لازِم آخُد مِن هوْن تأوصل ع__؟
How far is it?	*ʔaddē b3īd min hōn?*	قدّيْ بْعيد مِن هوْن؟
I'm looking for this address.	*3am nábbiš 3a ha-l3inwēn.*	عم نبِّش عَ هالعِنْوان.
Can you show me on the map?	*fīk tdíllni 3a-lxarīṭa?*	فيك تْدِلّْني عالخريطة؟

◇

Turn right.	*ksūr/frūʔ yamīn.*	كْسور/فْروق يمَين.
Turn left.	*ksūr/frūʔ šmēl.*	كْسور/فْروق شْمال.
Go straight.	*rūħ díɣri.*	روح دِغْري.
Go over the bridge and take the second offramp on the right.	*ţlā3 fōʔ iljísir w xōd tēni názli 3a-lyamīn.*	طْلاع فوْق الجِسِر وخُد تانى نزْلِة عَاليَمين.
Go through the tunnel and as soon as you're out, turn onto the third street on the right.	*fūt bi-t[ᶠtunnel]/ bi-nnáfaʔ w áwwal ma tíţla3, xōd tēlit šēri3 3a īd ilyamīn.*	فوت بِالتّونيْل/بِالنّفق، وأوّل ما تِطْلع، خوْد تالِت شارِع عَ إيد اليَمين.
You'll find it by the big green sign over there.	*bitlēʔi ħadd ilyāfţa -lxúdra hunīk.*	بِتْلاقي حدّ اليافْطة الخُضْرا هونيك.
I don't know really. You can ask at the shop next to me.	*ma bá3rif wálla. fīk tísʔal ilmaħáll -lli ħáddi.*	ما بعْرِف والله. فيك تِسْأل المحلّ اللي حدّي.
I have no idea. I'm not from around here.	*ma 3índi fíkra wálla. mánni min hōn.*	ما عِنْدي فِكْرة والله. منّي مِن هوْن.
Where did he tell you exactly?	*wēn ʔállak bi-ẓẓábiţ/ 3a-lmaẓbūţ?*	وِيْن قالّك بِالظّبِط/ عالمظْبوط؟
Where do you want to go?	*la-wēn báddak trūħ?*	لَويْن بدّك تْروح؟
It's ten minutes on foot.	*3ášr dʔēyiʔ máši.*	عشْر دْقايِق مشي.
You're going in the wrong direction.	*ínta rāyiħ bil-ittijēh ilɣálaţ.*	إنْتَ رايِح بِالاِتِّجاه الغلط.

Taking a Bus بِالباص

Traveling by باص *bāṣ* (or بوْسْطة *bōsṭa*) **bus** is probably the cheapest way to get around in Lebanon. Taking a bus in Lebanon is pretty much the same as taking one in most other places around the world: it is not glamorous, but it gets you where you need to go. Unless a bus is new and has recently been leased, it won't be very well-maintained, but it will still get the job done. Riders range from students to the elderly, and everyone except the very rich has probably been on a bus at some point in their lives. A public bus in Lebanon can be either government-owned or privately-owned. (This might be a bit confusing, as they're still considered public transportation, even though they're privately owned.) The government-owned buses are black, red, and white; the others could be any color, but there are many blue and white privately-owned buses. Both are reliable and mostly safe. But people, including locals, usually like to take the government-owned buses, since the drivers are government employees, and there's someone to hold accountable if anything goes wrong. While buses have a set route, they will stop wherever they're flagged down, which makes riding the bus even more convenient, though slightly unpredictable, timing-wise, because you can never be sure how many people will be on the bus or the number of stops it will make.

Finding your bus at the station

○ عفْواً، إذا بدّي أوصل عالدَّوْرة، أيّا باص لازِم آخُد؟

◇ الباصات الحُمْر هونيك. طْلعي بِيَلّي عم بيعبّوا رِكّاب هلّق.

(after reaching the bus)

○ لَوْ سمحِت، واصِل عالدَّوْرة؟[1]

◇ أيْه، طْلعي. فالّين بعْد نِتْفِة.[2]

○ Excuse me, if I want to get to Dawra, which bus should I take?

◇ The red buses over there. Get on one that is boarding.

(after reaching the bus)

○ Excuse me, does this go to Dawra?

◇ Yes, get on. We're leaving in a few minutes.

○ *3áfwan, íza báddi ūşal 3a-ddáwra, áyya bāş lēzim ēxud?*

◇ *-lbāşāt ilɧúmur hunīk. ţlá3i bi-yálli 3am bi3ábbu rikkēb hálla?.*

(after reaching the bus)

○ *law samáɧit, wāşil 3a-ddáwra?*[1]

◇ *ē, ţlá3i. fēllīn ba3d nítfi.*[2]

[1] = عفْواً، رايِح عالدَّوْرة؟ *3áfwan, rāyiɧ 3a-ddáwra?*

[2] لأ، مِش عطريقي. *la?, miš 3a ţarī?i.* **No, it's not on my route.**

Buses aren't on a schedule or as punctual as they are in places like the U.S. or Europe, but a website has been put together by bus riders and public transport users to try and make sense of the system and help others. You can access it at www.busmap.me.

Traffic, in general, is terrible in Lebanon. And this also affects buses, of course, because they can't just weave in between cars as some smaller vehicles can. With this in mind, you've probably gathered that buses are not the way to go if you need to be at a certain place at a certain time, unless you leave very early.

2

Paying the fare

o قدّيْ عالشّخِص، لَوْ سمحِت؟
◇ لَويْن واصْلِة[1]؟
o بُرْج حمّود.
◇ ألْف وخمْسْمية ليرة.
o تْفضّل.
◇ عم تِحْكي عن جدّ مادام؟ أكيد ما معي صْرافِةْ خمْسين دوْلار عَ باص عالخطّ.[2]

o How much is the fare, please?
◇ Where will you get off?
o Burj Hammoud.
◇ Then 1,500 L.L.
o Here you go.
◇ Are you serious, ma'am? Of course, I don't have change for $50 on a city bus!

o *ʔaddē 3a-ššáxiṣ, law samáɦit?*
◇ *la-wēn wāṣli[1]?*
o *burj ɦammūd.*
◇ *alf w xamsmīt līra.*
o *tfáḍḍal.*
◇ *3am tíɦki 3an jadd, [Fmadame]? akīd ma má3i ṣrāfit xamsīn dólar 3a bāṣ 3a-lxáṭṭ.[2]*

[1] = رايْحة؟ *rāyiɦ*

[2] مدام، ما معِك أزْغر؟ *[Fmadame], ma má3ik ázɣar?* **Ma'am, don't you have anything smaller** [a smaller bill]**?**

When you pay a driver, he might thank you by saying يْعوِّضُن *y3áwwiḍun,* **may [God] return** it, which is avery common blessing that implies "may God return this amount you just spent to you."

3

Making sure you are on the right bus

○ مرْحبا مْعلِّم، رايِح عَ طْرابْلُس؟

◇ أهْلا. لأ مدام. بسّ واصِل عَ جْبيْل.

○ إذا رِحِت معك عَ جْبيْل، بْلاقي باصات رايْحة عَ طْرابْلُس؟

◇ معْقولِة.[1] بسّ بِنْصحِك تاخْدي باص مِن هوْن. رح يْكون كْتير أصْعب تْلاقي باص مِن جْبيْل.

○ اه أوْكي. مرْسي كْتير.

◇ وَلا يْهِمِّك.

○ Hello, sir. Are you going to Tripoli?

◇ Welcome. No, ma'am. I'm only going to Jbeil.

○ If I go with you to Jbeil, will I find buses going to Tripoli?

◇ You might, but I recommend you catch one here; it's going to be much harder to find one from Jbeil.

○ Oh, okay. Thank you so much.

◇ Don't mention it.

○ *márɦaba m3állim, rāyiɦ 3a ţrāblus?*

◇ *áhla. laʔ, [ᶠmadame]. bass wāşil 3a jbēl.*

○ *íza ríɦit má3ak 3a jbēl, blēʔi bāşāt rāyɦa 3a ţrāblus?*

◇ *ma3ʔūli.*[1] *bass bínşaɦik tēxdi bāş min hōn. raɦ ykūn ktīr áş3ab tlēʔi bāş min jbēl.*

○ *āh okē. [ᶠmerci] ktīr.*

◇ *wála yhímmik.*

[1] معْقولِة *ma3ʔūli* (lit. reasonable, possible) is feminine here not because he's talking to a woman, but because it refers to the implied noun حالِة *ɦāli* **situation**. People also say معْقول *ma3ʔūl* in the masculine, likely in reference to a synonymous masculine noun, such as وَضِع *wáḍi3*.

Telling the driver where you want to get out

○ عفْواً خيّي. ويْن وودين باكْري؟ قالولي إنّو عَ طريقْنا.

◇ رح نوصل عَ وودين باكْري، بسّ هِيِّ عَ تاني مَيْلِة مْن الطّريق، وكْتير خِطْرة تِقْطع الطّريق.

○ شو بعْمِل؟

◇ أنا بِرأْيي خلّيك عالباص شْوَيّ، رح نمْرُق مِن حدّ جِسِر مُشاة. بْتِقْطعو بِسلامِة، وبْتِمْشي شي ميتيْن مِتْر وبْتوصل عالوودين.

○ أوْكي، بسّ پْليز ما تِنْساني.

◇ تِكْرم عَيْنك صديقي.

○ Excuse me, brother, where's Wooden Bakery? I was told this bus will pass by it on the way.

◇ We're almost at Wooden Bakery, but it's on the other side of the road, and it's very dangerous to cross.

○ What should I do?

◇ I advise you to stay on for a few minutes, as we'll drive by a pedestrian bridge shortly. You can then cross the freeway safely, and walk a couple hundred meters to Wooden Bakery.

○ Okay, just don't forget about me, please.

◇ You got it, my friend.

○ *3áfwan xáyyi. wēn [Wooden Bakery]? ʔālūli ínnu 3a ṭarīʔna.*

◇ *raḥ nūṣal 3a [Wooden Bakery], bass híyyi 3a tēni máyli mn iṭṭarīʔ, w ktīr xíṭra tiʔṭá3 iṭṭarīʔ.*

○ *šū bá3mil?*

◇ *ána bi-ráʔyi, xallīk 3a-lbāṣ šwayy, raḥ nímruʔ min ḥadd jísir mušē. btíʔta3u bi-salēmi, w btímši šī mītēn mitr w btūṣal 3a-l[Wooden].*

○ *okē, bass [please] ma tinsēni.*

◇ *tíkram 3áynak ṣadīʔi.*

5

Dealing with other passengers (1)

○ سوْري [1]، فِيي إقْعُد حدِّك؟ [2]
◇ أيْه أكيد. عِنْدِك مِشْكْلِة تِقِعْدي حدّ الشِّبّاك؟ لِأنّو بْتِلْعى نفْسي إذا أنا قعدِت. [3]
○ أيْه ما في مشْكل.
◇ مرْسي. وفْتحي الشِّبّاك إذا بدِّك. ما بِنْزِعِج.
○ هلّق ماشي الحال، بِفْتحو بعْد شْوَيّ إذا شوّبِت.
◇ أوْكي، مِتِل ما بِدِّك [4].

○ Excuse me, can I sit next to you?
◇ Yes, of course. Do you mind taking the window seat, though? I get nausea otherwise.
○ Sure, no problem.
◇ Thanks. And, feel free to open the window. That doesn't bother me.
○ Oh I'm okay for now. I will in a bit, if it gets too hot.
◇ Okay, as you wish.

○ *[sorry][1], fíyi íʔ3ud ɦáddik?[2]*
◇ *ē, akīd. 3índik míškli tiʔí3di ɦadd iššibbēk? li-ánnu btíl3a náfsi íza ána ʔa3ádit.[3]*
○ *ē, ma fī máškal.*
◇ *[Fmerci]. w ftáɦi -ššibbēk íza báddik. ma binzí3ij.*
○ *hállaʔ mēši -lɦāl, bíftaɦu ba3d šwayy íza šáwwabit.*
◇ *okē, mítil ma báddik[4].*

[1] = عفْواً *3áfwan* = عن إذْنِك *3an íznik* = لَوْ سمحْتي *law samáɦti* / [2] = فِيي إقْعُد جنْبِك؟ *fíyi íʔ3ud jánbik?* / [3] لأ معْليش، هَيْدا المكان محْجوز. *laʔ, ma3līš, háyda -lmakēn maɦjūz.* **No, sorry. This seat is reserved.** (Usually, people in Lebanon put a purse or something on an empty seat to indicate that it is reserved, usually for a spouse or friend who isn't on the bus yet and will be getting on later. / [4] = عَ راحْتِك *3a rāɦtik*

6

DEALING WITH OTHER PASSENGERS (2)

o پْليز[1] فيك تِطْفي السّيغارة؟

◇ وليْه بدّي طفّيا؟[2]

o لِأنّو ريحِتا بِتْقرِّف، ونِحْنا بِباص عامّ، ومكْتوب ممْنوع التّدْخين.

◇ هاها الهَيْقة جْديدِة هوْن. هَوْدي الأرمات منُّن إجْباري.[3]

(moves to another seat further away from the guy with the cigarette)

o منّي عم صدِّق قدّيْ وِقح هَيْدا.

o Excuse me. Can you please put out your cigarette?

◇ And why would I do that?

o Because it smells terrible, and we're on a public bus, and it says no smoking.

◇ Haha, sounds like you're new here. These signs aren't compulsory.

(moves to another seat further away from the guy with the cigarette)

o I can't believe how rude he is!

o *[please][1], fīk títfi -ssīgāra?*

◇ *w lē báddi ṭaffíya?*[2]

o *li-ánnu rīħíta bitʔárrif, w níħna bi-bāṣ 3āmm, w maktūb mamnū3 ittidxīn.*

◇ *ha ha, -lháyʔa jdīdi hōn. háwdi -lʔarmēt mánnun ijbāri.*[3]

(moves to another seat further away from the guy with the cigarette)

o *mánni 3am ṣáddiʔ ʔaddē wíʔiħ háyda.*

1 = عفْواً *3áfwan* = عْموْل معْروف *3mōl ma3rūf* = لوْ سمحِت *law samáħit*

2 أيْه أكيد. سوْري إذا زعجْتِك. *ē akīd. [sorry] íza za3ájtik.* **Yes, of course. Sorry if it bothered you.**

3 سوري، ما نْتبهِت *[sorry], ma ntabáhit* **Sorry, I didn't pay attention [to the sign].**

Extended Dialogue

○ بدّي أوصل عَ عمْشيت. أيّا باص لازِم آخُد؟

◇ عمْشيت منّا مدينِة كْبيرِة. فالباصات ما بيروحوا لهونيك. بدِّك تاخْدي باص عَ جْبيْل، بْترِجْعي بْتاخْدي تاكْسي أَوْ سرْفيس مِن هونيك.

○ اه أوْكي. أيّا باص لازِم آخُد؟

◇ الباص الأحْمر هونيك.

(approaches the red bus)

○ مرْحبا[1]، قالولي إنْتَ رايِح عَ جْبيْل؟

◇ أيْه، إن الله راد. تْفضّلي.

○ مرْسي. قدّيْ بِترْيد لهونيك؟

◇ ألْف وخمْسْمية بسّ.

○ يَعْني دوْلار واحد، ما هيْك؟ تْفضّل.

◇ مظْبوط. مرْسي مدام.

○ فيك پْليز تْقِلّي بسّ نوصل عَ جْبيْل؟ وَلا مرّة رايْحة قبِل وبدّي آخُد تاكْسي مِن هونيك عَ عمْشيت.

◇ أيْه، ما تِعْطلي همّ، رح نزّلِك حدّ التّاكْسِيات، وبْخلّي واحد مِن أصْحابي شوْفوريِةْ التّاكْسي يِهْتمّ فيكي.

○ أوْكي مْعلِّم. مرْسي كْتير. كلِّك ذوْق!

◇ وَلا يْهِمِّك. وَلَوْ.[2] مِن عَيْنيّ.[3]

○ الله يْخلّيك.

◇ وإنْتي كمان عَيْني. يَلّا منْفِلّ بعْد نِتْفِة.[4]

○ مرْسي كْتير![5]

- o I want to get to Amchit, which bus should I take?
- ◇ Amchit is not a major city, so buses don't go there directly. You'll have to take a bus to Jbeil, and then take a taxi or service from there.
- o Oh, okay! Which one should I take?
- ◇ The red one over there.

(approaches the red bus)

- o Hi there, I was told you're going to Jbeil?
- ◇ Yes, God willing. Get on.
- o Thank you, sir. How much is the fare for there?
- ◇ Just 1,500 L.L.
- o That's one dollar, correct? Here you go.
- ◇ Exactly. Thank you, ma'am.
- o Will you please tell me when we get to Jbeil? I've never been, and I need to catch a taxi from there to Amchit.
- ◇ Yes, don't you worry. I'll drop you off by the taxi stand and ask one of my driver friends to take care of you.
- o Okay, sir. Thank you so much. That's so kind.
- ◇ Don't mention it. It's my pleasure.
- o God bless you.
- ◇ You, too, dear. We'll be leaving in a few minutes.
- o Thanks a lot!

- o *báddi ūṣal 3a 3amšīt. áyya bāṣ lēzim ēxud?*
- ◇ *3amšīt mánna madīni kbīri. fa-lbāṣāt ma birūħu la-hunīk. báddik tēxdi bāṣ 3a jbēl, btírja3i btēxdi táksi aw [ᶠservice] min hunīk.*
- o *āh okē. áyya bāṣ lēzim ēxud?*
- ◇ *-lbāṣ ilʔáħmar hunīk.*

(approaches the red bus)

- o *márħaba*[1]*, ʔālūli ínta rāyiħ 3a jbēl?*
- ◇ *ē, in álla rād. tfáḍḍali.*
- o *[ᶠmerci]. ʔaddē bitrīd la-hunīk?*
- ◇ *alf w xamsmíyyi bass.*
- o *yá3ni dólar wāħad, ma hēk? tfáḍḍal.*

◇ *maẓbūṭ. [ᶠmerci], [ᶠmadame].*
○ *fīk [please] tʔílli bass nūṣal 3a jbēl? wála márra rāyḩa ʔábil w báddi ēxud táksi min hunīk 3a 3amšīt.*
◇ *ē, ma tí3ṭali hamm, raḩ názzlik ḩadd ittáksiyēt, w bxálli wāḩad min aṣḩābi šōfūríyyit ittáksi yihtámm fīki.*
○ *okē m3állim. [ᶠmerci] ktīr. kíllak zōʔ!*
◇ *wála yhímmik. waláw.*[2] *min 3áynayyi.*[3]
○ *álla yxallīk.*
◇ *w ínti kamēn 3áyni. yálla minfíll ba3d nítfi.*[4]
○ *[ᶠmerci] ktīr!*[5]

1 يَعْطيك العافْيِة *ya3ṭīk il3āfyi* **May God give you good health!** (a common greeting to someone working)

2 وَلَو *waláw* **you're welcome, no problem.**

3 = تِكْرمي *tíkrami*

4 = رح نِمْشي بعْد شْوَيّ *raḩ nímši ba3d šwayy*

5 = يِسْلمو *yíslamu* = شُكْراً *šúkran*

Vocabulary

bus	*bāṣ* *bōsṭa*	باص بوْسطة
to take a bus	*áxad (yēxud) bāṣ*	أخد (ياخُد) باص
to change buses	*báddal (ybáddil) bāṣāt* *ɣáyyar (yɣáyyir) bāṣāt*	بدّل (يْبدِّل) باصات غيّر (يْغيِّر) باصات
minibus	*míni bāṣ* *[van]*	ميني باص ڤان
door	*bēb (bwēb)*	باب (بْواب)
window	*šibbēk (šbēbīk)*	شِبّاك (شْبابيك)
seat	*máʔ3ad (maʔē3id)*	مقْعد (مقاعِد)
direction	*ittijēh*	اِتِّجاهْ
map	*xarīṭa (xarāyiṭ)*	خريطة (خرايِط)
sign	*yāfṭa*	يافْطة
stairs	*dáraj*	درج
pedestrian sidewalk	*manáṣṣa*	منصّة
exit	*máxraj* *ḍáhra*	مخْرج ضهْرة
entrance	*mádxal* *fáwti*	مدْخل فَوْتِة
boarding, getting on	*rukūb* *ṭál3a*	رُكوب طلْعة

to get on; to ride	*ríkib (yírkab)* *ţíli3 (yíţla3)*	رِكِب (يِركب) طِلِع (يِطْلع)
getting off	*nzūl* *názli*	نْزول نزْلِة
to get off	*nízil (yínzal)*	نِزِل (يِنْزل)
to load up (with passengers)	*ɦámmal (yɦámmil)* *3ábba (y3ábbi)*	حمّل (يْحمِّل) عبّى (يْعبّي)
front seat (next to the driver)	*máʔ3ad ʔidmēni*	مقْعد قِدْماني
tunnel	*náfaʔ (anfēʔ)*	نفق (أنْفاق)
express, direct	*díɣri* *[Fdirect]*	دِغْري ديريْكْت
first class	*-ddáraji -lʔūla*	الدّرجِة الأُولى
second class	*-ddáraji -ttēnyi*	الدّرجِة التانْية
air-conditioned	*mukáyyif*	مْكيِّف
inspector	*mufáttiš*	مْفتِّش
fine	*ɣarāmi* *ẓábiţ*	غرامِة ظبِط
to be fined	*áxad (yēxud) ẓábiţ* *ákal (yēkul) ẓábiţ*	أخد (ياخْد) ظبِط أكل (ياكُل) ظبِط

Expressions

Where is the bus to __?	*wēn ilbāṣ 3a __?*	وين الباص عَ __؟
Does this bus go to __?	*háyda -lbāṣ birūḥ šī 3a __?*	هَيْدا الباص بيروح شي عَ __؟
I'm going to __. Which bus should I take?	*rāyiḥ 3a __, ayy bāṣ lēzim ēxud?*	رايِح عَ __، أيّ باص لازِم آخُد؟
What time does this bus leave?	*áyya sē3a byímši háyda -lbāṣ/ háydi -lbōsṭa?*	أيّا ساعة بْيِمْشي هَيْدا الباص/ هَيْدي البوْسْطة؟
How much is it to go to __?	*ʔaddē íza báddi rūḥ 3a __?*	قدّيْ إذا بدّي روح عَ __؟
Two seats to __, please.	*maʔ3adēn 3a __, law samáḥit.*	مقْعدين عَ __ لَوْ سمحِت.
The bus is full. We can't take anymore passengers.	*-lbāṣ mfáwwal. ma fīna nēxud rikkēb.*	الباص مْفوّل. ما فينا ناخُد رِكّاب بقى.
(paying) I don't have anything smaller.	*ma má3i ázɣar.*	ما معي أزْغر.
You need to give me back 2,000 L.L.	*báddak tríddli alfēn līra.*	بدّك تْرِدْلي ألْفيْن ليرة.
How much longer to __?	*ʔaddē báddna wáʔit la __?* *ʔaddē báddna wáʔit ta-nūṣal 3a __?*	قدّيْ بدْنا وَقِت لـ__؟ قدّيْ بدْنا وَقِت تنوصل عَ __؟
Drop me off at the nearest place to __.	*nazzílni 3a áʔrab máṭraḥ/maḥáll la __.*	نزّلْني عَ أقْرب مطْرح/محلّ لـ__.

I want to get out near/at __.	*báddi ínzal ɦadd/3a...*	بدّي إنْزل حدّ/عَ __.
I want to get out here, sir.	*báddi ínzal hōn, ráyyis.*	بدّي إنْزل هوْن، ريِّس.
Anywhere here.	*ɦayálla máṭraɦ/ maɦáll hōn.*	حَيَلّا مطْرح/محلّ هوْن.
Drop me off by the tunnel.	*nazzílni ɦadd it[ᶠtunnel]/innáfaʔ.*	نزِّلني حدّ التّونيْل/النّفق .
Excuse me, can I get by? I'm getting off in a bit.	*[sorry], fíyi ímruʔ? nēzil ba3d nítfi/ba3d šwayy.*	سوْري، فِيي إمْرُق؟ نازِل بعْد نِتْفِة/بعْد شْوَيّ.

◇

This isn't the bus you should be on. Get off, cross the pedestrian bridge, and take the bus in the opposite direction.	*háyda miš ilbāṣ -lli lēzim tkūn 3lē. nzēl, ʔṭā3 jísir ilmušēt, w ṭlā3 3a bāṣ bi-lʔittijēh ittēni.*	هَيْدا مِش الباص اللي لازِم تْكون عْليْه. نْزال، قْطاع جِسِر المُشاةْ، وطْلاع عَ باص بِالاتِّجاه التّاني.
Yes, we still have some room for passengers. Get on.	*ē, ba3d 3ínna máṭraɦ la-kám rēkib. ṭlā3.*	أيْه، بعْد عِنّا مطْرح لكم راكِب. طْلاع.
A couple more passengers, then we'll be on our way.	*ba3d kam rēkib, w mnímši.*	بعْد كم راكِب، ومْنِمْشي.
You pay when you get on, not as you're getting off.	*btídfa3 ínta w ṭāli3 3a-lbāṣ/3a-lbōsṭa, miš ínta w nēzil/fēlil.*	بْتِدْفع إنْتَ وطالع عالباص/عالبوْسْطة، مِش إنْتَ ونازِل/فالِل .

At the Airport عالمطار

مطار رفيق الحريري الدُّوَلي *maṭār rafīʔ ilḥarīri -ddúwali* **Rafic Hariri International Airport**, also known colloquially as مطار بَيْروت *maṭār bayrūt* **the Beirut Airport**, is the only commercial airport in Lebanon. It is decent and somewhat modern, but it is not very organized relative to major international airports in the U.S. or Europe. With tourism being Lebanon's largest source of income, you might expect the airport to be equipped to welcome large numbers of passengers coming and going. But this is simply not the case. It is often extremely crowded, and passengers, Lebanese citizens and foreigners alike, have often taken to social media their calls for renovations and more order; so much so, that the government is working on building an extension (as of press time) that would meet these needs. At customs, you can expect to see different: one for Lebanese passport holders, and one for foreigners. Visitors from over 80 countries, including the likes of the U.S. and the U.K., can obtain visitor visas upon arrival and can stay for one month (extendable to two). It's best to check the website of the Lebanese Embassy or Consulate in your country for visa rules prior to traveling. Also, the airport's website has some good information on visas and rules www.aeroport-beyrouth.com/en/visa_on_arrival_lebanon.php

Going through security

◇ السّيْلوليرْ واللابْتوْپ بِالتّراي ورْجاع مْروق

o مِشي الحال؟[1]

◇ سوْري رْجاع فوت شْلاح صُبّاطك ورْجاع مْروق.[2]

◇ Cell phone and laptop on the tray, then pass through.

o Am I all right?

◇ Sorry, go back through and take off your shoes and pass through again.

◇ *-s[^F cellulaire] w il[laptop] bi-t[tray] w rjā3 mrūʔ*

o *míši -lḫāl?*[1]

◇ *[sorry] rjā3 fūt šlāḫ ṣubbāṭak w rjā3 mrūʔ.*[2]

[1] = مْنيح هيْك؟ *mnīḫ hēk?*

[2] أيْه مِشي الحال، تْفضّل. *ē míši -lḫāl, tfáḍḍal.* **Yes, all good. Go ahead.**

It is recommended that you book a taxi before landing in Beirut, and specify that you want the driver to wait for you with a plaque with your name on it in English. It's the smoothest way to get a ride from the airport. Otherwise, you'll have to find a taxi outside. And, while they're abundant, it is such a hassle to go about it that way. They will all try to get you to book their services by screaming from every direction, and it is not pleasant.

2

Checking in

◇ بْتحِبّي مقْعد عالشِّبّاك أَوْ عالطّرف[1]؟

o عالشِّبّاك پْليز.

◇ تمام. بسّ هَيْدا المُرْطْبان ما فيكي تاخْدي بِشنْطِة إيدِك.

o بسّ منّو سايِل[2]. بسّ في مْربّى.

◇ وإذا. ما فيكي تاخْدي معِك.

◇ Would you like a window or aisle seat?

o A window seat, please.

◇ Okay. But that jar cannot be taken as carry on.

o It's not liquid; it's just jam.

◇ You still can't take it.

◇ *bitḥíbbi máʔ3ad 3a-ššibbēk aw 3a-ṭṭáraf[1]?*

o *3a-ššibbēk, [please].*

◇ *tamēm. bass háyda -lmurṭbēn ma fīki tēxdi bi-šánṭit īdik.*

o *bass mánnu ṣēyil[2]. bass fī mrábba.*

◇ *w íza. ma fīki tēxdi má3ik.*

1 = عالممرّ *3a-lmamárr*

2 = ليكيد *[Fliquide]*

3

Checking in baggage

◇ هَيْدي الشّنْطة تِسْعة وعِشْرين كيلو. ما فينا نمرِّقا هيْك.[1]

○ أوْكي دْمْوازيْل، سِتِّة كيلو زْيادِة. مِش مْصيبِة.[2]

◇ عم قلِّك منّا وارْدِة[3]. جرّبي قصّميا عَ شنْطتيْن.

○ بسّ التّانْيِة كْتير زْغيرِة مِتِل منِّك[4] شايْفِة.

◇ طْلعي مْن الصّفّ فإذاً. ظبّطِينْ وقصّمِينْ عن جْديد ورْجعي لعِنْدي.

◇ This suitcase is 29 kilograms and cannot be checked in like this.

○ Okay, ma'am, it's only six kilograms over. No big deal.

◇ I'm telling you, it's not possible. Try to divide it into two suitcases.

○ But the other one is too small, as you can see.

◇ Take a step back, adjust and redistribute them, then come back again.

◇ *háydi -ššánṭa tís3a w 3išrīn kīlu. ma fīna nmárriʔa hēk.*[1]

○ *okē, [Fdemoiselle], sítti kīlu zyēdi. miš mṣībi.*[2]

◇ *3am ʔíllik mánna wērdi*[3]*. járrbi ʔaṣṣmíya 3a šanṭtēn.*

○ *bass ittēnyi ktīr zɣīri mítil mánnik*[4] *šēyfi.*

◇ *ṭlá3i mn iṣṣáff fa-ízan. ẓabbṭíyun w ʔaṣṣmíyun 3an jdīd w rjá3i la-3índi.*

[1] معك وَزن زايد. *má3ik wázin zēyid.* **Your bags are too heavy.**

[2] = مِش مِشْكْلِة *miš míškli*

[3] = وَلا مُمْكِن *wála múmkin*

[4] مَنّك *mánnak* can mean **you are not**. However, here, it is another way of saying colloquially ما إنْتَ *ma ínta*. So مِتِل مَنِّك شايْفِة *mítil mánnik šāyfi* means مِتِل ما إنْتي شايْفِة *mítil ma ínti šāyfi* **as you see**.

At passport control (1)

o لَوْ سمحْتي. فيكي تْقِليلي إذا واقْفِة بِالصّفّ المظْبوط؟

◇ پاسْپوْرك لِبْناني أَوْ أجْنبي؟[1]

o أجْنبي. أميْركاني.

◇ فإذاً لازِم توقفي بِالصّفّ يَلّي هونيك. هَيْدا الصّفّ هوْن للپاسْپوْرات اللِّبْنانية.[2]

o Excuse me, can you tell me if I'm standing in the right line?

◇ Are you here on a Lebanese passport or a foreign passport?

o A foreign passport. American.

◇ In that case, you should stand in that line over there. This one is for Lebanese passport holders.

o *law samáħti. fīki tʔilīli íza wēʔfi bi-ṣṣáff ilmaẓbūṭ?*

◇ *paspōrik libnēni aw ájnabi?*[1]

o *ájnabi. amerkēni.*

◇ *fa-ízan lēzim tūʔafi bi-ṣṣáff yálli hunīk. háyda -ṣṣaff hōn la-lpaspōrāt illibnēníyyi.*[2]

[1] حضرْتِك لِبْنانية أَوْ أجْنبية؟ *ħáḍirtik libnēníyyi aw ajnabíyyi?* **Are you Lebanese or a foreigner?**

[2] أيْه مظْبوط، هَيْدا الصّفّ للْپاسْپوْرات الأجْنبية. *ē, maẓbūṭ, háyda -ṣṣaff la-lpaspōrāt ilʔajnabíyyi.* **Yes, this is the line for foreign passport holders.**

5

At passport control (2)

◇ پاسْپوْرِك لَوْ سمحْتي.

o تْفضّل.

◇ بسّ شكْلِك كْتير مْغيرّ.

o قصّيْت شعْري بسّ.

◇ اه أوْكي. وهَيْدا الپاسْپوْر ختمْناه. توصلي بِالسّلامِة.

◇ Your passport, please.
o Here you are.
◇ But you look so different.
o I've cut my hair. That's all.
◇ Ah, I see. Here's your stamped passport. Have a good trip!

◇ *paspōrik, law samáħti.*
o *tfáḍḍal.*
◇ *bass šáklik ktīr mɣáyyar.*
o *ʔaṣṣēt šá3ri bass.*
◇ *āh okē. w háyda -lpaspōr xatamnē. tūṣali bi-ssalēmi.*

There are some unwritten tipping rules you should keep in mind at the airport. For instance, الشيّالين *-ššiyyēlīn* **baggage handlers** expect to be tipped, even if there's no set fee, as you'd expect in some other airports. Their expectations have gone up from a couple of U.S. dollars to about $5 now. Anything less will likely be frowned upon, and that, of course, varies from handler to handler. Cleaning staff keep the airport, especially the bathrooms, sparkling clean; and, while it is not mandatory to tip them, they would be grateful if you did, even if just a dollar or two.

6

FINDING YOUR GATE

o كيف فِيي أوصل عَ جايْتِ[1] رقِم تْنعْش؟

◇ خلّيكي ماشْيِة وخِدي تالِت يمَين.[2]

o أوْكيْ! مِرْسي كْتير.[3]

◇ تِكْرم عَيْنِك. بسّ سْتعْجْلي شْوَيّ تتوصلي عالوَقِت.

o How can I reach gate number 12?

◇ Keep walking and take the third right.

o Okay, thanks a lot.

◇ You're welcome. But hurry to make it [in time].

o *kīf fíyi ūṣal 3a [gate][1] ráʔim tna3š?*

◇ *xallīki mēšyi w xídi tēlit yamīn.[2]*

o *okē! [Fmerci] ktīr.[3]*

◇ *tíkram 3áynik. bass stá3jli šwayy ta-tūṣali 3a-lwáʔit.*

1 = بُوّابِة *buwwēbi*

2 روحي دِغْري، رْجعي فْرِقي يمين. *rūħi díɣri rjá3i fríʔi yamīn.* **Go straight then turn right.**

3 = يِسْلمو *yíslamu* = شُكْراً *šūkran* = كِلّك ذوْق *kíllik zōʔ*

Extended Dialogue

◇ هَيْدي أوّل مرّة بِتْغُطّي[1] بمِطار بَيْروت؟

o لأ بْروح وبِجي عْلَيْه كْتير.

◇ الهَيْقة بْتِجي عالمنْطقة كْتير؟

o صرْلي كم سِنِة عايْشِة بِلِبْنان، وبِرْجع عَ بلدي بِالفُرص.

◇ اه حِلو كْتير. لازِم تْحُطّي السّيْنْتور لأِنّو رح نْغُطّ[2] بعْد نِتْفِة[3].

o بِتْحِبّي تاخْدي عِلْكِة؟

◇ يِسْلمو! الأرْجح[4] نْعوزا![5]

(The plane lands.)

◇ حمْدِالله عالسّلامِة![6]

o الله يْسلْمِك.

◇ بِتْحِبّي ساعْدِك بِالشِّنط؟

o يا ريْت، بْكون ممْنونْتِك.[7]

(They disembark together and wait for their luggage at baggage claim.)

o شو؟! بطّل في شِنط؟

◇ لأ، وبعْد في إلي شنْطة الظّاهِر ما كانِت عالطّيّارة.

o وأنا ذات الشّي.[8]

◇ أوْكي لْحقيني. أنا دايْماً هيْك بيصير معي.

o شو مْنعْمِل هلّق؟

◇ مِنروح عَ شِبّاك الشِّنط الضّايْعة ومِنْبلِّغ عنْن. إجْمالاً بْيوصلوا عالطّيّارة اللي بعْدا.

o انْشالله![9]

◇ انْشالله. خلّينا نْبلِّغ عنْن بِالأوّل ومِنْشوف شو بيصير.

◇ Is this your first time landing at Beirut airport?
o No, I travel to and from it a lot.
◇ Looks like you're in the region often?
o I've actually been living here in Lebanon for a few years, and I just go back home on vacations.
◇ Very nice. You'd better fasten your seatbelt. We're about to land.
o Would you like some gum?
◇ Thank you. We probably need it.

(The plane lands.)

◇ Thank God you arrived safely!
o Bless you!
◇ Would you like any help with the luggage?
o Yes, I'd really appreciate that!

(They disembark together and wait for their luggage at baggage claim.)

o What!? No more suitcases?
◇ Nope... And I still have one suitcase that apparently wasn't on the plane.
o Same for me.
◇ All right, follow me. This always happens to me.
o What shall we do now?
◇ We'll go to the lost luggage window and report them. Sometimes they'll arrive on the next plane.
o I hope so!
◇ Hopefully! Let's report it first and see what happens.

◇ *háydi áwwal márra bitɣúṭṭi*[1] *bi-maṭār bayrūt?*
o *laʔ brūḫ w bíji 3lē ktīr.*
◇ *-lháyʔa btíji 3a-lmánṭaʔa ktīr?*
o *ṣárli kam síni 3āyši bi-libnēn, w bírja3 3a báladi bi-lfúraṣ.*
◇ *āh, ḫílu ktīr. lēzim tḫúṭṭi -s[*[F]*ceinture] li-ánnu raḫ nɣuṭṭ*[2] *ba3d nítfi*[3].
o *bitḫíbbi tēxdi 3ílki?*
◇ *yíslamu! -lʔárjaḫ*[4] *n3ūza!*[5]

(The plane lands.)

◇ *ḫamdílla 3a-ssalēmi!*[6]
o *álla ysállmik.*

◇ *bitḫíbbi sē3dik bi-šínaṭ?*
O *ya rēt, bkūn mamnūntik.*[7]
(They disembark together and wait for their luggage at baggage claim.)

O *šū?! báṭṭal fī šínaṭ?*
◇ *la?, w ba3d fī íli šánṭa -ẓẓāhir ma kēnit 3a-ṭṭayyāra.*
O *w ána zēt iššī.*[8]
◇ *okē lḫa?īni. ána dēyman hēk biṣīr má3i.*
O *šū mná3mil hálla??*
◇ *minrūḫ 3a šibbēk iššínaṭ iḍḍāy3a w minbálliɣ 3ánun. ijmēlan byūṣalu 3a-ṭṭayyāra -lli bá3da.*
O *nšálla!*[9]
◇ *nšálla. xallīna nbálliɣ 3ánun bi-l?áwwal w minšūf šū biṣīr.*

[1] = بْتِنْزلي *btínzali* = بْتِهْبْطي *btihíbṭi*

[2] = نِنْزل *nínzal* = نِهْبُط *níhbuṭ*

[3] = بعْد شْوَيّ *ba3d šwayy*

[4] الأرْجح *-l?árjaḫ* **probably**

[5] لأ يِسْلمو، كِلَّك ذوْق. *la?, yíslamu, kíllik zō?.* **No, thank you.** كِلّك ذوْق *kíllak zō?* is a common expression that means **you have good manners**, and, here, implies, that it was nice of you to offer.

[6] = حمْدِالله عَ وْصولِك بِالسّلامِة! *ḫamdílla 3a wṣūlik bi-ssalēmi!*

[7] أيْ، عْمِلي معْروف *ē, 3míli ma3rūf*

[8] = وأنا نفْس الشّي *w ána nafs iššī*

[9] = يا ريْت! *ya rēt!*

Vocabulary

airport	*maṭār*	مطار
hall	*ṣāli*	صالِة
arrivals	*-lmajīʔ*	المجيء
departure	*-lfálli*	الفلّة
ticket	*tázkara (tazēkir)*	تذْكرة (تذاكِر)
airline	*šírkit ṭayarān*	شِركْةِ طَيَران
worker	*šaɣɣīl*	شغّيل
suitcase	*šánṭa (šínaṭ)*	شنْطة (شِنط)
luggage	*šínaṭ sáfar*	شِنط سفر
luggage cart	*karrājit šínaṭ*	كرّاجِةْ شِنط
wrapping (suitcases with silicon wrap)	*taɣlīf*	تغْليف
weight	*wázin (awzēn)*	وَزِن (أَوْزان)
over the weight limit	*fōʔ ilwázin ilmasmūḥ* *wázin zēyid*	فوْق الوَزِن المسْموح وَزِن زايِد
forbidden	*mamnū3*	ممْنوع
liquids	*sawēyil*	سَوايِل
blade, sharp object	*ēli ḥāddi*	آلِة حادِّة
conveyor belt; baggage carousel	*sēr*	سيرْ
conveyor belt; baggage carousel	*ʔšāṭ*	قْشاط
passport control	*(tadʔīʔ il)jawēzēt*	(تدْقيق الـ)جَوازات

stamp	*xítim*	خِتِم
officer	*ẓābiṭ*	ظابِط
inspection, search	*tiftīš*	تِفْتيش
(penalty) fine	*ɣarāmi*	غرامِة
shuttle bus	*[shuttle]*	شاتل
gate	*[gate]* *buwwēbi*	جايْت بُوّابِة
plane	*ṭayyāra*	طيّارة
boarding	*[boarding]*	بوْرْدينْج
window	*šibbēk (šbēbīk)*	شِبّاك (شْبابيك)
corridor	*[corridor]*	كوْريدوْر
take-off	*iʔlēʒ*	إقْلاع
landing	*hubūṭ*	هُبوط
belt	*ʔšāṭ* *[ᶠceinture]*	قْشاط سينْتور
to fasten	*rábaṭ (yírbuṭ)* *ɦaṭṭ (yɦuṭṭ)*	ربط (يِرْبُط) حطّ (يْحُطّ)
flight attendant	*muḍīf*	مُضيف
pilot	*ṭayyār*	طيّار
captain	*[captain]*	كابْتِن
trip, flight	*ríɦli* *sáfra*	رِحْلِة سفْرة

transit	*[transit]*	ترانْزيت
to arrive	*wíṣil (yūṣal)*	وِصِل (يوصل)
to travel	*sēfar (ysēfir)*	سافر (يْسافِر)

Expressions

○

I would like to wrap this suitcase [in silicon], please.	*báddi ɣállif háydi -ššánṭa, 3mōl ma3rūf.*	بدّي غلِّف هَيْدي الشّنْطة عْموْل معْروف.
Excuse me. This suitcase is heavy. Can you put it on the conveyor belt for me?	*[sorry], -ššánṭa tʔíli. fīk tsē3ídni ḫúṭṭa 3a-liʔšāṭ.*	سوْري، الشّنْطة تْقيلِة. فيك تْساعِدْني حُطّا عالِقْشاط؟
There's a suitcase [of mine] that hasn't arrived.	*fī šánṭa ma waṣálit.*	في شنْطة ما وَصلِت.

◇

Jacket and shoes in the tray, please.	*-l[Fjaquette] w ilbōt 3a-ṣṣaníyyi.*	الجاكيتّ والبوت عَالصّنية.
Raise your arms, please.	*3áli īdēk, 3mōl ma3rūf*	علي إيديْك عْموْل معْروف.
Could you take off your belt?	*fīk tíšlaḫ is-[Fceinture]?*	فيك تِشْلح السّيْنْتور؟
Chicken or beef?	*djēj aw láḫmi?*	دْجاج أَوْ لحْمِة؟
Cola or juice?	*kōla aw 3aṣīr?*	كوْلا أَوْ عصير؟
What does the suitcase look like?	*kīf šakl iššánṭa?*	كيف شكْل الشّنْطة؟

At a Restaurant بِالمطْعم

Food is such a big part of Lebanese culture that it's hard to think of an outing that doesn't involve eating. It probably has to do with the fact that الأكِل اللِّبْناني -lʔákil illibnēni **Lebanese cuisine** is so exquisite–and that is a fact! Lebanese cuisine is popular the world over. While you can still find foreign cuisines in Lebanon, they're not nearly as popular as they are in the U.S. or Europe; Lebanese tend to prefer their own cuisine.

In Lebanon, أرْجيلِة *árgili* **hookah (shisha, waterpipe)** is just as much an integral part of the culture as is eating out. Given the choice, many people will choose smoking hookah over eating! Most restaurants offer hookah on their menus. There are lots of flavors to choose from. تِفّاحْتين *tiffēɧtēn* **two apples** is a popular one named for its green and red apple flavoring; another popular flavor is حامُض ونعْنع *ɧāmuḍ w ná3na3* **mint and lemon**. Note that hookahs are not only at restaurants; they're also at bakeries (See the Bakery chapter on p. 73), cafés, bars, etc. Hookahs are so popular in Lebanon that, for a few years now, there have been hookah home delivery services where not only do you get your hookah, but they can also replenish your coal and tobacco.

Ordering food (1)

- o پْليز، بدّي طاووق وبطاطا مِقْلية.
- ◇ بِتْحِبّي تاخْدي[1] صحِن حُمُّص معُن؟
- o لأ بِلا حُمُّص[2]، بسّ باخُد بابا غنوج، إذا بِتْريد. وفِيي كمان آخُد أرْغيلِة؟ حامُض ونعْنع.
- ◇ تِكْرم عَيْنِك![3]

- o I'd like an order of chicken skewers with fries.
- ◇ Would you like an order of hummus with that?
- o No hummus, but I'd like some baba ghanoush, please. And can I also have a hookah, please? The mint and lemon flavor.
- ◇ Coming right up!

- o *[please], báddi ţāwū? w baţāţa mi?líyyi.*
- ◇ *bitɧíbbi tēxdi*[1] *şáɧin ɧúmmuş má3un?*
- o *la? bála ɧúmmuş*[2]*, bass bēxud bāba ɣanūj, íza bitrīd. w fíyi kamēn ēxud argīli? ɧāmuḑ w ná3na3.*
- ◇ *tíkram 3áynik!*[3]

[1] = بدِّك *báddik*

[2] أيْ، عْموْل معْروف *ē, 3mōl ma3rūf* = أيْ إذا بِتْريد *ē, íza bitrīd* **Yes, please.**

[3] = مِن هالعينْ قبِل هالعينْ *min ha-l3ēn ?ábil ha-l3ēn* = مِن عْيوني *min 3yūni* = حاضِر *ɧāḑir*

2

Ordering Food (2)

◇ شو بِتْحِبّو تِطِلْبو شباب؟[1]

○ بدّْنا نْعذّْبك[2] ريِّس بِعِشْرين وِحْدِةْ شَوَرْما دْجاج وخمسْتعْشر وِحْدِةْ شَوَرْما لحْمِة.

◇ بِتْحِبّوا[3] توم مع شوَرْما الدّْجاج وطْحينِة مع شوَرْما اللّحْمِة؟

○ أيْه إذا بِتْريد. بدّْنا كِلّ شي فِيُنْ.[4] إذا فيك تْلبّينا عالسّريع، مِنْكون ممْنونين لِأنّو كْتير جوعانين.

◇ What would you like to order, gentlemen?

○ Listen, boss, we want 20 chicken shawarmas and 15 beef shawarmas.

◇ Would you like garlic sauce with the chicken shawarma and tahini with the beef shawarmas?

○ Yes, please! All the works! If you could make them quickly, that would be great because we are starving!

◇ *šū bitḫíbbu tiṭílbu šabēb?*[1]

○ *báddna n3ázzbak*[2] *ráyyis bi-3išrīn wíḫdit šawárma djēj w xamstá3šar wíḫdit šawárma láḫmi.*

◇ *bitḫíbbu*[3] *tūm ma3 šawárma -ddjēj w ṭḫīni ma3 šawárma -lláḫmi?*

○ *ē, íza bitrīd. báddna kill šī fíyun.*[4] *íza fīk tlabbīna 3a-ssarī3, minkūn mamnūnīn li-ánnu ktīr jū3ānīn.*

[1] جاهْزين آخُد الأوْرْدر؟ *jēhzīn ēxud il?[order]?* **Are you ready for me to take your order?** / [2] أيْ جاهْزين، بلْيز كْتوب عِنْدك... *ē jēhzīn, [please] ktūb 3índak...* **Yes, we're ready. Please write down...** / [3] = بْحِطِّلْكُن *bḫiṭṭílkun* **Shall I put...?** / [4] لأ، بلا توم. راجْعين عالشّغِل، ما بدّْنا تْكون ريحِةْ تمنا توم. *la?, bála tōm. rāj3īn 3a-ššíɣil, ma báddna tkūn rīḫit támana tōm.* **No, garlic sauce. We're going back to work and don't want to smell like garlic.**

3

ORDERING FOOD (3)

○ بِقْدر آخُد سانْدْويشْتينْ فلافِل، مع طْحينِة عَ جنب، عْمِلي معْروف؟
◇ إجانا كبيس كْتير طازة. بِتْحِبّي حِطِّلّك بِالسّانْدْويش؟
○ مِش كْتير بْحِبّ الكبيس، بسّ فيكي تْحِطّيلّي شْوَيّ عَ جنب بركي رْفيقْتي تْحِبُّن؟ وفينا كمان ناخُد فحِم[1] للأرْغيلِة؟
◇ أكيد، تِكْرم عَيْنِك.

○ I'd like two falafel sandwiches and tahini on the side, please.
◇ We also have very fresh pickles. Would you like some on the sandwiches?
○ I'm not a great fan of pickles, but can I get some on the side, in case my friend would like some? Also, can we get some coal for the hookah?
◇ Absolutely!

○ *bíʔdar ēxud [(F)sandwich]tēn falēfil, ma3 ţђīni 3a jánab, 3míli ma3rūf?*
◇ *ijēna kabīs ktīr ţāza. bitђíbbi ђiţţíllik bi-s[(F)sandwich]?*
○ *miš ktīr bђibb ilkabīs, bass fīki tђiţţílli šwayy 3a jánab, bárki rfīʔti tђíbbun? w fīna kamēn nēxud fáђim[1] la-lʔargīli?*
◇ *akīd, tíkram 3áynik.*

[1] فحِم *fáђim* **embers/coal** keeps the smoke coming. When the hookah seems to be dying out, you can ask for more embers if the waiter isn't already tending to the embers periodically.

4

ORDERING FOOD (4)

o عْملي معْروف، فِيي إطْلُب تْنينْ تبّولِة كْبار؟
◇ أكيد! عَ بالِك شي بطاطا أَوْ حُمُّص معُن؟
o لأ مرْسي. بسّ التبّولِة پْليز.[1]
◇ أكيد مِتِل ما بدِّك[2].

o Could I get two large orders of tabbouleh, please?
◇ Sure, would you like some extra fries or extra hummus with it?
o No, thank you. Just the tabbouleh, please.
◇ Of course, as you wish!

o *3míli ma3rūf, fíyi íṭlub tnēn tabbūli kbār?*
◇ *akīd! 3a bēlik šī baṭāṭa aw ḫúmmuṣ má3un?*
o *la? [Fmerci]. bass ittabbūli, [please].*[1]
◇ *akīd mítil ma báddik*[2].

[1] لأ، بسّ إذا في فتّوش، باخُد واحد كْبير عْمِلي معْروف. *la?, bass íza fī fattūš, bēxud wāḫad kbīr, 3míli ma3rūf.*

[2] تِكْرم عَيْنِك = *tíkram 3áynik*

As you've probably noticed, the Lebanese have adopted quite a few French words in their everyday language (for the simple reason that Lebanon was once a French colony). For example, **waiter** is غارْسوْن *[Fgarçon]*, or more commonly in recent years, ميْتر *[Fmaître]*. And you can simply say دْموازيْل *[Fdemoiselle]* (lit. miss) for a **waitress**. That said, it's becoming less and less acceptable to call your server anything. Instead, just raise your hand to politely get your server's attention.

5

Ordering food (5)

◇ تْفضّلي المِيْنو دُمْوازيْل.
○ فِيي إطْلُب كوكْتيْل شِقف، پْليز؟
◇ أيّا قْياس بِتْحِبّي؟[1]
○ الزِّغير، عْمول معْروف.
◇ بِتْحِبّي تاخْدي شي تاني؟[2]
○ فِيي آخُد قنينِة ميّ مْسقّعة، عْموْل معْروف؟

◇ Here's the menu, miss!
○ I'd like to order one chunky fruit cocktail, please.
◇ And what size would you like?
○ Just a small one, please.
◇ Would you like anything else?
○ Can I have a cold bottle of water, please?

◇ *tfáḍḍali -l[menu], [ᶠdemoiselle].*
○ *fíyi íṭlub [cocktail] ší?af, [please]?*
◇ *áyya ?yēs bitḫíbbi?*[1]
○ *lizzɣīr, 3mōl ma3rūf.*
◇ *bitḫíbbi tēxdi šī tēni?*[2]
○ *fíyi ēxud ?anīnit mayy msá??3a, 3mōl ma3rūf?*

[1] مِش مِتْوَفِّر اليوم. في عصير فْرِش إذا بدِّك. *miš mitwáffir ilyōm. fī 3aṣīr [fresh], íza báddik.* **It's not available today, but we have fresh juice if you want.**

[2] فيك تعْطيني مِيْنو الدّيسّيرْ عْموْل معْروف؟ *fīk ta3ṭīni [menu] id[ᶠdessert], 3mōl ma3rūf.* **Could you pleae give me the dessert menu?**

6

Getting the Bill

o سوْري، فِيي آخُد الفاتورة پْليز؟[1]

◇ تْفضّلي،[2] انْشالله حبّيْتي الأكِل.

o أيْه الأكِل بيجنِّن، بسّ الخُضْرا ما كانِت طازة مِتِل ما بِتْكون عادةً.

o Excuse me! I'd like the check!

◇ Here you are! I hope you liked the food.

o Yes, the food is great, but the vegetables in the salad weren't as fresh as usual.

o *[sorry], fíyi ēxud ilfātūra, [please]?*[1]

◇ *tfáddali.*[2] *nšálla ɧabbáyti -lʔákil.*

o *ē, -lʔákil bijánnin, bass ilxúdra ma kēnit ţāza mítil ma bitkūn 3ādatan.*

[1] = الحْساب عْمِلي معْروف. *liɧsēb, 3míli ma3rūf.*

[2] بِتْحِبّي تاخْدي شي تاني؟ *bitɧíbbi tēxdi šī tēni?* **Do you want to order anything else?**; بِتْحِبّي تْضيفي شي قبِل ما إطْبع الفاتورة؟ *bitɧíbbi tdīfi šī ʔábil ma íţba3 ilfatūra?* **Would you like to add anything before I print the check?**

[3] صراحة ما كْتير عجبْني اليوْم. مْغيرّين الشّيْف شي؟ *şarāɧa, ma ktīr 3ájabni -lyōm. myáyyrīn iš[Fchef] šī?* **Honestly, I didn't like it much today. Did you change chefs?**

There's no set tipping scheme in Lebanon like there is in the U.S., where the standard is 20-25%. It's acceptable to tip as little as a couple of bucks at a café, and as much as $5 for a meal at a restaurant. While tipping more than that is appropriate and greatly appreciated, it is not expected.

Extended Dialogue

- o سوْري، فِيي إطْلُب مِن مينو الترِّوْيقة[1]؟
- ◇ أيْه أكيد. فيكي تِطِلْبي ترْويقة لحدّ السّاعة وِحْدِة.[2]
- o كْتير مْنيح. عِنْدْكُن بيْض مِقْلي؟
- ◇ أيْه أكيد عِنّا.[3]
- o أوْكيْ فينا پْليز ناخُد بيْض مِقْلي، لبْنِة، خُضْرة، وخِبِز؟
- ◇ بْتِشْربوا شي؟[4]
- o لأ، برْكي بعْد الترِّوْيقة.
- ◇ أوْكيْ، أكيد.
- o عِنْدْكُن شي كْريْپ؟
- ◇ أيْه، مدام، في.
- o عظيم[5]، مْناخُد تْنيْن كْريْپ.
- ◇ بْتِحِبّوْن مع عسل أَوْ نوتيْلّا؟[6]
- o نوتيْلّا وجوْز عْموْل معْروف.

(30 minutes later)

- ◇ بْتِحِبّوا تِشْربوا شي هلّق؟
- o أيْه، إذا بْتِرْيد، فينا ناخُد واحد كاپوشينو وَسط وواحد شوْكوْلا شوْ؟[7]
- ◇ بْتِحِبّوا تاخْدوا قنينِةْ ميّ كمان؟
- o لأ مرْسي،[8] بسّ مْناخُد الفاتورة پْليز، لأِنّو فالّين بعْد شْوَيّ.

(10 minutes later)

- o لَوْ سمحِت، في غلْطة بِالفاتورة.
- ◇ شو هِيِّ؟ ويْن بِالظّبِط[9]؟
- o محْطوط[10] إنّو طلبْنا مشْروب مع الترِّوْيقة، غيْر يَلّي طلبْناهُن بعْديْن.

◇ أيْه، لِأنّو بْيِنْحسب المشْروب مع فورْمول الترّْويقة.[11]

○ ليْه ما وَضّحْتِلْنا مِن قبِل؟[12]

◇ ما تْواخْذيني مدام. وَلا يْهِمّك، عْطيني خمْس دقايِق وبْصلّحْلِك الفاتورة.

○ Excuse me, I'd like to know if I can still order off the breakfast menu?

◇ Yes, it's available until 1 p.m.

○ Okay, great. Do you have fried eggs?

◇ Yes, of course.

○ Okay, can we please have some fried eggs, labneh, vegetables, and bread?

◇ Would you like something to drink with it?

○ No, maybe after breakfast.

◇ Certainly.

○ Are there any crepes?

◇ Yes, ma'am, there are.

○ Great, we would like two [orders].

◇ With honey or Nutella?

○ Nutella and walnuts, please.

(30 minutes later)

◇ Would you like something to drink now?

○ Yes, please. We would like one medium cappuccino and one hot chocolate.

◇ Would you like a bottle of water, too?

○ No, thanks. We just need the check because we are going to leave soon.

(10 minutes later)

○ Excuse me, there is a mistake on the check.

◇ What is it? Where exactly?

○ It says that we ordered some drinks with the breakfast in addition to those we ordered later.

◇ Yeah! Because they're already included in the breakfast set.

○ Why didn't you clarify this in the first place?

◇ I'm sorry, ma'am. No worries, just give me five minutes, and I'll correct the check.

○ *[sorry], fíyi íṭlub min [menu] -ttirwīʔa*[1]*?*

◇ *ē, akīd. fīki tiṭílbi tirwīʔa la-ḥádd issē3a wíḥdi.*[2]

○ *ktīr mnīḥ. 3índkun bēḍ míʔli?*

◇ *ē, akīd 3ínna.*[3]

○ *okē, fīna [please] nēxud bēḍ míʔli, lábni, xúḍra, w xíbiz?*

◇ *btíšrabu šī?*[4]

○ *laʔ, bárki ba3d ittirwīʔa.*

◇ *okē, akīd.*

○ *3índkun šī [F crēpe]?*

◇ *ē, [F madame], fī.*

○ *3aẓīm*[5]*, mnēxud tnēn [F crēpe].*

◇ *bitḥibbúwun ma3 3ásal aw [Nutella]?*[6]

○ *[Nutella] w jōz, 3mōl ma3rūf.*

(30 minutes later)

◇ *bitḥíbbu tíšrabu šī hálla??*

○ *ē, íza bitrīd, fīna nēxud wāḥad [cappuccino] wásaṭ w wāḥad [F chocolat chaud]?*[7]

◇ *bitḥíbbu tēxdu ʔanīnit mayy kamēn?*

○ *laʔ [F merci].*[8] *bass mnēxud ilfātūra [please], li-ánnu fēllīn ba3d šwayy.*

(10 minutes later)

○ *law samáḥit, fī ɣálṭa bi-lfātūra.*

◇ *šū híyyi? wēn bi-ḍḍábiṭ*[9]*?*

○ *maḥṭūṭ*[10] *ínnu ṭalábna mašrūb ma3 ittirwīʔa, ɣēr yálli ṭalabnēhun ba3dēn.*

◇ *ē, li-ánnu byinḥásab ilmašrūb ma3 [F formule] ittirwīʔa.*[11]

○ *lē ma waḍḍaḥtíllna min ʔábil?*[12]

◇ *ma twēxzīni, [F madame]. wála yhímmik, 3ṭīni xams dʔāyiʔ w bṣallíḥlik ilfātūra.*

[1] = الفْطور -lfṭūr

2 بِعْتِزِر، وَقّفنا سرْڤيس التّرْويقة مْن ساعة. هلّق وَقْت غدا. *bi3tízir, wa??áfna [ᶠservice] -ttirwī?a mn sē3a. hálla? wa?t ɣáda.* **I appologize, but we stopped serving breakfast an hour ago. It's now lunch time.**

3 لِلأسف لأ. بِتْحِبّي شي تاني؟ *li-l?ásaf la?. bitɦíbbi šī tēni.* **Unfortunately, no. Would you like something else?**

4 بْتاخْدوا شي سِخِن؟ *btēxdu šī síxin?* **Would you like a hot drink?**

5 = تمام *tamēm* = كْتير مْنيح *ktīr mnīɦ*

6 كيف بِتْحِبّوهُن؟ *kīf bitɦibbūhun?* **How would you like them?**

7 لأ، قرّرْنا ما عاد نِشْرب شي. فينا ناخُد الفاتورة بسّ؟ *la?, ?arrárna ma 3ād níšrab šī. fīna nēxud ilfātūra bass?* **No, we've decided that we're not going to have anything to drink. Can we just get the bill, please?**

8 أيْ پْليز، بسّ تْكون مْسقّعة. *ē [please], bass tkūn msá??3a.* **Yes, please, but a very cold one.**

9 = بالتّحْديد *bi-ttaɦdīd*

10 = مكْتوب *maktūb* = مْسجّل *msájjal*

11 ما تْواخْذيني مدام، عْطيني بسّ خمْس دْقايِق وبْصلّحْلِك ياها. *ma twēxzīni [ᶠmadame], 3ţīni bass xams d?ēyi? w bşallíɦlik yēha.* **My apologies, ma'am. Just give me five minutes, and I'll fix it for you.**

12 = ليْه ما قِلْتِلْنا مْن الأوّل؟ *lē ma ?iltíllna mn il?áwwal.*

Vocabulary

restaurant	*máţ3am (maţā3im)*	مطْعم (مطاعِم)
kiosk, stand	*kyōsk [ᶠkiosque]*	كْيوْسْك
waiter	*garsōn (garasīn)*	غارْسوْن (غاراسين)
waitress	*[waitress]* *[ᶠdemoiselle]*	ويْتْريْس دُمْوازيْل
cook	*ţabbāx*	طبّاخ
menu	*[menu]*	ميْنو
set meal	*[ᶠformule]*	فورْمول
check, bill	*ɧsēb* *fātūra*	حْساب فاتورة
order	*[order]* *ţalabíyyi*	أوْرْدر طلبية
mistake	*ɣálţa*	غلْطة
pizza	*[ᶠpizza]*	بيتْزا
hamburger	*[hamburger]*	همْبُرْجر
French fries	*baţāţa miʔlíyyi*	بطاطا مِقْلية
salad	*sálaţa* *[ᶠsalade]*	سلطة سلاد
cheese	*jíbni*	جِبْنِة
ketchup	*kátšab*	كاتْشب
mayonnaise	*[ᶠmayonnaise]*	مايوْنيْز

grilled chicken	*djēj míšwi*	دْجاج مِشْوي
Lebanese sausages	*maʔēniʔ* *sijúʔʔ*	مقانِق سِجُقّ
grilled meat[1]	*mašēwi*[1]	مشاوي[1]
fried fish	*sámak míʔli*	سمك مِقْلي
grilled fish	*sámak míšwi*	سمك مِشْوي
shrimp	*ʔráydis*	قْرَيْدِس
lobster	*kárakand*	كركنْد
crab	*silṭa3ūn*	سِلْطعون
intestines	*ɣámmi*	غمِّة
liver	*kíbid (kbūd)*	كِبِد (كْبود)
rice with beef/chicken	*rizz 3a láḥmi/djēj*	رِزّ عَ لحْمِة/دْجاج
ful (mashed fava beans)	*fūl*	فول
falafel	*falēfil*	فلافِل
dolmas, stuffed vine leaves	*wáraʔ 3arīš*	وَرق عريش
omelette	*3íjji*	عِجِّة
potato stew	*yíxnit baṭāṭa*	يِخْنِة بطاطا
fattah (meat soup with rice and crispy flatbread)	*fátti*	فتِّة
tahini	*ṭḥīni*	طْحينِة
baba ganoush (pureed, grilled eggplant)	*bāba ɣanūj*	بابا غنوج

pickled vegetables	*kabīs*	كبيس
tea	*šāy*	شاي
coffee	*ʔáhwi*	قهْوِة
juice	*3aṣīr*	عصير
Pepsi	*[Pepsi]*	پيپْسي

See also the vocabulary for Visiting Someone's Home on p. 115.

[1] مشاوي *mašēwi* is the umbrella term for any grilled meat on a skewer, including tawouk (chicken), kebab, kofta (meatballs with parsley), and makanek (sausages).

Expressions

I'd like a table for five, please.	*báddi ṭāwli la-xáms ašxāṣ, 3mōl ma3rūf.*	بدّي طاوْلِة لخمْس أشْخاص عْموْل معْروف.
Could I reserve a table for 5 p.m.?	*fíyi íɦjiz ṭāwli la-ssē3a xámsi -l3áṣir?*	فِيي إحْجِز طاوْلِة للسّاعة خمْسِة العصِر؟
Waiter!	*law samáɦit!*	لَوْ سمحِت!
Can I have the pizza without mushrooms?	*fíyi ēxud [ᶠpizza] bála [ᶠchampignon]/fíṭr.*	فِيي آخُد پيزا بلا شامْپينْيوْن/فِطْر؟
The food is cold. Could you please reheat it?	*-lʔákil msáʔʔa3. fīk tírja3 tsáxxinu, [please]?*	الأكِل مْسقّع. فيك تِرْجع تْسخِّنو پْليز؟
I'd like to order another bowl of hummus.	*báddi íṭlub ṣáɦin ɦúmmus tēni.*	بدّي إطْلُب صحِن حُمُّص تاني.

Can I have extra bread?	*fíyi ēxud ba3d xíbiz?*	فِيي آخُد بعْد خِبِز؟
Excuse me, these pickles are off/spoiled.	*law samáɦit, -lkabīs manzū3.*	لَوْ سمحِت، الكبيس منْزوع.
Check, please!	*liɦsēb, [[F]please]!*	الِحْساب پْليز!
Excuse me, there's a mistake on the check.	*[sorry], fī míškli bi-liɦsēb.*	سوْري، في مِشْكْلِة بِالِحْساب.
Do you take credit cards?	*btēxdu [credit cards]/biṭāʔa?*	بْتاخْدوا كْرديت كارْدْز/بِطاقة؟
Could you put it on this card?	*fīk tɦúṭṭa 3a háyda -l[[F]carte]/-l[card]?*	فيك تْحُطّا عَ هَيْدا الكارْت/الكارْد؟

At a Bakery بِالفُرْن

A فُرُن *fúrun* **bakery** in Lebanon doesn't mean quite the same thing as it does in the West. While bakeries[1] do have sweets, they are most popular for their Lebanese منْقوشِة *manʔūši* (مناقيش *manaʔīš*) **mankousheh**, is flat bread topped with thyme, cheese, or ground meat. It is usually described to Westerners as 'Lebanese pizza.' Bakeries are an affordable way to eat while in Lebanon. A standard زعْتر *zá3tar* **thyme sauce** mankousheh can cost as little as half a dollar. The price is slightly higher if you customize it by adding vegetables or labneh, or if you want different kinds of manakeesh with cheese or minced meat. Depending on how big a bakery is, it might sell a variety of savory foods, besides manakeesh, have a large seating area, and sometimes offer hookahs.

[1] Bakeries that only sell sweets are referred to by the french word پاتيسْري *[Fpâtisserie]*.

ORDERING (1)

- ○ صباحو![1]
- ◇ أهْلاً[2] إسْتاذ. شو بْتُؤْمُر؟[3]
- ○ فِيي پْليز آخُد[4] منْقوشةْ زعْتر، منْقوشةِ جِبْنِة، ووِحْدِة لحْم بْعجين؟
- ◇ تِكْرم عَيْنك![5]
- ○ وفينا كمان نْزيد تنْكْتيْن پيپْسي وتنْكِةْ سيڤِن-آب؟

- ○ Good morning!
- ◇ Yes sir, how can I help you?
- ○ Can I please have one thyme mankousheh, one cheese mankousheh, and one minced meat?
- ◇ Coming right up!
- ○ And can we also add a couple cans of Pepsi and one 7up?

- ○ *ṣabāḫu!*[1]
- ◇ *áhla*[2] *istēz. šū btúʔmur?*[3]
- ○ *fíyi [please] ēxud*[4] *manʔūšit zá3tar, manʔūšit jíbni, w wíḫdi laḫm b-3ajīn?*
- ◇ *tíkram 3áynak!*[5]
- ○ *w fīna kamēn nzīd tanktēn [Pepsi] w tánkit [Seven-Up]?*

[1] = صباح الخيْر *ṣabāḫ ilxēr* = يَعْطيق العافْيِة *ya3ṭīʔ il3āfyi*

[2] = صباح النّور *ṣabāḫ innūr* = أهْلين *ahlēn*

[3] = كيف فيني إخْدْمك؟ = أُمُرْني؟ *ʔmúrni?*

[4] فيك تعْطيني پْليز... *fīk ta3ṭīni [please]...* **Can you please give me...?**

[5] = تحْت أمْرك! *taḫt ámrak!*

2

Ordering (2)

○ صباحو ريِّس!

◇ أهْلا مرْوان. مِتِل العادِة؟

○ ما طالِع عَ بالي[1] منْقوشِةْ جِبْنِة اليوْم. فِيي آخُد منْقوشِةْ زعْتر؟

◇ بدّك تعْمِلا إكْسْترا مع لبْنِة، نعْنع، بندورة، خْيار، وزَيْتون؟

○ أيْه، پْليز.[2] باخُد كمان فِنْجان شاي.

○ Morning, boss!

◇ Morning, Marwan. The usual?

○ I'm not feeling like a cheese mankousheh today. Can I have a zaatar mankousheh instead?

◇ Do you want to make it extra, with labneh, mint, tomatoes, cucumbers, and olives?

○ Yes, please. And I'll also have a cup of tea.

○ *ṣabāḫu ráyyis!*

◇ *áhla marwān. mítil il3ādi?*

○ *ma ṭāli3 3a bēli*[1] *manʔūšit jíbni ilyōm. fíyi ēxud manʔūšit zá3tar?*

◇ *báddak tá3mila [extra] ma3 lábni, ná3na3, banadūra, xyār, w zaytūn?*

○ *ē, [please].*[2] *bēxud kamēn finjēn šāy.*

[1] = ما جايي عَ بالي *ma jēyi 3a bēli*

[2] لأ، بسّ زعْتر عَ الحِل *laʔ, bass zá3tar 3a -lḫil* **No, just a regular zaatar.** (عَ الحِل *3a -lḫil* **pure, unmixed**)

3

ORDERING (3)

○ لَوْ سمحِت، بدّي وِحْدِة لحْم بْعجين وشرْحِةْ[1] حامُض.

◇ دْقايِق وبِتْكون جاهْزِة.[2]

○ مرْسي كْتير.

○ Excuse me, I'd like one minced meat mankousheh and a lemon wedge.

◇ Coming right up!

○ Thank you.

○ *law samáħit, báddi wíħdi láħm b-3ajīn w šárħit[1] ħāmuḍ.*

◇ *dʔāyiʔ w bitkūn jēhzi.*[2]

○ *[ᶠmerci] ktīr.*

[1] = ترْانْش *[ᶠtranche]* **slice**

[2] بسّ رح ياخْدوا شْوَيِّةْ وَقِت بِالفُرُن. *bass raħ yēxdu šwáyyit wáʔit bi-lfúrun.* **But it'll take some time in the oven.**

4

Ordering (4)

○ عفْواً، عِنْدْكُن شي مينْو قهْوِة؟

◇ أيْه أكيد، تْفضّلي مدام.

○ مرْسي، فِيي پْليز آخُد كاپوشينو؟ هلّق بِتْطلّع عَ مينْو الأكِل وبِطْلُب بعْد نِتْفِة[1].

○ Excuse me do you have a coffee menu?

◇ Yes, of course. Here you go ma'am.

○ Thank you. Can I please have a cappuccino? I'll look at the food menu and order shortly.

○ *3áfwan, 3índkun šī [menu] ʔáhwi?*

◇ *ē, akīd, tfáḍḍali, [F madame].*

○ *[F merci], fíyi [please] ēxud [cappuccino]? hállaʔ bitṭálla3 3a [menu] -lʔákil w bíṭlub ba3d nítfi[1].*

[1] = بعْد شْوَيّ *ba3d šwayy*

5

ORDERING (5)

o مسا الخيرْ!
◇ مسا النّور!
o بدّْنا نعْمِل طلبية كْبيرِة. فيك تْلبّينا؟[1]
◇ فِيي جرِّب! شو الطّلبية؟
o بدّْنا عِشْرين منْقوشِةْ زعْتر، تْلاتين منقوشِةْ جِبْنِة، تْلاتين وِحْدِةْ لحِم بْعجين، أرْبْعة پيزا فاميلي، ووِحْدِةْ پيزا جِبْنِة.
◇ اسْمالله، بدّْكُن تْطعّْموا جيْش؟!
o هاها هيْك شي.

o Good evening!
◇ Good evening!
o We need to place a large order. Can you fulfill it?
◇ I can try! What's the order?
o 20 zaatar manakeesh, 30 cheese manakeesh, 30 mince meat manakeesh, and 4 family-size pizzas, and one cheese pizza.
◇ God bless, are you feeding an army?
o Haha! Something like that.

o *mása -lxēr!*
◇ *mása -nnūr!*
o *báddna ná3mil ṭalabíyyi kbīri. fīk tlabbīna?*[1]
◇ *fíyi járrib! šū -ṭṭalabíyyi?*
o *báddna 3išrīn manʔūšit zá3tar, tlētīn manaʔūšit jíbni, tlētīn wíḫdit láḫim b-3ajīn, árb3a [Fpizza] [family], w wíḫdit [Fpizza] jíbni.*
◇ *smálla, báddkunn tṭá33mu jēš?!*
o *ha ha! hēk šī.*

[1] = فيك تاخُد الأوْرْدر؟ *fīk tēxud il[order]?* **Can you take the order?**

[2] أُمْروني! *ʔmurūni!* **At your service!**

[3] دِقّ عالخشب. بلا حسيدِة. *di?? 3a-lxášab. bála ɧasīdi.* **Knock on wood! No envy.** In Lebanese culture, people believe in عينْ الحاسود *3ēn ilɧāsūd* **the evil eye** (lit. eye of the envious). If someone points out the beauty or large quantity of something, they should precede by اسْمالله *smálla* **in the name of God** to let the other person know that they will not curse them or their possessions with the envious evil eye. In this dialogue, the waiter comments on the large quantity of food ordered, so the client might be afraid of getting sick (from food poisoning). Whether the waiter said اسْمالله *smálla* or not, some people still insist on mentioning this "knock on wood" phrase to ward off the omen of the evil eye. People also use this expression jokingly to accuse them of being envious.

6

ORDERING A HOOKAH

○ لَوْ سمحِت، عِنْدْكُن أرْغيلِة؟

◇ لأ سوْري والله.[1] لِأنّو الفُرْن عِنّا منّو بِالهَوا الطِّلق وما عِنّا قعْدات برّا، منّو مسْموح قانونِيّاً نْحُطّ أرْغيلِة.

○ بسّ مْبارِح بِاللّيْل رِحِت عَ مطْعم كان عِنْدو أرْغيلِة وما كِنّا قاعْدين برّا!

◇ الأرْجح[2] كِنْتوا قاعْدين بِإكْسْتانْشون مْغطّايِة. هَوْدي بْيُعْتبروا برّا وتقْريباً مسْموحين.

○ أيْه معك حقّ، قعدْنا بِالإكْسْتانْشون. طيِّب، فينا بسّ ناخُد پيزا فاميلي؟

○ Excuse me, do you guys have hookahs?

◇ No, sorry. Because we're not an open-air bakery and have no outdoor spaces, we're not legally allowed to.

- o But I went to a restaurant last night that had them. And we weren't sitting outside!
- ◇ You must have been sitting in a covered extension. Those are technically considered outdoors, and are somewhat okay.
- o Yes, you're right. We did sit in the extension. All right. Can we just have a family size pizza?

- o *law samáћit, 3índkun argīli?*
- ◇ *laʔ [sorry] wálla.*[1] *li-ánnu -lfúrun 3ínna mánnu bi-lháwa -ṭṭúliʔ w ma 3ínna ʔa3dēt bárra, mánnu masmūћ qānūníyyan nћúṭṭ argīli.*
- o *bass mbēriћ bi-llēl ríћit 3a máṭ3am kēn 3índu argīli w ma kínna ʔā3dīn bárra!*
- ◇ *-lʔárjaћ*[2] *kíntu ʔā3dīn bi-[extension] mɣaṭṭāyi. háwdi byu3tábaru bárra w taʔrīban masmūћīn.*
- o *ē, má3ak ћaʔʔ, ʔa3ádna bi-lʔ[extension]. ṭáyyib, fīna bass nēxud [ᶠpizza] [family]?*

[1] أيْ أكيد، بسّ بيصير لازِم تْنِقْلوا عالقعْدات يَلّي برّا. *ē akīd, bass biṣīr lēzim tníʔlu 3a-lʔa3dēt yálli bárra.* **Of course, but you'll have to move to the outdoor seating.**

[2] = الهَيْئة *-lháyʔa*

In 2011, a law was imposed forbidding restaurants and cafés from offering hookah in enclosed spaces, which meant that only places with an outdoor space were allowed to offer them, but in the winter, that isn't even an option. But, leave it to Lebanese entrepreneurs to find a loophole. Restaurants and cafés started adding extensions to their establishments covered with tent-like material, which helped them get around the rule. Since these extensions are, technically, not enclosed by walls, you can smoke hookah, but they're also covered enough to protect customers from rain in the winter.

7

Refreshing your Hookah

o لَوْ سمحِت، بدّي فحِم للأرْغيلِة.
◇ يَلّا ثَواني.
o سوْري، وأنا كمان بدّي غيِّر التّنْبك بِتبعي.

- o Excuse me, I want fresh embers/coal.
- ◇ Coming right up.
- o Excuse me, and I want to freshen up the tobacco in mine.

- o *law samáɦit, báddi fáɦim la-lʔargīli.*
- ◇ *yálla sawēni.*
- o *[sorry], w ána kamēn báddi ɣáyyir ittánbak bi-tába3i.*

[1] فحِم *fáɦim* **embers/coal** keeps the smoke coming. When the hookah seems to be dying out, you can ask for more embers if the waiter isn't already tending to the embers periodically.

⚠ Smoking hookah is harmful to your health. The dialogues and vocabulary for smoking hookah are only included for educational purposes, but we do not advocate smoking. All of the commonly known dangers in regards to nicotine addiction and the cancer-causing properties of tobacco also hold true for the hookah. The water may cool the smoke, making it less irritating, but it does not filter out harmful chemicals. The sweet flavors can also make you feel like smoking hookah is milder than smoking cigarettes. But in actuality, when you smoke hookah for one hour, the volume of smoke inhaled is equivalent to that of over 100 cigarettes! Furthermore, sharing a hookah mouthpiece can spread disease.

8

Settling the Bill

o لَوْ سمحِت، قدّيْ بدّك مِنّا؟[1]

◇ خلّيا عْلَيْنا[2] هَيْدي المرّة!

o مرْسي. كِلّك ذوْق. بسّ عن جدّ، قدّيْ بدّك مِنّا؟

◇ تْلاتّعْشر ألْف.

o هَيْدي خمْستْعْشر ألْف. خلّي الباقي.

o Excuse me, how much do we owe you?
◇ It's on the house this time!
o Thank you. So kind. But, really, how much?
◇ 13,000 L.L.
o Here's 15,000 L.L. Keep the change.

o *law samáɧit, ʔaddē báddak mínna?*[1]
◇ *xallíya 3láyna*[2] *háydi -lmárra!*
o *[ᶠmerci]. kíllak zōʔ. bass 3an jadd, ʔaddē báddak mínna?*
◇ *tlēttá3šar alf.*
o *háydi xamstá3šar alf. xálli -lbēʔi.*

[1] = قدّيْ بِترْيد؟ *ʔaddē bitrīd?*

[2] = خلّيا عَ حْسابْنا *xallíya 3a ɧsēbna.* These expressions are not meant to be taken literally. Your waiter does expect you to settle your bill. This is just a set expression to show hospitality. After saying thank you, you may need to ask for the bill a second time.

Extended Dialogue

○ خلّينا نِقْعُد هوْن، في طاوْلِة فاضْيِة.

◇ أوْكيْ. تمام.

(to waiter)

○ ميترْ!

◇ شو فِيِ جِبِلْكُن؟[1]

○ بدْنا تْنيْن شاي أخْضر پْليز. تبعي ما يْكون حِلو. وإنْتَ شرْبِل؟

◇ باخُد تبعي حِلو وَسط.

◇ أوْكيْ، شْوَيّ وبيْحْضروا.

○ مْناخُد أرْغيلِة؟

◇ أيْه ليْه لأ.

(waiter brings drinks)

◇ مْناخُد أرْغيلْتيْن كمان.

◇ أيّا نوْع؟[2]

◇ تِفّاحْتيْن إلي.

○ وأنا بدّي حامْض ونعْنع.

(later, after they've been smoking a while)

◇ ميترْ! وفينا نْغيرِّ الفحِم بِالأراغيل؟

◇ ثَواني.

○ وأنا بدّي تيپ تاني پْليز. تبعي مكْسور.

◇ تِكْرم عَيْنك.

(a while later)

○ قدّيْ بدّك مِنّا؟

◇ خلِّيا عْلَيْنا هَيْدي المرّة.

◇ الله يْخلّيك، مرْسي.

o بسّ عن جدّ قدّيْ بدّك مِنّا؟[3]

◇ عِشْرين ألْف.

◇ خلّيني أنا إدْفع هَيْدي المرّة.[4]

o أكيد لأ حبيبي. ضْيافْتي أنا. بعْدك دافع عالغدا مِن شْوَيّ!... تْفضّل. خلّي الباقي.

◇ نوّرْتونا. انْشالله نِرْجع نْشوفْكُن عِنّا.[5]

o أكيد، يِسْلموا.

◇ باي!

◇ مع السّلامِة.

o Let's sit over here. There's a free table.

◇ Okay.

(to waiter)

o Waiter!

◇ How can I help you?

o We'd like two green teas, please. Unsweetened for me. And you, Charbel?

◇ I'll take mine medium sweet.

◇ All right, coming right up.

o Should we get hookahs?

◇ Sure, why not?

(waiter brings drinks)

◇ We'll take two hookahs, too.

◇ What kind?

◇ 'Two apples' for me.

o And I want lemon and mint.

(later, after they've been smoking a while)

◇ Waiter, could we change out the coals on our hookahs?

◇ Right away.

o And a new tip for me, please. This one is broken.

◇ At your service.

(a while later)

○ How much do we owe?

◇ It's on us this time.

◇ God protect you, thanks.

○ How much do we owe really?

◇ 20,000 L.L.

◇ Let me pay this time.

○ No way, buddy. It's my treat! You paid for our lunch earlier... Here you are. Keep the change.

◇ We are blessed by your presence and are looking forward to seeing you again.

○ Of course, thanks.

◇ Goodbye!

◇ Goodbye!

○ *xallīna níʔ3ud hōn, fī ţāwli fāḑyi.*

◇ *okē. tamēm.*

(to waiter)

○ *[Fmaître]!*

◇ *šū fíyi jíbilkun?*[1]

○ *báddna tnēn šāy áxḑar, [please]. tába3i ma ykūn ɦílu. w ínta, šárbil?*

◇ *bēxud tába3i ɦílu wásaţ.*

◇ *okē, šwayy w byíɦḑaru.*

○ *mnēxud argīli?*

◇ *ē, lē laʔ.*

(waiter brings drinks)

◇ *mnēxud argīltēn kamēn.*

◇ *áyya nō3?*[2]

◇ *tiffēɦtēn íli.*

○ *w ána báddi ɦāmuḑ w ná3na3.*

(later, after they've been smoking a while)

◇ *[Fmaître]! fīna nɣáyyir ilfáɦim bi-lʔarāgīl?*

◇ *sawēni.*

○ *w ána báddi [tip] tēni, [please]. tabá3i maksūr.*

◇ *tíkram 3áynak.*

(a while later)

- O *ʔaddē báddak mínna?*
- ◇ *xallíya 3láyna háydi -lmárra.*
- ◇ *álla yxallīk, [ᶠmerci].*
- O *bass 3an jadd, ʔaddē báddak mínna?*[3]
- ◇ *3išrīn alf.*
- ◇ *xallīni ána ídfa3 háydi -lmárra.*[4]
- O *akīd laʔ ɧabībi. ḍyāfti ána. bá3dak dēfi3 3a-lɣáda min šwayy!... tfáḍḍal. xálli -lbēʔi.*
- ◇ *nawwartūna. nšálla nírja3 nšūfkun 3ínna.*[5]
- O *akīd, yíslamu.*
- ◇ *[bye]!*
- ◇ *ma3 issalēmi.*

[1] = كيف فِيي إخْدِمْكُن؟ *kīf fíyi ixdímkun?*

[2] = أيّا نكْهة؟ *áyya nákha?*

[3] = قدّيْ بِترْيد؟ *ʔaddē bitrīd?*

[4] = أنا عازِم اليوْم. *ána 3āzim ilyōm.*; خلّي الِحْساب عْليّي. *xálli liɧsēb 3láyyi.*

[5] = أهْلا وسهْلا فيكُن، شرّفْتونا. عيدوها. *áhla w sáhla fīkun, šarraftūna. 3īdūha.* (عيدوها *3īdūha* **do it again**)

Vocabulary

bakery	*fúrun (afrān, frān)*	فُرْن (أفْران، فْران)
baker	*farrān, xabbēz*	فِرّان، خِبّاز
labneh	*lábni*	لبْنِة
mankousheh ('Lebanese pizza')	*manʔūši (manaʔīš)*	منْقوشِة (مناقيش)
tomatoes	*banadūra*	بندورة
cucumber	*xyār*	خْيار
thyme sauce	*zá3tar*	زعْتر
drink, beverage	*mašrūb*	مشْروب
hot	*síxin*	سخِن
cold	*msáʔʔa3* *bērid*	مْسقّع بارِد
coffee	*ʔáhwi*	قهْوِة
Turkish coffee	*ʔáhwi tirkíyyi*	قهْوِة تِرْكية
tea	*šāy*	شاي
mint	*ná3na3*	نعْنع
anise, aniseed	*yēnsūn*	يانْسون
sugar	*síkkar*	سِكّر
cinnamon	*ʔírfi*	قِرْفِة
fruit(s)	*fwēki*	فْواكِه
flavor	*nákha*	نكْهة
apple	*tiffēḩ*	تِفّاح

grape	*3ínab*	عِنب
blueberry	*tūt ázra?*	توت أزْرق
cigarette	*sīgāra (sagíyir)*	سيغارة (سغايِر)
to smoke	*dáxxan (ydáxxin) sīgāra*	دخّن (يْدخِّن) سِغارة
smoking	*tidxīn*	تِدْخين
shisha, hookah, waterpipe	*argīli*	أرْغيلِة
to smoke a hookah	*árgal (y?árgil)* *šírib (yíšrab) argīli*	أرْجل (يْأرْجِل) شِرِب (يِشْرب) أرْغيلِة
hookah mouthpiece	*[tip]*	تيپ
coal, embers	*fáɦim*	فحِم

Expressions

Two mana'eesh, please.	*man?ūštēn, 3mōl ma3rūf.*	منْقوشْتينْ عمْول معْروف.
Where's the restroom?	*wēn ilɦammēm?*	ويْن الحمّام؟
Do you have a lighter?	*má3ak ?addēɦa?*	معك قدّاحة؟
We'd like two hookahs.	*bádda argīltēn.*	بدْنا أرْغيلْتينْ.
Can I have another mouthpiece [for my hookah]?	*fíyi ēxud [tip] tēni la-l?argīli?*	فِيي آخُد تيپ تاني للأرْغيلة؟

◇

Would you like a hot or cold drink?	*bitḫíbb šī msáʔʔa3 aw síxin?*	بْتْحِبّ شي مْسقّع أَوْ سخِن؟
We have mana'eesh zaatar, cheese, and minced meat.	*3ínna manaʔīš zá3tar, jíbni, w láḫim b-3ajīn.*	عِنّا مناقيش زعْتر، جِبْنِة، ولحِم بْعجين.
Would you like a hot or cold drink?	*bitḫíbb šī msáʔʔa3 aw síxin?*	بْتْحِبّ شي مْسقّع أَوْ سخِن؟
Here's the menu.	*háyda -l[menu]. tfáḍḍal il[menu].*	هَيْدا الميْنو. تْفضّل الميْنو.

Making Small Talk دَرْدشِة

Lebanese pride themselves on their hospitality, and one way to show this is through مْسايرة *msēyara* **small talk**–whether or not it's always welcome! But the Lebanese are very curious. Don't be surprised if you are asked questions which may, to you, seem a bit too personal for someone you've just met. *Are you married? Why not? What's your religion? How much do you earn?* They are not trying to pry or be rude. Such questions are perfectly acceptable in Lebanon. Remember that, as a foreigner, you are automatically interesting. But such questions get asked to everyone, including locals, especially by those who have never left Lebanon and don't know about foreign sensitivities. Typically, the further out you are from the main cities, the more personal the questions tend to be. If you ever express your distaste to such questions, you may be told something along the lines of ما تْواخِذْني كِنِت بسّ عم سايِر *ma twēxízni, kínit bass 3am sēyir* **My apologies, I was just making small talk.**

Where are you from?

◇ كْتير بْتِحْكي عربي مْنيح. مِن وين حضِرْتِك[1]؟

o مرْسي! كِلّك ذوْق. أنا مْن الصّين، بسّ عم بِدْرُس[3] عربي هوْن.

◇ You know Arabic very well. Where are you from?

o Thank you! So kind of you to say. I'm from China, but I'm studying Arabic here.

◇ *ktīr btíħki 3árabi mnīħ. min wēn ħáḍirtik[1]?*

o *[ᶠmerci][2]! kíllak zōʔ. ána mn iṣṣīn, bass 3am bídrus[3] 3árabi hōn.*

[1] = إنْتي *ínti*. حضِرْتك *ħáḍirtak* / حضِرْتِك *ħáḍirtak* are the more formal variants of إنْتَ *ínta* / إنْتي *ínti* and are used to convey respect for superiors and for strangers.

[2] = شُكْراً *šúkran*

[3] = بِتْعلّم *bit3állam*

2

Why are you in Lebanon?

◇ شو جابِك عَ لِبْنان؟[1]

○ عم بْعلِّم إنْجْليزي بِمعْهد لُغات.[2]

◇ واوْ حِلو كْتير. ورح تِبْقي بِلِبْنان مِن بعْد هيْك[3]؟

○ لأ، بسّ لفترْةْ العقِد، وراجْعة عَ أميرْكا.[4]

◇ And what brought you here to Lebanon?

○ I'm working here as an English teacher at a language institute.

◇ Oh wow, and will you stay in Lebanon long term?

○ No, just for the duration of the contract, and then I'm going back home again.

◇ *šū jēbik 3a libnēn?*[1]

○ *3am b3állim inglīzi bi-má3had luɣāt.*[2]

◇ *wāw ḥílu ktīr. w raḥ tíbʔi bi-libnēn min ba3d hēk*[3]*?*

○ *laʔ, bass la-fátrit il3áʔid, w rēj3a 3a amērka.*[4]

[1] = شو عم تعْمِل/تْساوي عِنّا بِلِبْنان؟ *šū 3am tá3mil/tsēwi 3ínna bi-libnēn?*

[2] عم بِشْتِغِل هوْن مْعلْمِة. *3am bištíɣil hōn m3állmi.* **I'm working here as a teacher.**

[3] = عن عَ طول *3an 3a ṭūl*

[4] أيْه مبْدئِيّاً، بسّ أكيد بِرْجع زْيارات عَ أميرْكا. *ē, mabdaʔíyyan, bass akīd bírja3 zyarāt 3a amērka.* **Yes, most likely, but I'll definite be going back to the U.S. to visit.**

3

Where do you live?

◇ ساكْنِة وَحْدِك هوْن؟[1]

o أيْه، ساكْنِة بِسْتوديْوْ وَحْدي.

◇ ويْن ساكْنِة بِالظّبِط[2]؟

o بِداوْنْتاوْن بَيْروت.

◇ حِلو كْتير هونيك![3] زِرْتي المتْحف الوَطني شي؟ مْرمِّمينو جْديد!

o لأ بعْد ما رِحِت، بسّ أكيد رح روح.[4]

◇ And are you living here by yourself?

o Yes, I'm in a studio apartment.

◇ Where in the city are you staying?

o In downtown Beirut.

◇ It's beautiful there! Have you visited the National Museum yet? It's been rennovated recently!

o I haven't yet, but I'll definitely check it out.

◇ *sēkni wáħdik hōn?*[1]

o *ē, sēkni bi-[studio] wáħdi.*

◇ *wēn sēkni bi-ẓẓábiṭ*[2]*?*

o *bi-[downtown]bayrūt.*

◇ *ħílu ktīr hunīk!*[3] *zírti -lmátħaf ilwáṭani šī? mrammimīnu jdīd!*

o *laʔ, ba3d ma ríħit, bass akīd raħ rūħ.*[4]

[1] = عايْشِة/مُقيمِة لحالِك هوْن؟ *3āyši/muʔīmi la-ħālik hōn?*

[2] = بِالتّحْديد *bi-ttaħdīd*

[3] بسّ كْتير غالي هونيك. *bass ktīr ɣāli hunīk.* **But it's really expensive there.**

[4] أيْه رِحِت مْبارِح! رَوْعة! *ē, ríħit mbēriħ! ráw3a!* **Yes, I went yesterday. It's amazing!**

4

ARE YOU MARRIED?

◇ زْيارة بسّ؟ أَوْ عايْشِة هوْن؟

○ مْجوّزِة[1]، وساكْنِة هوْن مع جَوْزي.

◇ معْناتا[2] أكيد جَوْزِك لِبْناني.

○ مظْبوط، كِنّا ساكْنين بِالإمارات، بسّ رْجِعْنا عَ لِبْنان.

◇ مبْصوطة[3] بلِبْنان؟

○ حمْدِالله، بعْدْني عم بِتْعوّد عالجَوّ.[4]

◇ So, are you just visiting or living here in Lebanon?

○ I'm married and living here with my husband.

◇ Your husband must be Lebanese then.

○ Yes, he is. We used to live in the U.A.E., but we came back to Lebanon.

◇ Are you happy in Lebanon?

○ Praise God... I'm still getting used to it.

◇ *zyāra bass? aw 3āyši hōn?*

○ *mjáwwazi*[1]*, w sēkni hōn ma3 jáwzi.*

◇ *ma3nēta*[2] *akīd jáwzik libnēni.*

○ *mazbūt, kínna sēknīn bi-lʔimarāt, bass rji3na 3a libnēn.*

◇ *mabsūta*[3] *bi-libnēn?*

○ *ħamdílla, bá3dni 3am bit3áwwad 3a-ljáww.*[4]

1 = مْزوّجِة *mzáwwaji*

2 يَعْني *yá3ni*

3 مِرتاحة *mirtāħa* **comfortable**; تْأقْلَمْتي *tʔaʔlámti* **you acclimatized**

4 كْتير حمْدِالله! كْتير بْحِبّ لِبْنان! *ktīr, ħamdílla! ktīr bħibb libnēn.* **Yes! Praise God! I love Lebanon so much!**; بعْد ما تْأقْلمِت عَلى الجَوّ. *ba3d ma tʔaʔlámit 3la -ljaww.* **I still haven't gotten used to it.**

5

What is your religion?

◇ ليْه بدِّك تْزوري الجامِع؟ إنْتي مِسِلْمِة؟

o لأ، بسّ بْحِبّ زور مَوَاقع أثرية وإتْعرّف عَ غيرْ دِيانات.

◇ إنْتي شو فإذاً؟[1] مسيحية؟

o عَيْلْتي مسيحية، بسّ أنا منّي كْتير مِتْديِّنِة.

◇ And why do you want to visit this mosque? Are you a Muslim?

o No, but I like visiting and seeing archeological sites, and I like getting to know other religions, as well.

◇ Then what are you? Christian?

o My family is, but I'm not that religious.

◇ *lē báddik tzūri -ljēmi3? ínti misílmi?*

o *la?, bass bħibb zūr mawē?i3 asaríyyi w it3árraf 3a ɣēr diyēnēt.*

◇ *ínti šū fa-ízan?*[1] *masīħíyyi?*

o *3áylti masīħíyyi, bass ána mánni ktīr mitdáyyni.*

[1] شو دينِك؟ *šū dīnik?* **What's your religion?**

6

Do you have children?

◇ عِنْدِك وْلاد؟

○ أيْه[1]، عِنْدي صبي عايِش بِسْويسْرا وبِنْت عايْشِة بِفْرنْسا.

◇ ليْه ما جِبْتِينْ معِك؟

○ عِنْدُن حَياتُن الخاصّة هلّق وكْتير مشْغولين. جيت لهوْن مع جَوْزي سِياحة.

◇ And do you have children?

○ Yes, I have a son living in Switzerland, and a daughter studying in France.

◇ Why didn't you bring them over with you then?

○ No, they have their own lives now and are too busy. I came with my husband for a tour.

◇ *3índik wlēd?*

○ *ē̤[1], 3índi ṣábi 3āyiš bi-swīsra w bint 3āyši bi-fránsa.*

◇ *lē ma jíbtiyun má3ik?*

○ *3índun ḫayētun ilxāṣṣa hálla? w ktīr mašɣūlīn. jīt la-hōn ma3 jáwzi siyēḫa.*

[1] لأ، ما عِنْدي وْلاد. *la?, ma 3índi wlēd.* **No, I don't have children.**

◇ شو إسْمِك؟

○ أليكْسانْدْرا. وإنْتَ؟

◇ إسْمي شرْبِل. شو بْتعْمْلي هوْن؟

○ أنا حكيمِة بمِسْتشْفى الجامْعة الأميرْكية.

◇ وشو عم تعْمْلي بِجْبيْل؟

○ عِنْدي كم يوْم فُرْصة، فقلِت بعْمِل شْوَيِّةْ سِياحة بِالويك أنْد.

◇ نقَّيْتي أحْلى مطْرح!

○ هيْك قالولي! خبّروني إنّو البحِر والكنايِس هوْن بيعقّْدوا!

◇ مظْبوط! إذا بْتِمْشي شْوَيّ، بِتْلاقي جامِع وكْنيسِة جدّ[1] بعْضُن. منْظر مِش كِلّ يوْم بِتْشوفي[2].

○ حِلو كْتير. شو في غيرْ مطارِح شوفا[3] أنا وهوْن؟ باقْيِة يَوْمين.

◇ فيكي تْروحي عَ متْحف الشّمِع، قلْعِةْ جْبيْل، و المينا، وللأكِل بِنْصحِك تْروحي عَ پيپي عبِد، إذا بْتِحِبّي السّمك، أَوْ إلموْلينو للأكِل المِكْسيكي، أَوْ فينيقْيا للأكِل اللِّبْناني.

○ واوْ. أيْه أكيد بْشوفُن.

◇ وتِمْشي[4] بِسوق العتيق. الشّوارِع ضيْقة وحِلْوِة.

○ كْتير حابِّة شوفُن[5]، أكيد بْروح.

◇ جْبيْل رَوْعة[6] بِاللّيْل كمان. مِش مِن زمان، صارِت جْبيْل وِجْهة للسّهر. كْتير في پابات، وبارات، ومطاعِم. كِلُّن فيكي توصليلُن مشي مِن هوْن.

○ عظيم. حابِّة إسْهر!

◇ بْيِدْفعولِك[7] مْنيح بِالأي يو بي؟

○ سوْري بسّ هَيْدا سُؤال كْتير شخْصي.[8]

◇ ما تْواخْذيني، كان بسّ قصْدي سايِر. مْجوّزِة؟

○ أيْه نعم. مْجوّزِة وعِنْدي وَلديْن.

◇ اه اسْمالله الله يِحْمِينُ. هِنِّ كمان بلِبْنان؟ وِلّا[9] بِأميرْكا؟

○ هِنِّ بِأميرْكا مع بيُّن، كمان حكيم. رح يِنِقْلوا قريباً لهوْن كِلُّن.

◇ بْتِحْكي عربي كْتير مْنيح!

○ مرْسي! درسِت كْتير قبِل ما جيت[10] عَ لِبْنان، ومِن وَقِت ما جيت كْتير تْحسّنِت[11].

◇ What's your name?

○ Alexandra, and yours?

◇ My name is Charbel. And what do you do here?

○ I'm a doctor at the American University of Beirut Medical Center (AUBMC).

◇ And what brings you to Byblos?

○ I have a few days off, so I thought of touring around on the weekend.

◇ Well, you choose the nicest place!

○ So I've heard! I was told the beaches and churches here are mind-blowing.

◇ True! If you walk a little that way, you'll even see a mosque and a church side-by-side. It's not a sight you see everyday.

○ Very nice. What other places can I visit? I'm staying here for two days.

◇ You can go to the Wax Museum, the Citadel of Byblos, the Marina, and I highly recommend Pepe Abed for seafood, El Molino for Mexican, or Phoeniqia for Lebanese food.

○ Fantastic! I'll be sure to check them out.

◇ Make sure you also take a stroll in the old souq area; the streets are narrow and beautiful.

○ I'd love to see that. I'll be sure to go.

◇ Byblos at night is gorgeous, as well. It recently became a destination for nightlife. There are many bars, pubs, and restaurants, all within walking distance.

○ Great! I'd like to go out there.

◇ So, are they paying you well at AUB?

○ Sorry, that's a very personal question.

◇ Pardon me. I'm just making conversation. Are you married then?

○ Yes, married with two children!

◇ Wow, bless them. Are they in Lebanon, too, or back in the US?

○ They are back in the US with their father, who is also a doctor. They will be relocating soon to join me.

◇ Your Arabic is so fluent!

○ Thank you! I studied a lot before I came to Lebanon, and after I moved here, it improved a lot.

◇ *šū ísmik?*

○ *[Alexandra]. w ínta?*

◇ *ísmi šárbil. šū btá3mli hōn?*

○ *ána ɧakīmi bi-mistášfa -ljēm3a ilʔamērkíyyi.*

◇ *w šū 3am tá3mli bi-jbēl?*

○ *3índi kam yōm fúrṣa, fa-ʔílit bá3mil šwáyyit siyēɧa bi-l[weekend].*

◇ *naʔʔáyti áɧla máṭraɧ!*

○ *hēk ʔālūli! xabbarūni ínnu -lbáɧir w ilkanēyis hōn bi3áʔʔdu!*

◇ *maẓbūṭ! íza btímši šwayy, bitlēʔi jēmi3 w knīsi ɧadd*[1] *bá3ḍun. mánẓar miš kill yōm bitšūfi*[2]*.*

○ *ɧílu ktīr. šū fī ɣēr maṭāriɧ šūfa*[3] *ána w hōn? bēʔyi yawmēn.*

◇ *fīki trūɧi 3a mátɧaf iššámi3, ʔál3it jbēl, w ilmīna, w la-lʔákil binṣáɧik trūɧi 3a pēpē 3ábid, íza bitɧíbbi -ssámak, aw [El Molino] la-lʔákil ilmeksīki, aw fīnīʔya la-lʔákil illibnēni.*

○ *wāw. ē, akīd bšūfun.*

◇ *w tímši*[4] *bi-sūʔ il3atīʔ. -ššawēri3 ḍáyyʔa w ɧílwi.*

○ *ktīr ɧābbi šūfun*[5]*, akīd brūɧ.*

◇ *jbēl ráw3a*[6] *bi-llēl kamēn. miš min zamēn, ṣārit jbēl wíjha la-ssáhar. ktīr fī [pub]ēt, w bārāt, w maṭā3im. kíllun fīki tūṣalīlun máši min hōn.*

○ *3aẓīm. ɧābbi íshar!*

◇ *byidfa3ūlik*[7] *mnīḫ bi-l[AUB]?*
○ *[sorry] bass háyda suʔāl ktīr šáxṣi.*[8]
◇ *ma twēxzīni, kēn bass ʔáṣdi sēyir. mjáwwazi?*
○ *ē, ná3am. mjáwwazi w 3índi waladēn.*
◇ *āh, smálla álla yíḫmiyun. hínni kamēn bi-libnēn? wílla*[9] *bi-amērka?*
○ *hínni bi-amērka ma3 báyyun, kamēn ḫakīm. raḫ yiníʔlu ʔarīban la-hōn kíllun.*
◇ *btíḫki 3árabi ktīr mnīḫ!*
○ *[ᶠmerci]! darásit ktīr ʔábil ma jīt*[10] *3a libnēn, w min wáʔit ma jīt ktīr tḫassánit*[11].

[1] = جنْب *jamb*

[2] مِش مألوف *miš maʔlūf* **unfamiliar**

[3] ويْن فِيي روح؟ *wēn fíyi rūḫ?* **Where can I go?**; شو فِيي زور؟ *šū fíyi zūr?* **What can I visit?**

[4] = تمْشّي *tmášši*

[5] زورُن *zūrun* **I visit them**

[6] = بِتْجنِّن *bitjánnin*

[7] معاشِك *ma3āšik* **your salary**

[8] حمْدِلله! *ḫamdílla* **Praise God!** In this context, the expression can be used to indicate that you're making a decent amount, but you don't want to specify, out of modesty or to avoid the evil eye.

[9] = ولّا *wálla* = أَوْ *aw*

[10] = قبِل ما إجي *ʔábil ma íji*

[11] تقْدّمِت *tʔáddamit* **it progressed**

Vocabulary

to chat, have a conversation	*tsēyar (yitsēyar)* *dárdaš (ydárdiš)*	تْسايَر (يِتْسايَر) درْدش (يْدرْدِش)
conversation, chat	*ħadīs* *dárdaši* *msēyara*	حديث درْدشِة مْسايرة
talk, talking	*ħáki*	حكي
getting to know one another	*ta3āruf*	تعارُف
question	*suʔāl (ásʔila)*	سُؤال (أسْئِلة)
answer	*jawēb*	جَواب
reason	*sábab*	سبب
friendship	*ṣúħbi*	صُحْبِة
married	*mjáwwaz* *mitjáwwiz*	مْجوّز مِتْجوِّز
single (male)	*á3zab*	أعْزب
single (female)	*3ázba*	عزْبِة
madam, ma'am, Mrs. (married woman)	*[Fmadame]*	مدام
ma'am, Ms. (formal when you do not know if she's married or not)	*sitt*	سِتّ
sir, Mr.	*istēz*	إسْتاذ
my husband	*jáwzi*	جَوْزي

my wife	*márti* *[ᶠmadame]ti*	مرْتي مدامْتي
child	*wálad (wlēd)*	وَلد (وْلاد)
son	*íbin*	إبِن
daughter	*bínit (banēt)*	بِنت (بنات)
Muslim	*míslim*	مِسْلِم
Christian	*masīħi*	مسيحي
Jewish	*yahūdi*	يَهودي
religious	*mitdáyyin*	مِتْديّن
non-religious	*miš mitdáyyin*	مِش مِتْديّن
mosque	*jēmi3 (jawēmi3)*	جامِع (جَوامِع)
church	*knīsi (kanēyis)*	كْنيسِة (كنايِس)
temple, synagogue	*má3bad*	معْبد

Expressions

○

Beirut is crowded but beautiful.	*bayrūt fíya 3áj?a bass ħílwi.*	بَيْروت فِيا عجْقِة بسّ حِلْوِة.
I'd rather not say.	*bfáḍḍil ma íħki.*	بْفضِّل ما إحْكي.
What religion are you?	*šū dīnak?* *ínta min áyya diyēni?*	شو دينك؟ إنْتَ مِن أيّا دِيانِة؟
Are you married?	*mjáwwaz?*	مْجوّز؟
That's personal.	*háyda šī šáxṣi.*	هَيْدا شي شخْصي.

Where do you live?	*wēn 3ēyiš?* *wēn sēkin?*	وينْ عايِش؟ وينْ ساكِن؟

◇

Do you like Beirut?	*bitḫíbb bayrūt?*	بِتْحِبّ بَيْروت؟
You have to try Malak Al Tawouk (restaurant).	*lēzim tjárrib málik iṭṭāwūʔ.*	لازِم تْجرِّب ملِك الطّاووق.
Have you tried __?	*šī márra jarrábit __?*	شي مرّة جرّبِت __؟
You have to come over to my place sometime.	*lēzim tíbʔa tíji la-3índi.*	لازِم تِبْقى تِجي لعِنْدي.
Wait, I'll show you myself. I'm not doing anything anyway.	*láḫẓa, ána bfarjīk. ma 3índi šī áṣlan.*	لحْظة، أنا بْفرْجيك. ما عِنْدي شي أصْلاً.
You have to take your kids to the Baalbek Castle.	*lēzim tēxud wlēdak 3a ʔál3it b3álbak.*	لازِم تاخُد وْلادك عَ قلْعِةْ بعلْبك.
How much do you spend on rent?	*ʔaddē btídfa3 ājār?*	قدّيْ بْتِدْفع أجار؟
How much do you earn (a month)?	*ʔaddē btíʔbaḍ?*	قدّيْ بْتُقْبُض؟

Visiting Someone's Home زْيارة

There are very few things that Lebanese people enjoy doing more than feeding you. So expect to be invited to people's homes for a meal, and don't even think about saying no! You may also get invited over to someone's house عالنّسْكافيْه *3a-n[Nescafé]* **to have Nescafé**, which has replaced, to a large extent, the more traditional Turkish coffee, especially amongst young people. When you do get invited over to someone's home, it is always appropriate to take something with you. In Lebanon, we say ما تْروح إيديْك فاضْيِين *ma trūḫ idēk fāḏyīn* (to a man) and ما تْروحي إيدَيْكي فاضْيِين *ma trūḫi idáyki fāḏyīn* (to a woman) **Don't go empty-handed**. 'What shall I take,' you may ask? What you bring should ideally be complementary to what you're invited to. For example, if you're invited to dinner, take a dessert. If you're invited over to have Nescafé, bring cookies. It used to be the case that people would take only Lebanese sweets, such as بقْلاوِة *báqlawi* **baklava** or نمّورة *nammūra* **nammura**, when visiting friends. These days, people also bring things that may be considered more Western, such as كايْك *[cake]* or نْبيد *nbīd* **wine** (but only if you know that your hosts drink alcohol).

Accepting an Invitation

◇ هاي! عازْمِتك جِمْعِةْ الجايِة[1] عالغدا عِنْدي بِالبيْت!
o مرْسي كْتير! كِلّك ذوْق![2]
◇ شوفي أيّا نْهار بِناسْبِك، ورِدّي عْلَيي خبر.
o بِفْتكِر التّلاتا بيكون كْتير مْنيح.[3]
◇ أوْكيْ! وأنا كمان فِيي[4] التّلاتا. لكان رح أُنْطْرِك السّاعة أرْبْعة ومْنِتْغدّى سَوى.

◇ Hey, you're invited to lunch next week at my place.
o Bless you! Thanks!
◇ Check which day suits you and let me know.
o I think Tuesday would be okay.
◇ Okay, I'm free on Tuesday, too. So I'll be expecting for you at 4 p.m. to have lunch together.

◇ *[hi]! 3āzmítik jím3it iljēyi[1] 3a-lɣáda 3índi bi-lbēt!*
o *[Fmerci] ktīr! kíllik zōʔ![2]*
◇ *šūfi áyya nhār bi-nēsbik, w ríddi 3láyi xábar.*
o *bíftikir ittalēta bikūn ktīr mnīḫ.[3]*
◇ *okē! w ána kamēn fíyi[4] -ttalēta. lakēn raḫ únṭrik issē3a árb3a w mnitɣádda sáwa.*

[1] = الأُسْبوع الجايي *-lʔusbū3 iljēyi*

[2] كلّك ذوْق، بسّ مشْغولِة الأُسْبوع الجايي. *kállik zōʔ, bass mašɣūli -lʔusbū3 iljēyi.* **That's very kind, but I'm busy next week.**

[3] بْظِنّ التّنيْن بيْظْبط. *bẓinn ittanēn byúẓbaṭ.* **I think Monday works.**; بْظِنّ الخميس ما عِنْدي شي. *bẓinn ilxamīs ma 3índi šī.* **I think I'm free on Thursday.**

[4] (lit. I can); فاضْيِة *fāḍyi* **free, unoccupied**

2

Arriving at someone's home

◇ يا أهْلا وسهْلا! حمْدِالله عالسّلامِة.

o الله يْسلْمِك.

◇ تْفضّلي فوتي، البيْت بيْتِك.

o مْنيح بعتيلي اللّوكايْشِن[1]. كْتير ساعدِتْني أوصل.[2]

◇ خيّ حمْدِالله. قِلِت أحْسن إبْعت اللّوكايْشِن لِأنّو العِنْوان صعْب شْوَيّ.

◇ Welcome, welcome! Thank God you arrived safely!

o God bless you.

◇ Come in. Make yourself at home.

o It's good you sent me the location. That made it much easier.

◇ Cool, thank God. I thought it best to send the location because the address is a bit tricky.

◇ *ya áhla w sáhla! ɦamdílla 3a-ssalēmi.*

o *álla ysállmik.*

◇ *tfáḍḍali fūti, -lbēt báytik.*

o *mnīɦ ba3atīli -l[location][1]. ktīr sē3adítni ūṣal.[2]*

◇ *xayy ɦamdílla. ʔílit áɦsan íb3at il[location] li-ánnu -l3inwēn ṣá3b šwayy.*

[1] المَوْقع *-lmáwʔi3*

[2] = كْتير فادْني. *ktīr fēdni.*

3

Sitting down to eat

◇ تْفضّلي عَ[1] أوضْةْ السُّفْرة.

o شو هَيْدا كِلّو؟ يَعْطيكي العافْيِة![2]

◇ منّي عامْلِة شي. كِلّو مِن حَواضِر البيْت![3] يَلّا قْعِدي.[4]

o عن جدّ تعّبْتي حالِك[5].

◇ Come on into the dining room.

o What is all this? Bless your hands!

◇ What did I do, girl? It's all simple stuff. Have a seat.

o You've really worn yourself out.

◇ *tfáḍḍali 3a*[1] *ūḍt issúfra.*

o *šū háyda kíllu? ya3ṭīki -l3āfyi!*[2]

◇ *mánni 3āmli šī. kíllu min ḫawāḍir ilbēt!*[3] *yálla ?3ídi.*[4]

o *3an jadd ta33ábti ḫālik*[5].

[1] = شرّْفي علْى *šárrfi 3la*

[2] = يِسْلمو إيدَيْكي! *yíslamu idáyki!*

[3] كِلّو أكِل جاهِز. *kíllu ákil jēhiz.* **It's all delivery food.**

[4] = يَلّا تْفضّلي *yálla tfáḍḍali*

[5] = عزّبْتي حالِك *3azzábti ḫālik*

4

FINISHING THE MEAL

○ يِسْلموا إيدَيْكي![1] عن جدّ الأكِل بيجنِّن.

◇ بِالكادِ[2] أكلْتي!

○ أنا ما أكلِت شي؟! نْفزرِت![3] انْشالله دايْماً بِالأفْراح.

◇ انْشالله يْكون الأكِل عَ ذَوْقِك! شو عم تعْمْلي؟! تْرِكي كِلّ شي محلّو. أنا بْعزِّل الطّاوْلِة.[4]

○ Bless your hands, really. The food is amazing!

◇ You barely ate anything!

○ I didn't eat anything?! I'm stuffed. An enduring dining table!

◇ I hope you enjoyed the food. What are you doing? Leave everything as it is. I'll clear the table.

○ *yíslamu idáyki!*[1] *3an jadd ilʔákil bijánnin.*

◇ *bi-lkēd*[2] *ákálti!*

○ *ána ma ákálit šī?! nfazárit!*[3] *nšálla dēyman bi-lʔáfrāɦ.*

◇ *nšálla ykūn ilʔákil 3a záwʔik! šū 3am tá3mli?! tríki kill šī maɦállu. ána b3ázzil iţţāwli.*[4]

[1] = يَعْطيكي العافْيِة! *ya3ţīki -l3āfyi!*

[2] = أنْجق *ʔánjaʔ*

[3] = نْتفخِت *ntafáxit*

[4] = انْشالله يْكون الأكِل عجبِك! شو عم تْساوي؟ ما تِدْقري شي. رْتاحي و أنا بِهْتمّ. *nšálla ykūn ilʔákil 3ájabik! šū 3am tsēwi? ma tídʔari šī. rtēɦi w ána bihtámm.*

5

Visiting a Sick Friend

○ حمْدِالله عالسّلامِة يا بطل!

◇ الله يْسلّمِك.

○ أوّل ما عْرِفْنا إنّك طْلِعِت مْن المِسْتشْفى، قِلْنا مْنِجي مِنْشِقّ عْليْك[1].

◇ يْخلّيلي ياكُن! شو جايْبين؟ ما كان في لْزوم تِتْعذّبوا![2]

○ أيّا عذاب! ما في شي بْيِحْرُز![3] المْهِمّ هلّق إنّو تْصير مْنيح[4] تَنْطمِّن بالْنا عْليْك.

○ Thank God you're okay, champ!

◇ God bless you!

○ As soon as we found out that you were out of the hospital, we thought we should come and check on you.

◇ Bless you! And what's this you've brought? You shouldn't have [gone to the trouble]!

○ What trouble? It's nothing really. What's important is that you get better, so we can feel reassured about your health.

○ *ɧamdílla 3a-ssalēmi ya báţal!*

◇ *álla ysállmik.*

○ *áwwal ma 3rífna ínnak ţlí3it mn ilmistášfa, ʔílna mníji minší?? 3lēk*[1].

◇ *yxallīli yēkun! šū jēybīn? ma kēn fī lzūm tit3ázzbu!*[2]

○ *áyya 3azēb! ma fī šī byíɧruz!*[3] *limhímm hállaʔ ínnu tşīr mnīɧ*[4] *ta-nţámmin bēlna 3lēk.*

[1] = مِنْطِلّ عْليْك *minţíll 3lēk* = مِنْزورك *minzūrak* **/** [2] ليْه عزّبْتوا حالْكُن؟ *lē 3azzábtu ɧālkun?* **Why did you trouble yourself?** **/** [3] ما شي هَيْدا! مِش مِن قيمْتك. *ma šī háyda! miš min ʔīmtak.* **It's nothing really.** (مِش مِن قيمْتك *miš min ʔīmtak* (lit. it's not worth your value) means "you deserve more than this." The expression is commonly used as a reply to someone thanking you for a gift you bought them. **/** [4] = أحْسن *áɧsan*

6

I HAVE TO GET GOING

○ طيِّب، أنا صار لازِم إمْشي.[1]

◇ ما بعْدِك واصْلِة! شو عِنْدِك؟

○ لأ عن جِدّ بْقيت زْيادِة عن اللّزوم وسهّرْتِك لَوَقْت مْأخّر.[2]

◇ أيّا زْيادِة عن اللّزوم؟ نْبسطِت فيكي قدّ الدِّني.[3] كانِت زْيارة كْتير حِلْوِة.

○ تِسْلميلي حبيبْتي. تاني مرّة عِنْدي إذا الله راد.

○ Well, it's about time I get going.

◇ But you just got here. What do you have to do?

○ No, seriously, I've overstayed my welcome, and I've kept you up late.

◇ What are you talking about? Your visit has made me happy. It was a really nice visit.

○ Bless you, sweetie. Next time, at my place, God willing.

○ *ṭáyyib, ána ṣār lēzim ímši.*[1]

◇ *ma bá3dik wāṣli! šū 3índik?*

○ *laʔ 3an jadd bʔīt zyēdi 3an illzūm w sahhártik la-wáʔt mʔáxxar.*[2]

◇ *áyya zyēdi 3an illzūm? nbasáṭit fīki ʔadd iddíni.*[3] *kēnit zyāra ktīr ḫílwi.*

○ *tislamīli ḫabībti. tēni márra 3índi íza álla rād.*

[1] = بِسْتأْذِن، صار لازِم فِلّ. *bistáʔzin, ṣār lēzim fill.* **Forgive me, but I have to leave.**

[2] = لأ، كْتير طوّلِت عْلَيْكي. *laʔ, ktīr ṭawwálit 3láyki.*

[3] = شرّفْتي *šarráfti*

Extended Dialogue

- ○ أهْلا وسهْلا! وْصِلْتي كْتير بْسِرْعة!
- ◇ أيْه حمْدِالله الطُّرْقات كانِت كْتير مْنيحة وتْذكّرْت العِنْوان مِن مرّةْ الماضْيِة.
- ○ مْنيح إنّو ما نْسيتي! يَلّا فوتي، الأكِل جاهِز، هلّق شِلْتو مْن الفُرُن.
- ◇ أوْكيْ حُطّي هَيْدا بِالبرّاد.
- ○ يا الله! ما كان في لْزوم![1]
- ◇ أيّا ما في لْزوم. ما بْيِحْرُز. مْناكْلو ديسّيْر.
- ○ مرْسي[2] حبيبْتي. يِسْلموا إيدَيْكي.[3]
- ◇ يِسْلموا إيدَيْكي إنْتي! بْساعْدِك بِشي؟
- ○ لأ، كِلّو جاهِز. غسّْلي إيدَيْكي، وتعي عَ أوضْةْ السُّفْرة.

(guest comes to the dining table)

- ○ واوْ! شو هالفخامِة هَيْدي![4]
- ◇ هَيْدا أقلّ شي حبيبْتي![5]
- ○ مِش كان أحْسن لَوْ كِلّ وِحْدِة عِمْلِت شي بدال ما إنْتي شْتغلْتي وتِعِبْتي وَحْدِك؟[6]
- ◇ أيْه عَ أساس إنْتي بْتعْرْفي تِطْبْخي. ما ضروري تْجرّْصينا يا بِنِت![7]
- ○ أوْكيْ بسّ خلّيكي مِتْذكّْرة إنّو أنا عرضِت علَيْكي خدماتي وإنْتي رفضْتيِنْ.[8]
- ◇ يَلّا طيِّب. بلّْشي كِلي، قبِل ما يْسقّْع الأكِل. شو بدِّك إسْكِبْلِك[9]؟[10]
- ○ لأ پْليز ما تِتْعذّبي. أنا بِسْكُب.
- ◇ أوْكيْ. بسّ پْليز تِعْتِبْري البيْت بَيْتِك. ما رح ضلّ إعْزُم.

(after finishing the meal)

- ○ عن جدّ يِسْلموا إيدَيْكي. الأكِل كان بيجنِّن![11]

◇ صحّْتينْ حبيبْتي. مطْرح ما يِسْروا يمِْروا! خلّينا نِشْرب نيسْكافيْه وناكُل الحِلو اللي جِبْتيه معُن.

○ لأ، أنا صار لازمِ إمْشي تلحِّق مَوْعد الحكيم.

◇ جايِة تاكْلي وتْفِلّي؟ بلا سئالِة. بعْمِل نيسْكافيْه عالسّريع.

○ أوْكي، بْضلّ بعْد شْوَيّ، بسّ ما فِيِ طوِّل.

◇ وَلا يْهِمِّك! بعْمِل النّيسْكافيْه إنْتي وعم بِتْغسّْلي إيدَيْكي.

◇ Welcome! You got here fast!

○ Yeah, thank God, the roads were good, and I remembered the address from last time.

◇ Well, that's good you didn't forget it. Come on then. The food is ready. I just took it off the stove.

○ Okay, put this in the refrigerator then.

◇ Oh my! You shouldn't have!

○ What do you mean! It's something simple we'll have for dessert.

◇ Thank you, dear! Bless your hands!

○ Bless your hands! Shall I help you with anything?

◇ No, everything is ready. Go wash your hands, then come to the dining room.

(guest comes to the dining table)

○ Wow! What's all this high-end work!

◇ It's the least I could do, hun!

○ Wouldn't it have been better if we had made it a potluck instead of you wearing yourself out like this?

◇ Yeah right! Like you even know how to cook! Keep that on the down low!

○ Okay! Just remember that I offered my services and you rejected them.

◇ Come on then. Start eating before it gets cold. What shall I dish out for you?

○ No, don't bother yourself. I'll do it myself.

◇ Okay, but please make yourself at home. I'm not going to keep offering.

(after finishing the meal)

○ Really, bless your hands! The food was amazing!

◇ My pleasure, dear! Let's have some nescafe and eat with it the dessert that you brought.

○ No, I should get going, so that I can make it in time to my doctor's appointment.

◇ So you're eating and running? Don't be ridiculous! I'll make the nescafe quickly.

○ All right, I'll stay a bit, but I can't be too late.

◇ Don't worry. I'll make the Nescafe while you go wash your hands.

○ *áhla w sáhla! wṣílti ktīr b-sír3a!*

◇ *ē, ђamdílla, -ṭṭurʔāt kēnit ktīr mnīђa w tzákkart il3inwēn min marrt -lmāḍyi.*

○ *mnīђ ínnu ma nsīti! yálla fūti, -lʔákil jēhiz, hállaʔ šíltu mn ilfúrun.*

◇ *okē ђúṭṭi háyda bi-lbarrād.*

○ *ya allāh! ma kēn fī lzūm!*[1]

◇ *áyya ma fī lzūm. ma byíђruz. mnēklu [F dessert].*

○ *[F merci]*[2] *ђabībti. yíslamu idáyki.*[3]

◇ *yíslamu idáyki ínti! bsē3dik bíši?*

○ *laʔ, kíllu jēhiz. ɣássli idáyki, w tá3i 3a ūḍt issúfra.*

(guest comes to the dining table)

○ *wāw! šū ha-lfaxāmi háydi!*[4]

◇ *háyda aʔáll šī ђabībti!*[5]

○ *miš kēn áђsan law kill wíђdi 3ímlit šī badēl ma ínti štaɣálti w ti3íbti wáђdik?*[6]

◇ *ē, 3a asēs ínti btá3rfi títbxi. ma ḍarūri tjarrṣīna ya bínit!*[7]

○ *okē bass xallīki mitzákkra ínnu ána 3aráḍit 3láyki xadamēti w ínti rafaḍtíyun.*[8]

◇ *yálla ṭáyyib. bállši kíli, ʔábil ma ysáʔʔi3 ilʔákil. šū báddik iskíblik*[9]*?*[10]

○ *laʔ [please] ma tit3ázzabi. ána bískub.*

◇ *okē. bass [please] ti3tíbri -lbēt báytik. ma raђ ḍall í3zum.*

(after finishing the meal)

○ *3an jadd yíslamu idáyki. -lʔákil kēn bijánnin!*[11]

◇ *ṣaħħtēn ħabībti. máṭraħ ma yísru yímru! xallīna níšrab [Nescafé] w nēkul ilħílu -lli jibtī má3un.*
○ *laʔ, ána ṣār lēzim ímši ta-láħħiʔ máw3ad ilħakīm.*
◇ *jēyi tēkli w tfílli? bála saʔāli. bá3mil [Nescafé] 3a-ssarī3.*
○ *okē, bḍall ba3d šwayy, bass ma fíyi ṭáwwil.*
◇ *wála yhímmik! bá3mil in[Nescafé], ínti w 3am bityássli idáyki.*

[1] ليْه مْعزّبي حالِك؟ *lē m3ázzbi ħálik?*

[2] = شكراً *šúkran*

[3] = كِلّك ذوْق *kíllik zōʔ* **You're too kind.**

[4] = يا عيْن! شو هالحِلو! *ya 3ēn! šū ha-lħílu!*

[5] = مِش مِن قيمْتِك حبيبْتي. *miš min ʔīmtik, ħabībti.*

[6] مِش كان أرْيَحْلِك لَوْ كِلّ وِحْدِة حضّرِت شي؟ *miš kēn aryáħlik law kill wíħdi ħáḍḍarit šī?* **Wouldn't it have been better if we had each prepared something?**

[7] لأ وَلَوْ! إنْتي ضيْفِة! *laʔ, waláw! ínti ḍīfi!* **No, come on! You're a guest!**; تْجرّصينا *tjarraṣīna* is an idiom that means 'you put us to shame, you embarass us.' Basically, one of the girls is telling her friend that if she had cooked, she would have embarassed herself because she's not great at cooking. Not that there's anyone else beside them, but the idiom is meant to sound like there are other people who are judging the situation, in addition to the two of them.

[8] ما في بيْناتْنا. أنا مْن البيْت. منّي غريبِة. *ma fī bēnētna.* (lit. there is nothing between us) *ána mn ilbēt. mánni ɣarībi.* These expressions are commonly used by a guest as a response to a host who just wants them to relax and not help in order to assure the host that such formalities are unnecessary.

[9] = صِبِّلّك *ṣibbíllik* = حِطِّلّك *ħiṭṭíllik*

[10] ما رح إعْزُم فيكي، رحْ خلّيكي عَ راحْتِك. *ma raħ í3zum fīki, raħ xallīki 3a rāħtik.* **I won't invite you; I will leave you with your comfort.** (meaning: I won't insist on you eating. I'll let you serve youreIf (to make you comfortable).)

[11] = كان كْتير طيِّب! *kēn ktīr ṭáyyib.*

Vocabulary

meal invitation	*3azīmi*	عزيمِة
breakfast	*tirwīʔa*	تِرْويقة
to have breakfast	*tráwwaʔ (yitráwwaʔ)*	تْروّق (يِترْوّق)
lunch	*ɣáda*	غدا
to have lunch	*tɣádda (yitɣádda)*	تْغدّى (يِتْغدّى)
dinner	*3áša*	عشا
to have dinner	*t3áššа (yit3áššа)*	تْعشّى (يِتْعشّى)
dessert	*ɦílu* *[ᶠdessert]*	حِلو ديسيرْ
to have dessert	*tɦálla (yitɦálla)*	تْحلّى (يِتْحلّى)
water	*mayy*	ميّ
tea	*šāy*	شاي
a glass of tea	*finjēn šāy*	فِنْجان شاي
coffee	*ʔáhwi*	قهْوِة
a cup of cofffee	*finjēn ʔáhwi*	فِنْجان قهْوِة
dining table	*ţāwlit súfra*	طاوْلِة سُفْرة
food	*ákil*	أكِل
hot	*síxin*	سخِن
cold, cool	*bērid* *msáʔʔa3*	بارِد مْسقّع
address	*3inwēn (3anawīn)*	عِنْوان (عناوين)

the way	*-ṭṭarīʔ*	الطّريق
late	*mitʔáxxir*	مِتْأخِّر
early	*bakkīr*	بكّير
to arrive	*wíṣil, yūṣal*	وُصِل، يوصل
to eat	*ákal (yēkul)*	أكل (ياكُل)
to gather up, clear away (dishes, etc.)	*lamm (ylimm)*	لمّ (يْلِمّ)
tray	*ṣaníyyi (ṣawēni)*	صنية (صَواني)
plate	*ṣáħin*	صحِن
fork	*šáwki (šúwak)*	شوْكِة (شُوَك)
spoon	*málʔa3a (malēʔi3)* *mál3ʔa (malē3iʔ)*	ملْقعة (ملاقع) ملْعْقة (ملاعِق)
pot	*ṭánjra*	طنْجْرة
ladle	*kábši*	كبْشِة
knife	*sikkīni (skakīn)*	سِكّينِة (سْكاكين)
cup	*finjēn (fanajīn)*	فِنْجان (فناجين)
bathroom	*ħammēm*	حمّام

Expressions

No, I'm paying this time.; It's on me this time.	*laʔ, ána báddi ídfa3 ha-lmárra.* *laʔ, xallíya 3láyi ána ha-lmárra.*	لأ، أنا بدّي إدْفع هالمرّة. لأ، خلِّيا علَيي أنا هالمرّة.
(to someone insisting on paying) Absolutely not. You do this every time.	*akīd laʔ. kill márra btá3mil hēk.*	أكيد لأ. كِلّ مرّة بْتعْمِل هيْك.
You've brought us joy (lit. enlightened us) and honored us.	*nawwartūna w šarraftūna.*	نوّرْتونا وشرّفْتونا.
(response) Your home is already enlightened by its inhabitants.	*-lbēt mnáwwar bi-áhlu.*	البيْت مْنوّر بِأهْلو.
Compliments to the chef! (lit. Bless your hands!)	*yíslamu idēk!* *ysállimun!*	يِسْلموا إيديْك! يْسلِّمُن!
An enduring dining table![1]	*súfra dēymi.*	سُفْرة دايْمِة.
May [this house] always be filled with food and guests.	*nšálla tḍálla -lʔáfrāḥ bi-diyārkun 3āmra.*	انْشالله تْضلّا الأفْراح بْدِيارْكُن عامْرة.
Thank God you are back / arrived safely / recovered.	*-lḥamdílla 3a-ssalēmi.*	الحمْدِالله عالسّلامِة.
(response) Thank you.	*álla ysállmak.*	الله يْسلّْمك.

[1] (lit. May this dining table always be filled with guests and food.)

◇

What's up with being right on time...? To the minute, wow!	*šū ha lmawā3īd lli 3a lwáʔit háydi? 3a ddaʔīʔa, wāw!*	شو هالمَواعيد اللي عالوَقِت هَيْدي؟ عالدقيقة، واوْ!
(sarcastic, to someone who is late) Such punctuality! Why don't you just come tomorrow?	*šū ha ddíʔʔa bi lmawā3īd? ínnu kínt jīt búkra.*	شو هالدِقّة بالمَواعيد؟ إنّو كِنِت جيت بُكْرا.
Would anybody like coffee or tea?	*ђáda 3a bēlu ʔáhwi aw šāy?*	حدا عَ بالو قهْوِة أَوْ شاي؟
Minds are lost for the sake of tummies.[1] Grab a chair and dig in.	*3ind ilbuṭṭūn ɖā3it il3ʔūl. jīb kírsi, w midd īdak.*	عِنْد البُطّون ضاعِت العْقول.[1] جيب كِرْسي، ومِدّ إيدك.
I hope you enjoyed the food.	*bi-lhána w -ššífa.*	بِالهنا والشِفا.
I cannot get enough of your presence.	*ʔa3dítkun ma byinšába3 mínna.*	قعْدِتْكُن ما بْيِنْشِبِع مِنّا.
Where are you going? It's still early.	*la-wēn rāyiђ? ba3d bakkīr.*	لَويْن رايِح؟ بعْد بكّير.

[1] This is a colloquial idiom you might jokingly say to or about who's not thinking straight because they're so hungry. You can even say it about yourself.

Making Appointments أخِد مَواعيد

One cannot talk about making مَواعيد *mawē3id* **appointments** without addressing the elephant in the room: the stereotype that Lebanese people are never on time. While that is true for many (okay, probably most) Lebanese, everyone's punctuality was not created equal. So, it's always best that you show up on time for appointments, even if the people you're meeting with are running late–because you never know. But expect to wait at least 10 minutes past the appointment time. And this applies not only to social settings but also to appointments with doctors, meetings at work, etc. When you're waiting for a friend or a colleague to show up for a meeting or a get-together, and you call to check on their whereabouts, you'll likely be told something like واصِل *wāṣil* **I'm just arriving**, or عالطّريق *3a-ṭṭarīʔ* **I'm on the way**, or ثَواني وبْكون عِنْدَك *sawēni w bkūn 3índak* **I'll be there in a few seconds**. But take all of these expressions with a grain of salt; they're rarely literal!

Setting a Formal Appointment

○ كان بدّي إحْكيك بِخْصوص المشْروع.

◇ سوْري بسّ مشْغول هلّق.[1]

○ أوْكي، فاضي[2] بعْد الضُّهُر؟[3]

◇ أيْه مفْروض السّاعة وِحْدِة بْتِظْبُط[4].

○ I wanted to talk to you about the project.

◇ Sorry, but I'm busy now.

○ All right, are you free this afternoon?

◇ Yes, 1 p.m. should be fine.

○ *kēn báddi iħkīk bi-xṣūṣ ilmašrū3.*

◇ *[sorry] bass mašɣūl hálla?.*[1]

○ *okē, fāḍi*[2] *ba3d iḍḍúhur?*[3]

◇ *ē, mafrūḍ issē3a wíħdi btíẓbuṭ*[4].

[1] حْكيني بعْديْن، مِش فاضي هلّق. *ħkīni ba3dēn, miš fāḍi hálla?.* **Talk to me later. I'm not free at the moment.**

[2] = بيناسْبك *binēsbak* (lit. it is convenient for you)

[3] بسّ المَوْضوع كْتير مِسْتعْجِل، ما بْيِنْطر. *bass ilmawḍū3 ktīr mistá3jil, ma byínṭur.* **But it is very urgent and cannot be put off.**

[4] عالوِحْدِة مْنيح؟ *3a-lwíħdi mnīħ?* **Is around one o'clock good?**

Lebanese people (and Middle Easterners in general) love meetings. They'll often meet to schedule another meeting to discuss a previous meeting. Because of this and other reasons, companies rarely run efficiently; so many roles are somewhat redundant, and many employees end up spending a good chunk of the day socializing. You see, work in Lebanon is not just about work; it's also about the relationships and friendships you build along the way–only the latter ends up taking a good portion of the day.

2

Making plans with a friend

o ليْك شو رأْيَك نْروح عالسّينِما بعْد الشِّغِل اليوْم؟

◇ هات لنْروح مِن عشية.[1]

o أوْكيْ، خلّينا نِحْضر عرْض السّاعة سبْعة.

◇ أوْكيْ، كْتير مْنيح. بْلاقيك عَ شِبّاك التّذاكِر عالسّبْعة إلّا رِبِع.

o Hey, how about we go to the movies after work today?

◇ Well, let's make it in the evening.

o Okay, let's see a seven-o'clock showing.

◇ All right, very good. I'll meet you there at the ticket window at a quarter to seven.

o *lēk šū ráʔyak nrūḫ 3a-ssīnema ba3d iššíɣil ilyōm?*

◇ *hēt la-nrūḫ min 3ašíyyi.*[1]

o *okē, xallīna níḫḍar 3arḍ issē3a sáb3a.*[2]

◇ *okē, ktīr mnīḫ. blēʔīk 3a šibbēk ittazēkir 3a-ssáb3a ílla ríbi3.*

[1] = تعا نْروح عشِيِّة. *tá3a nrūḫ 3ašíyyi.*

[2] طيِّبْ، فيك تِمْرُق تاخِدْني؟ *ṭáyyib, fīk tímruʔ tēxídni?* **Okay, can you come by and pick me up?**

3

Agreeing on a Time (Formal)

○ أوْكي، فاضْيِة الخميس السّاعة تْنعْش الضُهُر؟[1]

◇ لأ الخميس كْتير صعْبِة السّاعة تْنعْش. برْكي عشْرة الصُبُح، شو رأْيَك؟

○ لِلأسف عِنْدي اِجْتِماع[2] السّاعة عشْرة. برْكي اليوْم بعْد الضُّهُر إذا فاضْيِة؟

◇ لأ، كْتير مشْغولِة اليوْم، ويمِكِن فِلّ بكّير. شو رأْيَك بِالسّبِت؟[3]

○ أوْكي مدام. السّبِت كْتير مْنيح. بسّ قوليلي أيّا ساعة بِناسْبِك أكْتر شي.

○ Okay, are you free at 12 p.m. on Thursday?

◇ No, Thursday will be too difficult around noon. Maybe around 10 a.m. What do you think?

○ Unfortunately, I have a meeting at 10. Maybe this afternoon if you are free?

◇ No, I'm extremely busy today, and I might leave early. How about Saturday?

○ Okay, ma'am. Saturday will be perfect. Just tell me what time suits you best.

○ *okē, fāḍyi -lxamīs issē3a tna3š iḍḍúhur?*[1]

◇ *laʔ -lxamīs ktīr ṣá3bi -ssē3a tna3š. bárki 3ášra -ṣṣúbuḫ, šū ráʔyak?*

○ *li-lʔásaf 3índi ijtimē3*[2] *issē3a 3ášra. bárki -lyōm ba3d iḍḍúhur íza fāḍyi?*

◇ *laʔ, ktīr mašɣūli -lyōm, w yímkin fill bakkīr. šū ráʔyak bi-ssábit?*[3]

○ *okē, [*F*madame]. -ssábit ktīr mnīḫ. bass ʔūlīli áyya sē3a binēsbik áktar šī.*

1 = عِنْدِك/مِرْتِبْطة شي الخميس الضُّهُر؟ *3índik/mirtíbṭa šī -lxamīs iḍḍúḫur?*

2 اِرْتِباطات *irtibāṭāt* **commitments**

3 فاضْيِة، ما عندي شي. *fāḍyi, ma 3índi šī.* **I'm free. I don't have anything [going on then].**

4

AGREEING ON A TIME (INFORMAL)

◇ شو صاحْبي! أيّا ساعة رح نِتْلاقى اليوْم؟

o ضُهْرِيات. شو رأيَك نِتْغدّى سَوا؟

◇ لأ مان. إمّي عامْلِة أكْلِة بْتِقْتُل[1]. خلّينا نِتْلاقى مِن عشية.

o أوْكيْ،[2] بسّ بكّير شي السّاعة سبْعة لِأنّو بدّي إمْرُق عَ محلّ الكُمْبيوترِ قبِل ما روح عالبيْت وقبِل ما يْسكّروا.

◇ أيْه وَلا يْهِمّك، ما بيسكّروا قبِل الحِدعْش.

◇ Hey, dude! When are we meeting up today?

o Around noon. How about we have lunch together?

◇ No, man. My mom is making a killer meal today. Let's meet in the evening.

o Okay, but early, around 7 p.m. so I can get to the computer shop before going home and they close.

◇ Don't worry. They don't close until 11.

◇ *šū ṣāḫbi! áyya sē3a raḫ nitlēʔa -lyōm?*

o *ḍuhriyēt. šū ráʔyak nitɣádda sáwa?*

◇ *laʔ [man] . ímmi 3āmli ákli btíʔtul*[1]*. xallīna nitlēʔa min 3ašíyyi.*

o *okē,* [2] *bass bakkīr, šī -ssē3a sáb3a li-ánnu báddi ímruʔ 3a maḫáll il[computer] ʔábil ma rūḫ 3a-lbēt w ʔábil ma ysákkru.*

◇ *ē, wála yhímmak, ma bisákkru ʔábil liḫda3š.*

[1] = دمار *dmār* (lit. of destruction) = بِتْجنِّن *bitjánnin* (lit. that drives crazy) = بِتْعقِّد *bit3áʔʔid* (lit. gives you a complex) **/** [2] A response could be طب قِلّي تْفضَّل! *ṭab, ʔílli tfáḍḍal!* **At least, invite me!** (lit. So, say to me 'please, here you are') Here, the friend mentioned that his mom was cooking a tasty meal, so you could jokingly imply that you'd like to be invited to partake. Often someone who is, for example, eating a sandwich, might say تْفضّل *tfáḍḍal* as an invitation to share the food. But this is an empty courtesy to show good manners. It is not to be taken seriously, and you should not then help yourself to your friend's sandwich. Instead, say شُكْراً، صحّتينْ *šúkran, ṣaḫḫtēn* **Thank you. Bon appetit!**

5

RESCHEDULING

○ مرْحبا، كان عِنْدي مَوْعد مع دُكْتوْر هِشام نْهار الخميس السّاعة خمْسِة العصِر.

◇ أيْه مظْبوط دْمْوازيْل. كان بدّي دِقِّلِك تأكِّد المَوْعد.

○ أوْكي، فينا نعْمْلو أبْكر شْوَيّ، حَيَلّا نْهار، لِأنّو مْسافْرة الخميس؟

◇ لِلأسف دُكْتوْر هِشام مشْغول كْتير كِلّ هَيْدي الجِمْعة. بِهالحالِة خلّينا نعْمِل المَوْعد الجِمْعة الجايِة[1].

○ أوْكي، أيْه عْمِلي معْروف.

○ Hi, I had an appointment with Dr. Hisham at 5 p.m. on Thursday.

◇ Ah, yes, miss. I was going to call to confirm with you.

○ Okay, can we make it earlier on any other day because I'm traveling on Thursday?

◇ Unfortunately, Dr. Hisham is busy all week. In that case, we can set another appointment for next week.

○ Okay, yes, please!

○ *márḫaba, kēn 3índi máw3ad ma3 [ᶠdocteur] hišām nhār ilxamīs issē3a xámsi -l3áṣir.*

◇ *ē, maẓbūṭ, [ᶠdemoiselle]. kēn báddi diʔʔílik ta-ʔákkid ilmáw3ad.*

○ *okē, fīna ná3mlu ábkar šwayy, ḫayálla nhār, li-ánnu msēfra -lxamīs?*

◇ *li-lʔásaf [ᶠdocteur] hišām mašɣūl ktīr kill háydi -ljím3a. bi-ha-lḫāli xallīna ná3mil ilmáw3ad iljím3a ljēyi[1].*

○ *okē, ē, 3míli ma3rūf.*

[1] = الأُسْبوع الجايي *-lʔusbū3 iljēyi*

6

Canceling plans

○ بْتعْرْفي شو، روحوا بلايي عالكوْنْسِرْت اللَّيْلِة.

◇ ييه ليْه! شو صار؟

○ قسْطل مسْدود بِالحمّام، وجايي السّنْجري يْشوف شو القُصّة. ما بعْرِف أيّا ساعة بيخلِّص.

◇ ييه لأ! ما تِعْتلي همّ. بيصلِّحا، وإذا خلّص بكّير، لاقينا!

○ أوْكي، تنْشوف. انْشالله كِلّو يمِرْق عَ سلامِة[1].

○ You know what? You guys go ahead without me to the concert tonight.

◇ Why?! What happened?

○ A pipe is blocked in the bathroom and a plumber is coming to fix it. I have no idea what time he will finish.

◇ Oh no! Don't worry. Hopefully, he'll fix it, and if he finishes early, go ahead and join us.

○ Okay, we'll see. Hopefully, it'll go smoothly!

○ *btá3rfi šū, rūħu balēyi 3a-l[concert] illáyli.*

◇ *yī lē! šū ṣār?*

○ *ʔásṭal masdūd bi-lħammēm, w jēyi -ssangári yšūf šū -lʔúṣṣa. ma bá3rif áyya sē3a bixálliṣ.*

◇ *yī laʔ! ma tí3tali hamm. biṣallíħa, w íza xállaṣ bakkīr, lēʔīna!*

○ *okē, tanšūf. nšálla kíllu yímruʔ 3a salēmi*[1].

[1] = عَ خيرْ *3a xēr*

○ لَيْكي يا بِنِت! بِحياتْنا ما رح نِضْهر؟[1]

◇ يا ريْت والله! مِشْتاقِتْلِك كْتير![2]

○ أوْكي، شو رأيِك بالويك أنْد الجايي؟

◇ الجِمْعة عِنْدي رِحْلِة، بسّ السّبِت بْيِمْشي!

○ أوْكي، شو رأيك نِتْغدّى سَوى، ونِحْضر فيلْم؟

◇ خلّيا تِرْويقة[3]. شو رأيِك مِنْروح نِرْكُض عالكوْرْنيش، ومْنِرْجع مْنِتْروّق.

○ الكوْرْنيش؟ مِش مْسكّْرينو تَيْحضْروا للمهْرجان؟

◇ لأ ما بِفْتِكِر بيبلّْشوا لجِمْعِةْ الجايِة.

○ بْتعْرْفي شو؟ نْسي الرّكِض. ما إلي جْلادِة.[4]

◇ طيِّب. خلّينا نْروح نِتْغدّى ومْنِحْضر سينِما عالأرْبْعة.

○ لأ خلّينا نِتْغدّى عالأرْبْعة، ونِحْضر فيلْم عالسّبْعة.

◇ لحْظة شْوَيّ. شو التّاريخ السّبِت؟[5]

○ تْلاتة وعِشْرين أذار.

◇ لأ نوْ وايْ![6] نْسيت إنّو[7] عِنْدي مَوْعد عِنْد الحكيم.

○ عم تِمْزِجي.[8] أيّا ساعة؟

◇ خمْسِة العصِر.

○ طيِّب، فإذاً خلّينا نِتْروّق[9] ومْنِرْجع مِنْشوف إذا مِنْلحِّق نْروح عالسّينِما.

◇ أوْكي، خلّينا نْأكِّد لبعْضْنا[10] الجِمْعة مِن عشية.

○ Girl, aren't we ever going to go out?

◇ I really want to, girl. I miss you so much.

○ Well, how about next weekend?

◇ Next Friday, I have a trip, but Saturday works for me.

o Okay, how about we have lunch and go to the movies?

◇ Let's make it breakfast, or how about we go for a jog on the corniche and then have breakfast?

o The corniche? Isn't it closed down for the public as they prepare for the festival?

◇ No, I don't think they're starting until next week.

o You know what? Forget about jogging. I can't be bothered.

◇ Okay, let's have lunch and go to the cinema at 4 then.

o No, let's have lunch at 4 and watch a movie at 7.

◇ Wait a minute! What date is that Saturday?

o March 23.

◇ No way! I totally forgot that I have a doctor's appointment!

o You must be kidding! What time is it at?

◇ At 5 p.m.

o Then let's make it breakfast and then see if we can make it to the cinema.

◇ Okay, let's confirm with each other on Friday evening.

o *láyki ya bínit! bi-ɧayētna ma raɧ níɖhar?*[1]

◇ *ya rēt wálla! mištēʔítlik ktīr!*[2]

o *okē, šū ráʔyik bi-l[weekend] iljēyi?*

◇ *-ljím3a 3índi ríɧli, bass issábit byímši!*

o *okē, šū ráʔyik nitɣádda sáwa, w níɧɖar fīlm?*

◇ *xallíya tirwīʔa*[3]*. šū ráʔyik minrūɧ nírkuɖ 3a-lkōrnīš, w mnírja3 mnitráwwaʔ.*

o *-lkōrnīš? miš msakkrīnu ta-yɧáɖɖru la-lmahrajēn?*

◇ *laʔ ma bíftikir bibállšu la-jím3it iljēyi.*

o *btá3rfi šū? nsi -rrákiɖ. ma íli jlēdi.*[4]

◇ *ţáyyib. xallīna nrūɧ nitɣádda w mníɧɖar [cinema] 3a-lʔárb3a.*

o *laʔ xallīna nitɣádda 3a-lʔárb3a, w níɧɖar [^{F}film] 3a-ssáb3a.*

◇ *láɧẓa šwayy. šū -ttērīx issábit?*[5]

o *tlēta w 3išrīn azār.*

◇ *la? [no way]!*[6] *nsīt ínnu*[7] *3índi máw3ad 3ind ilɦakīm.*
○ *3am tímzaɦi.*[8] *áyya sē3a?*
◇ *xámsi -l3áṣir.*
○ *ṭáyyib, fa-ízan xallīna nitráwwaʔ*[9] *w mnírja3 minšūf íza minláɦɦiʔ nrūɦ 3a-ssīnema.*
◇ *okē, xallīna nʔákkid la-bá3ḍna*[10] *-ljím3a min 3ašíyyi.*

[1] ضاق خِلْقي بالْبيت! *ḍāʔ xílʔi bi-lbēt* **I'm boring (always) being at home!** (lit. my morale/mood is confined at home) = زْهِقِت مْن القعْدِة بِالبيْت! *zhíʔit mn ilʔá3di bi-lbēt.*

[2] أيْ بْشرفِك، يَلّا نِطْلع! *ē, b-šárafik, yálla níṭla3!* **Yes, absolutely! Let's go out!** (بْشرفك *b-šárafak* (lit. by your honor) is a common phrase used to emphasize or implore.)

[3] = فْطور *fṭūr*

[4] = ما إلي خِلِق *ma íli xíli?*

[5] = قدّيْ بيكون بِالْشّهِر اْلسّبِت؟ *ʔaddē bikūn bi-ššáhir, -ssábit?*

[6] = لأ عن جدّ؟ *laʔ! 3an jadd?*

[7] = راح عن بالي إنّو... *rāɦ 3an bēli ínnu...* **It slipped my mind that...**

[8] عمْ تِحْكي جدّ؟ *3am tíɦki jadd?* **Are you serious?**

[9] = نِفْطر *níftar*

[10] في تِلِفوْن بيْناتْنا *fī [ᶠtelephone] bēnētna* **we'll call each other** (lit. there is a call between us)

Vocabulary

appointment, meeting (time)	*máw3ad (mawā3īd)* *ijtimē3*	مَوْعد (مَواعيد) اِجْتِماع
to meet	*ʔēbal (yʔēbil)*	قابل (يْقابِل)
to book	*ɦájaz (yíɦjiz)*	حجز (يِحْجِز)
reservation	*ɦájiz*	حجِز

to confirm	*ákkad (yʔákkid)*	أكّد (يْأكِّد)
confirmation	*taʔkīd*	تأْكيد
phone; phone call	*[Ftéléphone]*	تِلِفوْن
phone call	*ittiṣāl*	اِتِّصال
to call	*daʔʔ (ydiʔʔ)*	دقّ (يْدِقّ)
hour	*sē3a*	ساعة
two hours	*sē3tēn*	ساعْتينْ
three hours	*tlēt sē3āt*	تْلات ساعات
one minute	*dʔīʔa wíħdi*	دقيقة وِحْدِة
five minutes	*xams dʔāyiʔ*	خمْس دْقايِق
ten minutes	*3ášr dʔāyiʔ*	عشِر دْقايِق
15 minutes, a quarter hour	*ríbi3 sē3a*	رِبِع ساعة
20 minutes	*tilt sē3a*	تِلْت ساعة
half an hour	*nuṣṣ sē3a*	نُصّ ساعة
a quarter to	*sē3a ílla ríbi3*	ساعة اِلّا رِبِع
one moment	*sēnyi wíħdi*	ثانْيِة وِحْدِة
Saturday	*-ssábit*	السّبِت
Sunday	*-lʔáħad*	الأحد
Monday	*-ttanēn*	التّنينْ
Tuesday	*-ttalēta*	التّلاتة
Wednesday	*-lʔírb3a*	الإرْبْعا
Thursday	*-lxamīs*	الخميس

Friday	*-ljím3a*	الجِمْعة
weekend	*[weekend]*	ويك إنْد
during the week, on weekdays	*nuşş iljím3a*	نُصّ الجِمْعة
in the morning	*-şşúbuħ*	الصُّبُح
at noon	*-ḑḑúhur*	الضُّهُر
in the (early) afternoon	*ba3d iḑḑúhur*	بعْد الضُّهُر
in the late afternoon	*-l3áşir*	العصِر
at sunset	*-lmáɣreb* *-lmaɣīb*	المغْرب المغيب
in the evening	*bi-ssáhra*	بِالسّهْرة
in the late evening, at night	*bi-llēl*	بِاللّيْل
early	*bakkīr*	بكّير
late	*mitʔáxxir*	مِتْأخِّر
to cancel	*láɣa (yílɣi)*	لغى (يِلْغي)
1:05	*wíħdi w xámsi*	وِحْدِة وخمْسِة
2:10	*tnēn w 3ášra*	تْنيْن وعشْرة
3:15	*tlēti w ríbi3*	تْلاتِة وربِع
3:20	*tlēti w tilt*	تْلاتِة وتِلْت
4:25	*árb3a w nuşş ílla xámsi*	أرْبْعة ونُصّ اِلّا خمْسِة
5:30	*xámsi w nuşş*	خمْسِة ونُصّ
6:35	*sítti w nuşş w xámsi*	سِتِّة ونُصّ وخمْسِة

7:40	*tmēni ílla tilt*	تمْانِة إلّا تِلْت
9:45	*3ášra ílla ríbi3*	عشْرة إلّا ربِع
10:50	*ɧdā3iš ílla 3ášra*	حْداعِش إلّا عشْرة
11:55	*tnā3iš ílla xámsi*	تْناعِش إلّا خمْسِة
12:00 a.m.	*tnā3iš bi-llēl*	تْناعِش بِاللّيْل
12:00 p.m.	*tnā3iš iḑḑúhur*	تْناعِش الضُّهُر
2:00 a.m.	*tnēn bi-llēl*	تْنين بِاللّيْل
2:00 p.m.	*tnēn iḑḑúhur*	تْنين الضُّهُر
1:00 a.m.	*wíɧdi bi-llēl*	وِحْدِة بِاللّيْل
1:00 p.m.	*wíɧdi -ḑḑúhur*	وِحْدِة الضُّهُر
4:00 a.m.	*árb3a -lfájir*	أرْبْعة الفجِر
4:00 p.m.	*árb3a -l3áşir*	أرْبْعة العصِر

Expressions

(on the phone) Who's speaking? (lit. Who is with me?)	*mīn má3i?*	مين معي؟
Meet me at the Dawra roundabout in 10 minutes.	*laʔīni 3a [ᶠrond point] iddáwra ba3d 3ašr dʔāyiʔ.*	لاقيني عَ روْنْد پْوانْت الدَّوْرة بعْد عشْر دْقايِق.
Can we move our appointment to Monday?	*fīna nʔájjil máw3adna la-ttanēn?*	فينا نْأجِّل مَوْعدْنا للتّْنين؟

Can we have the meeting an hour <u>earlier</u>?	*fīna ná3mil il[meeting] ʔábil bi-sē3a?* *fīna nbákkir ilʔijtimē3 sē3a?*	فينا نعْمِل الميتينْغ قبِل بِساعة؟ فينا نْبكِّر الاِجْتِماع ساعة؟
Can we make the meeting one hour <u>later</u>?	*fīna nʔáxxir -lʔijtimē3 sē3a?* *fīna nʔájjil -l[meeting] sē3a?*	فينا نْأخِّر الاِجْتِماع ساعة؟ فينا نْأجِّل الميتينْغ ساعة؟
Cancel with them today.	*lɣī má3un ijtimē3 ilyōm.*	لْغي معُن اِجْتِماع اليوْم.
The appointment was canceled.	*-lmáw3d ltáɣa.*	المَوْعد لْتغى.
The outing was postponed until next week.	*-ḍḍáhra tʔájjalit la-jím3it iljēyi/ la-usbū3 iljēyi.*	الضّهْرة تْأجّلِت لجِمْعةِ الجايةِ/ لأُسْبوع الجايي.
At what time?	*áyya sē3a?*	أيّا ساعة؟
What time is it?	*ʔaddē -ssē3a?*	قدّيْ السّاعة؟
How many hours?	*kam sē3a?*	كم ساعة؟
On which day?	*ayy yōm?* *ayy nhār?*	أيّ يوْم؟ أيّ نْهار؟

At a Language Institute بِمركز تِعْليم اللُّغات

Larger cities in Lebanon, especially the capital, have a number of معاهِد لُغات *ma3āhid luɣāt* **language institutes** to meet the need of not only expats but also Lebanese who grew up abroad. Language classes are relatively affordable, compared to what you would pay for them in the U.S. or Europe, averaging between $9 and $20 an hour, depending on the institute. Major Lebanese American universities, such as the American University of Beirut and the Lebanese American University, also conduct intensive Arabic programs, but these aren't offered by the hour; rather, students are charged a program tuition, which varies from school to school, and depends on whether you're studying Classical Arabic (MSA) or colloquial Arabic, the latter being cheaper.

Inquiring about courses

○ حابّة أعْرِف أكْتر عن صْفوف العربي اللي بِتْقدّمُوْن هوْن.[1]

◇ فُصْحى أَوْ دارِج؟

○ فيكي تْقوليلي شْوَيّ عن التّنينْ[2]؟

◇ إن كان فُصْحى أَوْ دارِج، في تْنعْشر مُسْتَوى بِالتّنينْ، وكِلّ مُسْتَوى أرْبْعة وعِشْرين ساعة.

○ I would like to find out more about the Arabic courses you give at your center.

◇ MSA or colloquial?

○ Can you tell me about both?

◇ Whether MSA or colloquial, both have 12 levels of 24 hours each.

○ *ḫābbi á3rif áktar 3an ṣfūf il3árabi -lli bitʔáddmuwun hōn.*[1]

◇ *fúṣḫa aw dērij?*

○ *fīki tʔūlīli šwayy 3an ittnēn*[2]*?*

◇ *in kēn fúṣḫa aw dērij, fī tná3šar mústawa bi-ttnēn, w kill mústawa árb3a w 3išrīn sē3a.*

1 فيك تعْطيني فِكْرة عن صْفوف العربي؟ *fīk ta3ṭīni fíkra 3an ṣfūf il3árabi?* **Can you give me an idea (some information) about the Arabic classes?**

2 التّنينْ *-ttnēn* = الِتْنينْ *litnēn*

2

ARRANGING PRIVATE LESSONS

○ لَوْ سمحْتي، بدّي صفّ بسّ لإلْنا تْنَيْناتْنا[1].

◇ بسّ هَيْدا بْيُعْتبر صفّ پْريفيْه[2]، وبيكون أغْلى[3] مِن صْفوف المجْموعة.

○ أيْه ما في مشْكل.[4] بسّ مْهِمّ إنّو يْكون الصّفّ بعْد الضُّهُر.

◇ أوْكيْ، خلّيني شوف[5] شو في عِنّا، وبْرِدّ عْلَيْكي خبر.

○ Excuse me, I'd like a class, just for the two of us.

◇ But that would be considered a private course and will cost more than a regular course.

○ That's okay, no problem. But most importantly, it should be in the afternoon.

◇ Okay, let me check if there are available times, and I'll call and let you know.

○ *law samáḫti, báddi ṣaff bass la-ílna tnaynētna[1].*

◇ *bass háyda byu3tábar ṣaff [ᶠprivé][2], w bikūn áɣla[3] min ṣfūf ilmajmū3a.*

○ *ē, ma fī máškal.[4] bass mhimm ínnu ykūn iṣṣáff ba3d iḍḍúhur.*

◇ *okē, xallīni šūf[5] šū fī 3ínna, w bridd 3láyki xábar.*

[1] تْنَيْناتْنا tnaynētna **both of us** (masculine and feminine)

[2] = خْصوصي *xṣūṣi*

[3] = بيكلِّف أكْتر *bikállif áktar*

[4] قدّيْ بيكلِّف؟ *ʔaddē bikállif?* **How much does it cost?**

[5] = شيِّك *šáyyik* (derived from the English 'check')

3

CANCELING A PRIVATE LESSON

o سوْري، بسّ ما رح فِيي إجي اليوْم عالصّفّ، وبدّي إلْغي الدّرِس.

◇ بِأيّا غْروپ[1] إنْتَ؟

o لأ منّي بِغْروپ. عِنْدي دْروس خْصوصية السّاعة أرْبْعة اليوْم مع إسْتاذ كريم.

◇ كان لازِم تْقِلْنا[2] قبِل بِنْهار. هلّق الصّفّ بْيِنْحسب[3] عْليْك.

o ما بيأثِّر.[4] لأِنّو ما رح فِيي إجي عَ كِلّ الحالات. بسّ خبْرِي إسْتاذ كريم تما يِجي عالفاضي.

o I'm sorry, but I won't be able to make it to the course today, and would like to cancel the lesson.

◇ Which group are you in?

o No, I have a private lesson at 4 today with Mr. Karim.

◇ Well, you should have notified us a day ahead. Now you'll be charged for the lesson.

o That's okay. I won't be able to make it anyway. Just let Mr. Karim know so that he doesn't come in [to work] for nothing.

o *[sorry], bass ma raɧ fíyi íji -lyōm 3a-ṣṣáff, w báddi ílɣi -ddáris.*

◇ *bi-áyya [group][1] ínta?*

o *laʔ mánni bi-[group]. 3índi drūs xṣūṣíyyi -ssē3a árb3a -lyōm ma3 istēz karīm.*

◇ *kēn lēzim tʔílna[2] ʔábil bi-nhār. hállaʔ íṣṣaff byinɧásab[3] 3lēk.*

o *ma biʔássir.[4] li-ánnu ma raɧ fíyi íji 3a kill ilɧālēt. bass xábbri istēz karīm ta-má yíji 3a-lfāḍi.*

[1] = مجْموعة *majmū3a*

[2] = تْخبرّْنا *txábbirna*

[3] = بْيِتْمرّك *byitmárrak* **it is marked** (derived from the English 'mark')

[4] = مِش مِشْكْلِة *miš míškli* **no problem**

4

PAYING FOR A COURSE

○ عفواً لَوْ سمحِت،[1] بدّي إدْفع لصفّ العربي الدّارِج، النّيڤوْ[2] التّالِت.

◇ أوْكيْ، أوّل درْس بيكون بُكْرا، إن الله راد[3].

○ كْتير مْنيح. خمْسة وسِتّين دوْلار، ما هيْك؟

◇ أيْه مظْبوط. خمْسة وسِتّين دوْلار عالصّفّ، وخمْسْتعْشر دوْلار للِكْتاب.

○ Excuse me, I'd like to pay for the Colloquial Arabic course, level 3.

◇ Okay, the first lesson will be tomorrow, God willing.

○ Yes, $65, right?

◇ Yes, exactly. $65 for the course and $15 for the book.

○ *3áfwan law samáḫit,*[1] *báddi ídfa3 la-ṣáff il3árabi -ddērij, in[ᶠniveau]*[2] *-ttēlit.*

◇ *okē, áwwal dars bikūn búkra, in álla rād*[3].

○ *ktīr mnīḫ. xámsa w sittīn dólar, ma hēk?*

◇ *ē, maẓbūṭ. xámsa w sittīn dólar 3a-ṣṣáff, w xamstá3šar dólar la-liktēb.*

[1] = إذا بتْريد *íza bitrīd* = عْمول معْروف *3mōl ma3rūf*

[2] = المُسْتَوى *-lmústawa*

[3] = انْشالله *nšálla*

5

FINISHING A COURSE

◇ أوْكيْ، المرّةِ الجايةِ بيكون آخِر صفّ إذا الله راد.

o أيْ متى مِنْبلِّش بِتاني مرْحلةِ؟

◇ قبِل هيْك في فحِص ساعْتينْ عَ مية نُقْطة.

o أيْ متى هَيْدا؟

◇ أُسْبوع مِن بعْد آخِر سيْشِن[1]. والنّتايِج بْتِطْلع جِمْعة مِن بعْد هيْك كمان. مِن بعْد هيْك، مِنْبلِّش نْظبِّط الِغْروب لتاني ليْقِل.

◇ Okay, next time will be our final class, God willing.

o When will the next level start?

◇ Well, first there will be a two-hour exam out of 100 points.

o When will that be?

◇ One week after the final lesson and the results will come out a week after that. Then, we start forming a group for the next level.

◇ *okē, -lmárra iljēyi bikūn ēxir ṣaff íza álla rād.*

O *áymata minbálliš bi-tēni márɦali?*

◇ *ʔábil hēk fī fáɦiṣ sē3tēn 3a mīt núʔṭa.*

O *áymata háyda?*

◇ *usbū3 min ba3d ēxir [session][1]. w innatēyij btíṭla3 jím3a min ba3d hēk kamēn. min ba3d hēk, minbálliš nẓábbiṭ li[group] la-tēni [level].*

[1] = حِصّة *ɦíṣṣa*

Final assessment

○ مِسّ[1] سارة، فِيي أعْرِف علامْتي، پْليز؟
◇ شو إسْمِك؟
○ ساندْرا ويلْيامْز.
◇ ساندْرا، جِبْتي خمْسة وتِسْعين. واوْ! لازِم تْكفّي عَ تاني مُسْتَوى.
○ عن جدّ؟ مُسْتَوايي مْنيح؟
◇ كْتير مْنيح. وصار عِنْدِك حصيلِةْ كِلْمات كْتير واسْعة. أوعا تْوَقّْفي!

○ Ms. Sara, can I find out my grade, please?
◇ What's your name?
○ Sandra Williams.
◇ Sandra, you got 95. Wow! You should continue on to the next level.
○ Really? Is my level good?
◇ Very good. And you have acquired a great amount of vocabulary. Don't stop!

○ *[miss][1] sāra, fíyi á3rif 3alēmti, [please]?*
◇ *šū ísmik?*
○ *[Sandra Williams].*
◇ *[Sandra], jíbti xámsa w tis3īn. wāw! lēzim tkáffi 3a tēni mústawa.*
○ *3an jadd? mustawēyi mnīɧ?*
◇ *ktīr mnīɧ. w ṣār 3índik ɧaṣīlit kilmēt ktīr wēs3a. ū3a twáʔʔfi!*

[1] Teachers are politely addressed as مِسْتر *[mister]* and مِسّ *[miss]*, which can optionally be followed by the teacher's first name.

◇ صباح الخيْر. أنا وائِل، وأنا رح علِّمْكُن العربي الدّارِج، المُسْتَوى الرّابِع. حابِب إتْعرِّف عْلَيْكُن.

○ إسْمي روْزْماري روْك.

◇ مِن ويْن إنْتي روْزْماري؟

○ مِن أميرْكا.

◇ تمام! وليْه عم تِتْعلّمي لِبْناني؟

○ عم بِشْتِغِل هوْن عَ كوْنْترا خمْس سْنين ولازِم إتْعلّم عربي لِبْناني، تفِي مشّي حالي.

◇ حِلو كْتير. وإنْتَ؟

○ أنا إسْمي مارْك مِن بْريطانْيا وعم بعْمِل ماجيسْتيرْ بِالعربي، بسّ حابِب إتْعلّم لِبْناني كمان.

◇ مُمْتاز. خلّيني خبرِّكُن كيف رح يمْشي الصّف.

○ في فرِق بِالصّفّ لأِنّو نِحْنا پْرايْڤِت؟

◇ لأ لأ، هِنِّ نفْس الفِكْرة. أرْبْعة وعِشْرين ساعة مقْسومين مرْتيْن بِالجِمْعة، كِلّ مرّة ساعْتيْن، عَ مِدِّةْ شهِر ونُصّ.

○ ساعْتيْن وَرا بعْضُن؟ ما في بْرايْك؟

◇ مِنْبلِّش كِلّ مرّة عالسّاعة أرْبْعة عالقدّ، إذا الله راد. مْنِرْجع مِنْوَقِّف عالخمْسِة إلّا عشْرة، مْناخُد بْرايْك قصير، ومْنِرْجع مِنْكفّي.

○ رح[1] ناخُد مَواضيع جْديدِة؟ أَوْ نْكفّي بِذات الكْتاب.

◇ رح نْبلِّش بِكْتاب جْديد. لازِم يْكون صار عِنْدْكُن ياه. رح نعْمِل فيه سِتِّة يونيتْس.

○ ديْجا شْترَيْتو. وفي أرْبْعة وعِشْرين يونيتْس.

◇ لازِم يْغطّي أرْبع مُسْتَويات. بِالأوّل، رح نعْمِل جزْء القِراية والاِسْتِماع، مْنرْجع بِتاني صفّ، مْنعْمِل الكتيبِة والحِوار، يَعْني مِنْخلِّص كِلّ يونيت بِصفّيْن.

○ مشْروع حِلو لِأنّو المُسْتَوى اللي قبِل، ما كان هالقدّ مْنظّم.

◇ انْشالله نمْشي عَ هَيْدا المشْروع. خلّينا نْبلِّش هلّق. مِنْبلِّش بِالاِسْتِماع تترِجْعوا تِتْذكّروا شْوَيّ. جاهْزين؟

◇ Good morning! I'm Mr. Wa'el, and I will be teaching you Colloquial Arabic, level 4. I would like to get to know you.

○ My name is Rosemary Rock

◇ Where are you from, Rosemary?

○ From the U.S.

◇ Great! And why are you learning Lebanese?

○ I'm working here on a 5-year contract. That's why I need to learn Lebanese Arabic, to be able to get by.

◇ Very nice. And What about you?

○ My name is Mark, from the U.K., and I'm pursuing a Master's Degree in Arabic, but I would like to learn the Lebanese dialect, as well.

◇ Excellent! Okay, let me first tell you how the course will go.

○ Will there be any difference since we're a private group?

◇ No, not at all. They're the same, 24 hours [of classes] twice a week for a month and a half. Each class is two hours long.

○ Two continuous hours? No break?

◇ We start right at 4 p.m. everytime, God willing, and then stop at 4:50 [ten to five], take break, then continue.

○ Are we going to take on new topics, or will we move on with the same book?

◇ We will start in a new book. You should have it now, and we will do 6 units.

o I already bought it, and it has 24 units.

◇ It should cover four levels. First, we will do the reading and listening [sections], and in the following class, writing and conversation. So, a unit is completed in two classes.

o Nice plan... because the previous level was not that systematic.

◇ Hopefully, we will stick to this plan. Let's start now. We will start with the listening to refresh a little bit. Are you ready?

◇ *şabāḩ ilxēr. ána wāʔil, w ána raḩ 3allímkun il3árabi -ddērij, -lmústawa irrābi3. ḩābib it3árrif 3láykun.*

o *ísmi [Rosemary Rock].*

◇ *min wēn ínti [Rosemary]?*

o *min amērka.*

◇ *tamēm! w lē 3am tit3allámi libnēni?*

o *3am bištíɣil hōn 3a [[F]contrat] xams snīn w lēzim it3állam 3árabi libnēni, ta-fíyi mášši ḩāli.*

◇ *ḩílu ktīr. w ínta?*

o *ána ísmi [Mark] min brīţānya w 3am bá3mil mājīstēr bi-l3árabi, bass ḩābib it3állam libnēni kamēn.*

◇ *mumtēz. xallīni xabbírkun kīf raḩ yímši -şşaf.*

o *fī fáriʔ bi-şşáff li-ánnu níḩna [private]?*

◇ *laʔ laʔ, hínni nafs ilfíkra. árb3a w 3išrīn sē3a maʔsūmīn marrtēn bi-ljím3a, kill márra sē3tēn, 3a míddit šáhir w nuşş.*

o *sē3tēn wára bá3ḑun? ma fī [break]?*

◇ *minbálliš kill márra 3a-ssē3a árb3a 3a-lʔádd, íza álla rād. mnírja3 minwáʔʔif 3a-lxámsi ílla 3āšra, mnēxud [break] ʔaşīr, w mnírja3 minkáffi.*

o *raḩ[1] nēxud mawāḑī3 jdīdi? aw nkáffi bi-zēt liktēb.*

◇ *raḩ nbálliš bi-ktēb jdīd. lēzim ykūn şār 3índkun yēh. raḩ ná3mil fī sítti [units].*

o *[[F]déjà] štaráytu. w fī árb3a w 3išrīn [units].*

◇ *lēzim yɣáţţi árba3 mustawayēt. bi-lʔáwwal, raḩ ná3mil jizʔ liʔrāyi w lʔistimē3, mnírja3 bi-tēni şaff, mná3mil ilkatībi w ilḩiwār, yá3ni minxálliş kill [unit] bi-şaffēn.*

○ *mašrū3 ḫílu li-ánnu -lmústawa -lli ʔábil, ma kēn ha-lʔádd mnáẓẓam.*
◇ *nšálla nímši 3a háyda -lmašrū3. xallīna nbálliš hállaʔ. minbálliš bi-lʔistimē3 tatírja3u titzákkaru šwayy. jēhzīn?*

[1] رح *raḫ* is also commonly pronounced لح *laḫ*. You will hear this word pronounced both ways in the audio, but we write رح *raḫ* for consistency.

Vocabulary

institute, academy	*má3had (ma3ēhid)*	معْهد (معاهِد)
(primary, secondary) school	*mádrasi (madēris)*	مدْرسِة (مدارِس)
course	*[course]* *[Fcours]* *dáwra*	كوْرْس كور دَوْرة
intensive course	*[course]/[Fcours] mukássaf/sarī3* *[Fcours intensif]*	كوْرْس/كور مُكثّف/سريع كور إينْتانْسيف
level	*mústawa (mustawayēt)*	مُسْتَوى (مُسْتوَيات)
Arabic	*3árabi* *lúɣa 3arabíyyi*	عربي لُغة عربية
Standard Arabic, MSA	*fúṣḫa*	فُصْحى
Colloquial Arabic	*3āmmíyyi* *dērij*	عامّية دارِج
Lebanese (Colloquial) Arabic	*libnēni*	لِبْناني

teacher (male)	*istēz*	إسْتاذ
teacher (female)	*m3állmi*	مْعلّْمِة
student (male)	*tilmīz (tlēmīz)* *ţālib (ţullāb)*	تلْميذ (تْلاميذ) طالِب (طُلّاب)
student (female)	*tilmīzi* *ţālbi*	تلْميذِة طالْبِة
class	*şaff*	صفّ
to cancel	*láɣa (yílɣi)*	لغى (يِلْغي)
to start	*bállaš (ybálliš)*	بلّش (يْبلِّش)
to learn	*t3állam (yit3állam)*	تْعلّم (يِتْعلّم)
to study, to be a student	*dáras (yídrus)*	درس (يِدْرُس)
to study, do (one's) homework	*3ímil (yá3mil)* *fárḑu/[ᶠdevoir]u*	عِمِل (يَعْمِل) فرْضو\دوڤْوارو
to take (a course, etc.)	*áxad (yēxud)*	أخد (ياخُد)
placement test	*imtiɧān/fáɧiş taɧdīd mústawa*	اِمْتِحان/فحِص تحْديد مُسْتَوى
beginner	*múbtadiʔ*	مُبْتدى
(level) basic, elementary	*ibtidēʔi*	اِبْتِدائي
intermediate	*wásaţ*	وَسط
advanced	*3āli*	عالي
to improve, get better	*tɧássan (yitɧássan)*	تْحسّن (يِتْحسّن)

to make progress in	t?áddam (yit?áddam) bi-	تْقدّم (يِتْقدّم) بِـ
to practice	tdárrab (yitdárrab) 3ála	تْدرّب (يِتْدرّب) على
book	ktēb (kútub)	كْتاب (كُتُب)
unit, chapter	[Fchapitre]	شاپيترْ
methodology	mánhaj (manēhij)	منْهج (مناهِج)
listening	smē3	سْماع
to listen to	sími3 (yísma3)	سِمِع (يِسْمع)
speaking, conversation	maɦādasi ɦadīs dárdaši ɦiwār ɦáki	محادْثِة حديث درْدشِة حِوار حكي
to speak	ɦíki (yíɦki)	حِكي (يِحْكي)
writing	kitēbi	كِتابِة
to write	kátab (yíktub)	كتب (يِكْتُب)
reading	?rēyi	قْرايِة
to read	?ára (yí?ra)	قرا (يِقْرا)
passage, text	má?ţa3 (ma?āţi3) [paragraph] naşş (nuşūş)	مقْطع (مقاطِع) پاراجْراف نصّ (نُصوص)
test, exam	musēba?a	مُسابقة
photocopy	násxa	نسْخة

topic	*mawḍū3*	مَوْضوع
fees	*rusūm*	رُسوم
price, fee, tuition	*táman* *sí3ir*	تمن سِعِر
private	*[private]* *[ᶠprivé]* *xāṣṣ*	پْرايْڤِت پْريڤيْه خاصّ
group	*majmū3a* *[group]*	مجْموعة غْروپ
break, rest time	*[brake]* *fúrṣa*	بْريْك فُرْصة
lecture hall	*qā3it ilmuħāḍarāt*	قاعِة المُحاضرات
classroom	*ṣaff (ṣfūf)*	صفّ (صْفوف)
restroom	*ħammēm*	حمّام
canteen	*[cafeteria]*	كافيتيرِيا

Expressions

○

I want to change to a new class, please.	*báddi ínʔul 3a ṣaff tēni, [please].*	بدّي أنْقُل عَ صفّ تاني پْليز.
Can you call me next month since I won't be able to start this month?	*fīk tiħkīni -ššáhir iljēyi? li-ánnu ma raħ fíyi bálliš háyda -ššáhir.*	فيك تِحْكيني الشّهِر الجايي؟ لأِنّو ما رح فِيي بلِّش هَيْدا الشّهِر.

I want an intensive course because I'm here temporarily.	*báddi -l[course] ilmukássaf, li-ánnu ána hōn mwáʔʔat.*	بدّي الكوْرْس المُكثّف، لِأنّو أنا هوْن مْوَقّت.
Who will be teaching the next level?	*mīn raђ y3állim il[level] ittēni?*	مين رح يْعلِّم اللّيْفل التّانْيِة؟
Is there a placement test?	*fi fáђiṣ taђdīd mústawa?*	في فحِص تحْديد مُسْتَوى؟
I want to change to a new class, please.	*báddi ínʔul 3a ṣaff tēni, [please].*	بدّي أُنْقُل عَ صفّ تاني پْليز.

◇

Your placement results indicate that you need to start in level 2.	*natēyij fáђiṣ taђdīd ilmústawa bitʔūl ínnu lēzim tbálliš mn ilmústawa -ttēni.*	نتايِج فحِص تحْديد المُسْتَوى بِتْقول إنّو لازِم تْبلِّش مْن المُسْتَوى التّاني.

At the Doctor's عِنْد الحكيم

Healthcare in Lebanon is one of the best, if not the best, in the region, so much so that nationals from neighboring countries and the Gulf come to Lebanon in pursuit of medical treatment. Lebanese doctors are required to go abroad to specialize and do their residencies and fellowships in the U.S. or in Europe, which elevates the caliber of care in the country. This also means that most doctors can speak English or French really well. As such, unless your Arabic is better than their English, it may be best to discuss your medical concerns and symptoms in English to avoid misunderstandings. The American University of Beirut Medical Center, Clemenceau Medical Center, and LAU Medical Center - Rizk Hospital, are the most prominent hospitals in the country and are the choice among foreigners in Lebanon, as well as for Lebanese who are able to afford these institutions. They tend to be more expensive than others but also attract la crème de la crème in terms of doctors and staff.

Checking in with the receptionist

o لَوْ سمحْتي، عِنْدي مَوْعِد[1] بِإسِم ندى أسْوَد.

◇ مظْبوط، عِنْدي إسْمِك هوْن. في مَوْعديْن قبْلِك.

o أوْكيْ. فِيي فوت عالتّواليْت[2]؟

◇ أكيد. التّواليْت مِن هوْن.[3]

o Excuse me, I've made an appointment under the name Nada Aswad.

◇ That's right. I have you right here. There are two patients ahead of you.

o Okay, may I use the restroom?

◇ Sure, it's this way.

o *law samáħti, 3índi máw3ad[1] bi-ísim náda áswad.*

◇ *maẓbūṭ, 3índi ísmik hōn. fī maw3adēn ʔáblik.*

o *okē. fíyi fūt 3a-t[ᶠtoilette][2]?*

◇ *akīd. -t[ᶠtoilette] min hōn.[3]*

[1] = حجِز *ħájiz*

[2] = عالحمّام *3a-lħammēm*

[3] تْفضّلي مِن هوْن. *tfáḍḍali min hōn.* **Right this way!**

It is important to note that foreigners are legally required to obtain health insurance while residing in Lebanon. More information about the law and its specifics could be found at:

www.general-security.gov.lb/en/posts/209.

You can make an appointment to see a doctor at a clinic, a polyclinic (which has more than one doctor), or at the hospital. The Lebanese relaxed take on punctuality also affects healthcare, and so you can expect to have an appointment at 4:00 p.m. and not be seen until 5:00 p.m. or even later... often because الحكيم بعْد ما وُصِل *-lħakīm ba3d ma wúṣil* **The doctor hasn't arrived yet**.

2

ASKING ABOUT A DOCTOR

o سوْري، بدّي شوف إذا الحكيم بْيَعْمِل زرِع سْنان؟

◇ لأ، اِخْتِصاص دُكْتوْر صعِب أعْصاب السْنان. بسّ في دُكْتوْر مْراد، بْيِجي التّنيْن والخميس، واِخْتِصاصو الجِراحة.

o وفي هُوِّ يَعْمِلّي جِراحِة سْنان؟

◇ فيكي تاخْدي مَوْعد معو، وهُوِّ بيقِلِّك إذا بدِّك زرِع.

o Excuse me. I wanted to find out if the dentist does dental implants?

◇ No, Dr. Saab's specialty is nerve treatment, but there is Dr. Mrad who comes on Mondays and Thursdays, and his specialty is surgery.

o And can he do a dental implant for me?

◇ You can book an appointment with him, and he'll tell you if an implant is right for you.

o *[sorry], báddi šūf íza -lḫakīm byá3mil zári3 snēn?*

◇ *laʔ, ixtiṣāṣ [Fdocteur] ṣá3ib a3ṣāb lisnēn. bass fī [Fdocteur] mrād, byíji -ttanēn w ilxamīs, w ixtiṣāṣu -ljirāḫa.*

o *w fī húwwi ya3mílli jirāḫit snēn?*

◇ *fīki tēxdi máw3ad má3u, w húwwi biʔíllik íza báddik zári3.*

Perhaps one of the best aspects of receiving care in Lebanon is that doctors spend more time with their patients than they would in the U.S., for example, where most of the time is spent with the assistant/nurse, and only the last part of the appointment is spent with the doctor. Making appointments with doctors in Lebanon is also much easier than it is in most places. You can expect to get an appointment within a week, in most cases, unless you are looking for a very specialized physician who only comes occasionally to Lebanon because they practice abroad.

③

BRINGING X-RAYS BACK TO THE DOCTOR

○ تْفضّل حكيم. هَوْدي الصُّوَر والفْحوصات اللي طلبْتُن.

◇ الصُّوَر مْناح الحمْدِالله. بسّ الفْحوصات ما كْتير عجبوني[1].

○ ليْه؟

◇ عِنْدِك شْوَيِّة نقِص بِالحديد[2]. رح أُوْصُفْلِك حديد عِلاج تْلات أُشْهُر. ومْنرْجع مِنْشوف.

○ Here you are, doctor: the x-rays and tests [analyses] you requested.

◇ The x-rays are good, thank God. But I don't like the results of the tests.

○ Why's that?

◇ You seem to be a bit iron-deficient. I'll prescribe an iron course for you for three months, and then we'll see.

○ *tfáḍḍal ħakīm. háwdi -ṣṣúwar w lifħūṣāt -lli ṭalábtun.*

◇ *-ṣṣúwar mnēħ, -lħamdílla. bass lifħūṣāt ma ktīr 3ajabūni*[1].

○ *lē?*

◇ *3índik šwáyyit náʔiṣ bi-lħadīd*[2]. *raħ uwṣúflik ħadīd 3ilēj tlēt úšhur. w mnírja3 minšūf.*

1 ما كْتير مْناح *ma ktīr mnēħ* **aren't very good**

2 = فِقْر دمّ *fiʔr damm* (lit. poverty of blood)

Explaining symptoms and getting a prescription

○ أكلِت سمك وديسيرْ شوكولا.[1] بسّ هاي[2] منّا أوّل مرّة باكُل هيْك، وأوّل مرّة بيصير معي هيْك شي[3].

◇ الحساسية إلا أسْباب كْتيرة غيرْ الأكِل.

○ شو لازِم أعْمِل[4] طيِّب؟

◇ رح أوْصُفْلِك كم دَوا. وأنْواع أكِل محْدودِة بِتْكون مسْموحة[5] عَ شهِر.

○ I had fish and a chocolate dessert. It isn't the first time I've eaten that, but it's the first time this has happened to me.

◇ Allergies can have many causes aside from food.

○ What should I do then?

◇ I'll prescribe some medications. And only limited kinds of food will be allowed for one month.

○ *akálit sámak w [ᶠdessert chocolat].[1] bass hay[2] mánna áwwal márra bēkul hēk, w áwwal márra biṣīr má3i hēk šī[3].*

◇ *-lħasāsíyyi íla asbēb ktīri ɣēr ilʔákil.*

○ *šū lēzim á3mil[4] ṭáyyib?*

◇ *raħ uwṣúflik kam dáwa. w anwē3 ákil maħdūdi bitkūn masmūħa[5] 3a šáhir.*

[1] There is a popular belief in Lebanon that eating seafood and dairy products (especially foods containing milk or yoghurt) on the same day can cause 'food poisoning.'

[2] = هَيْدي *háydi*

[3] = أوّل مرّة بِتْحسّس هيْك *áwwal márra bitħássas hēk*

[4] = ساوي *sēwi*

[5] نِظام غِذائي *niẓām ɣizēʔi* **diet, dietary program**

◇ مْبينّ إنّو دقّات قلْبِك كْتير مْنيحة والتّخْطيط كمان مْنيح.

o طيِّب وليْه مَوْجوعة هيْك؟ وليْه ما فِيي إتْنفّس طبيعي؟[1]

◇ الأرْجح اِلْتِهاب بِعضل الصّدِر، مِن هيْك ما عم فيكي تِتْنفّسي مْنيح وحاسِّة هيْك.

o وشو العِلاج حكيم؟[2]

◇ رح أُوْصُفْلِك[3] مرْهم تِدْهنيه وكم دَوا تاني عَ جِمِعْتيْن[4]. وإذا بيضلّ في وَجع، بِرْجع بْشوفِك.

◇ It seems like your heartbeat is fine, and the EKG is also clear.

o Then why do I feel this pain? And why can't I breathe normally?

◇ Most probably it's an inflammation in the chest muscles. That's why you cannot breathe properly and feel this way.

o And how can this be treated, doctor?

◇ I'll prescribe an ointment for you to use alongside with some medications for two weeks. And if the pain persists, I'll check you again.

◇ *mbáyyan ínnu daʔʔāt ʔálbik ktīr mnīḫa w ittaxṭīṭ kamēn mnīḫ.*

O *ṭáyyib, w lē mawjūʒa hēk? w lē ma fíyi itnáffas ṭabīʒi?*[1]

◇ *-lʔárjaḫ iltihēb bi-ʒáḍal iṣṣídir, min hēk ma ʒam fīki titnáffasi mnīḫ w ḫāssi hēk.*

O *w šū -lʒilēj, ḫakīm?*[2]

◇ *raḫ uwṣúflik*[3] *márham tidhanī w kam dáwa tēni ʒa jimiʒtēn*[4]*. w íza biḍáll fī wája3, bírja3 bšūfik.*

[1] ليْه طابِق عَ قلْبي هيْك؟ *lē ṭābiʔ 3a ʔálbi hēk?* **Why do I feel that my heart is so tight?** (to express heart pain and difficulty breathing) **/** [2] = و شو الحلّ دوكْتور؟ *w šū -lḫall, [Fdocteur]?* **/** [3] = إكْتِبْلِك *iktíblik* **/** [4] = أُسْبوعيْن *usbū3ēn*

6

A BROKEN BONE

o وْقعِت عَ إيدي وبِفْتِكِر مكْسورة. الوَجع كْتير قوَي.

◇ أوْكيْ، خلّينا نعْمِل صورة قبِل كِلّ شي. قِلّي[1] كيف وْقِعِت عْلَيا.

o كِنِت عم قوم مْن التّخِت بِالعتْم، ووْقِعِت وإجا كِلّ جِسْمي عَ إيدي.

(after the x-rays come back)

◇ طيِّب، خلّينا نْجبرِّا مْوقّت لبُكْرا الصُّبِح. وبعْديْن لازِم تْشوف أخِصّائي عضِم[2]، لِأنّو يمْكِن تْعوز عملية.

o ليْه عملية؟

◇ مْن الصّورة مْبيّن إنّو عِنْدك شي إسْمو كِسِر مْركّب، معْناتا العضْمِة نْكسرِت وغرزِت بِالجِلْدِة. مِن هيْك جرّاح العضِم هُوِّ يَلّي بدّو يْقرِّر شو لازِم يِنْعمل.

o I fell on my arm and it's probably broken. The pain is horrible.

◇ Okay, let's take an x-ray first before anything else. And tell me how you fell on it.

o I was getting up from bed in the dark and I fell with my whole body on top of my hand.

(after the x-rays come back)

◇ Okay, we'll make a temporary splint until tomorrow morning. And you'd better follow up with an orthopedic consultant because it might require surgery.

o Why surgery?

◇ The x-ray shows what we call a compound fracture, which means that the bone broke and pierced the skin. That's why the orthopedic surgeon is the one who will determine what needs to be done exactly.

- ○ *wʔá3it 3a īdi w bíftikir maksūra. -lwája3 ktīr ʔáwi.*
- ◇ *okē, xallīna ná3mil ṣūra ʔábil kill šī. ʔílli kīf wʔí3it 3láya.*
- ○ *kínit 3am ʔūm mn ittáxit bi-l3átm, w wʔí3it w íja kill jísmi 3a īdi.*

(after the x-rays come back)

- ◇ *ṭáyyib, xallīna njábbira mwáʔʔat la-búkra -ṣṣúbuḫ. w ba3dēn lēzim tšūf axiṣṣāʔi 3áḍim*[2]*, li-ánnu yímkin t3ūz 3amalíyyi.*
- ○ *lē 3amalíyyi?*
- ◇ *mn iṣṣūra mbáyyan ínnu 3índak šī ísmu kísir mrákkab, ma3nēta -l3áḍmi nkasárit w ɣarázit bi-ljíldi. min hēk jarrāḫ il3áḍim húwwi yálli báddu yʔárrir šū lēzim yín3amal.*

[1] = خبِّرْني *xabbírni*

[2] لازِم أخِصّائي عضِم يِفْحصك *lēzim axiṣṣāʔi 3áḍim yífḫaṣak* **a specialist needs to examine you**

While being a doctor is prestigious everywhere, it is taken to a whole other level in Lebanon, where people treat doctors like gods. The downside is that this gets into the head of some doctors and shows in the way they deal with patients. In fact, the common word for doctor in Levantine Arabic is حكيم *ḫakīm*, which literally translates as 'wise.' That said, most good doctors have excellent bed manners and people skills.

دُكْتور *[ᶠdocteur]* and حكيم *ḫakīm* are both used to mean **doctor**. Both can be used to talk about a doctor or to address them, but as a title before one's name, دُكْتور *[ᶠdocteur]* is preferred. For example, دُكْتوْر مْراد *[ᶠdocteur] Mrād* **Dr. Mrad** (not حكيم مْراد *ḫakīm mrād*).

Extended Dialogue

◇ شو المِشْكْلِة دُمْوازيْل سارة؟ بِشو عم بِتْحِسّي عالمظْبوط؟

○ إلي شهرين بِبَيْروت، ومِن وَقْت ما وْصِلت، عِنْدي مشاكِل بمِعْدْتي.

◇ فإذاً منِّك لِبْنانية ونقلْتي لهوْن مِش مِن زمان، صحّ؟

○ أيْه مظْبوط حكيم. كان عِنْدي مشاكِل بِالقوْلوْن، ومِن وَقْت ما جيت لهوْن، هَيْئِتو رِجِع.

◇ أوْكيْ، مُمْكِن التّغْيير بِالأكِل هُوِّ اللي عم بيسبِّب هالشّي؟

○ منّي مِتأكْدِة. يمْكِن. ويمْكِن السْتْريْس مِن كِلّ هالتّغْييرات؟

◇ شو العَوارِض اللي عم بِتْحِسّي فِيا عالمظْبوط؟

○ دايْماً حاسِّة بِنفْخة ومِعْدْتي دايْماً مزْعوجِة مِنّا.

◇ عم تعْمْلي عسِر هضِم؟

○ أيْه كْتير عم بِتْصير. باكُل عادي، وبْكون مْنيحة بْوَقْتا، بسّ تاني يوْم، مِعْدْتي بِتْوَجِّعْني كْتير.

◇ أوْكيْ حاسِّة شي بْحريق؟

○ لأ ما في، بسّ كْتير عم بِسْتفْرِغ[1].

◇ أوْكيْ، حسب النّاضور، القوْلوْن مِتْضخِّم وكْتير مِلْتِهِب.

○ معْقول يْكون هَيْدا اللي عم بيسبِّب النّفْخة.

◇ عم بِتْحِسّي بِالنّفْخة بعْد أكِل مْعينّ؟ أم ما إلا قاعْدِة؟[2]

○ إيّام بسّ آكُل نوْع أكِل مْعينّ[3]، وإيّام مْن السْتْريْس.

◇ طيِّب، خلّيني إكْتبْلِك كم فحِص تعْمْلِيْن، وتِرْجعي لعِنْدي مع النّتايِج.

○ طيِّب أوْكي، لازِم آخُد دَوا أَوْ شي؟[4]

◇ خلّينا نُنْطُر النّتايِج قبِل، ومِنْقرِّر عَ هالأساس العِلاج المْناسِب.

○ أوْكيْ رح أعْمِلْن وبِرْجع لعِنْدك بِأقْرب وَقِت.

◇ What seems to be the problem, Ms. Sarah? What are feeling exactly?

o I've been in Beirut for two months, and ever since I arrived, I've been having stomach problems.

◇ You're not Lebanese and [recently] moved here, huh?

o Yes, exactly, doctor. I used to have irritable bowel syndrome long ago, but it seems to have returned once I came here.

◇ Okay. Perhaps the difference in food is what is causing all of this?

o I'm not sure. Maybe, yes. And maybe it's the stress from all these changes.

◇ What are the symptoms you're suffering from exactly?

o A constant feeling of bloating and my stomach is always upset.

◇ Do you have indigestion?

o Yes, it happens a lot. I eat normally and it doesn't make me sick at the time, but the next day, I find my stomach hurting so much.

◇ Okay, is there any burning feeling?

o No, there isn't, but I throw up a lot.

◇ All right, I can see from the endoscope that the colon is enlarged and severely inflamed.

o That must be what's causing the constant bloating.

◇ Do you feel bloated after consuming a certain type of food? Or is there no pattern?

o Sometimes after certain types of food, and sometimes just from stress.

◇ Okay, let me write down some tests [analyses] for you to get, and bring the results to me.

o All right. Should I take any medicine or anything?

◇ Let's wait for the results first, and based on them, I'll prescribe the appropriate treatment.

○ Okay, I'll get them done and bring them to you as soon as possible.

◇ *šū -lmíškli, [[F]demoiselle] [Sarah]? bi-šū 3am bitḫíssi 3a-lmaẓbūṭ?*
○ *íli šahrēn bi-bayrūt, w min wáʔt ma wṣílit, 3índi mašēkil bi-mí3dti.*
◇ *fa-ízan mánnik libnēníyyi w naʔálti la-hōn miš min zamēn, ṣaḫḫ?*
○ *ē, maẓbūṭ ḫakīm. kēn 3índi mašēkil bi-lqōlōn, w min wáʔt ma jīt la-hōn, hayʔítu ríji3.*
◇ *okē, múmkin ittaɣyīr bi-lʔákil húwwi -lli 3am bisábbib ha-ššī?*
○ *mánni mitʔákkdi. yímkin. w yímkin is[stress] min kill ha-ttiɣyīrāt?*
◇ *šū -l3awāriḍ -lli 3am bitḫíssi fíya 3a-lmaẓbūṭ?*
○ *dēyman ḫāssi bi-náfxa w mí3dti dēyman maz3ūji mínna.*
◇ *3am tá3mli 3ásir háḍim?*
○ *ē, ktīr 3am bitṣīr. bēkul 3ādi, w bkūn mnīḫa b-wáʔta, bass tēni yōm, mí3dti bitwajjí3ni ktīr.*
◇ *okē ḫāssi šī b-ḫarīʔ?*
○ *laʔ ma fī, bass ktīr 3am bistáfriɣ*[1].
◇ *okē, ḫásab innāḍūr ilqōlōn mitḍáxxim w ktīr míltihib.*
○ *ma3ʔūl ykūn háyda -lli 3am bisábbib innáfxa.*
◇ *3am bitḫíssi bi-nnáfxa ba3d ákil m3áyyan? am ma íla qā3di?*[2]
○ *ʔiyyēm bass ēkul nō3 ákil m3áyyan*[3]*, w iyyēm mn is[stress].*
◇ *ṭáyyib, xallīni iktíblik kam fáḫiṣ ta3mlíyun, w tírja3i la-3índi ma3 innatēyij.*
○ *ṭáyyib okē, lēzim ēxud dáwa aw šī?*[4]
◇ *xallīna núnṭur innatēyij ʔábil, w minqárrir 3a ha-lʔasēs il3ilēj ilmunēsib.*
○ *okē, raḫ á3milun w bírja3 la-3índak bi-áʔrab wáʔit.*

1 = عم راجع *3am rāji3*

2 = أَوْ ما إلا خِصّة؟ *aw ma íla xíṣṣa?*

3 نوْع __ مْعيّن *nō3 __ m3áyyan* **certain kinds of __**

4 رح توصِفلي دَوا؟ *raḫ tūṣífli dáwa?* **Are you going to prescribe me medicine?**

hospital	*mistášfa*	مِسْتشْفى
clinic	*3iyēdi*	عِيادِة
private clinic	*3iyēdi xáşşa*	عِيادِة خاصّة
dispensary	*mustáwşaf*	مُسْتَوْصف
examination	*fáɧiş (fɧūşāt)*	فحِص (فْحوصات)
consultation	*istišāra*	اِسْتِشارة
emergency	*ţawāriʔ*	طَوارِئ
ambulance	*is3āf*	إسْعاف
insurance	*taʔmīn* *[ᶠassurance]*	تأْمين أسّورانْس
appointment	*máw3ad (mawā3īd)*	مَوْعد (مَواعيد)
doctor	*doktōr (dakētra)* *ɧakīm*	دُكْتوْر (دكاتْرة) حكيم
general practitioner	*ɧakīm ţibb 3āmm*	حكيم طِبّ عامّ
specialist	*ɧakīm axişāʔi*	حكيم أخْصائي
surgeon	*jarrāɧ*	جرّاح
internist	*ɧakīm ţibb dēxili*	حكيم طِبّ داخِلي
osteopath, orthopedist	*ɧakīm 3áđm*	حكيم عظْم
obstetrician	*ɧakīm nísa w wilēdi*	حكيم نِساء ووِلادِة
pediatrician	*ɧakīm aţfāl*	حكيم أطْفال
oncologist	*ɧakīm awrām*	حكيم أَوْرام

dentist	*ɦakīm snēn*	حكيم سْنان
nurse (male)	*mumárriḍ*	مُمرِّض
nurse (female)	*mumárriḍa*	مُمرِّضة
illness, sickness, disease	*máraḍ (amrāḍ)*	مرض (أمْراض)
ulcer	*ʔárɦa*	قرْحة
heartburn	*ɦárʔa*	حرْقة
indigestion	*3ásir háḍim*	عسِر هضِم
irritable bowel syndrome	*ʔolōn 3áṣabi*	قوْلوْن عصبي
tooth decay, cavities	*tasáwwus*	تسوُّس
pulling a tooth	*ʔábi3/ʔáli3 ḍíris*	قبِع/قلع ضِرِس
compound fracture	*kisr mḍā3af*	كِسْر مْضاعف
inflammation	*iltihāb*	اِلْتِهاب
injury, wound	*jirɦ*	جِرِح
chronic disease	*máraḍ múzmin*	مرض مُزْمِن
high blood pressure	*ḍáɣiṭ*	ضغِط
diabetes	*síkkari*	سِكّري
surgery	*3amalíyyi*	عملية
medicine	*ṭubb*	طُبّ
pill	*ɦábbit dáwa*	حبِّةْ دوا
treatment; medication	*3ilēj*	عِلاج
tests, analyses	*taɦalīl*	تحاليل

x-ray	*ṣūrit aší33a*	صورةْ أشِعّة
intensive care	*3inēyi mrákkazi* *3inēyi fēyʔa*	عِنايِة مْركّزِة عِنايِة فايْقة

Expressions

○

Excuse me, doctor, this medicine makes me feel ill.	*ma twēxízni, ḫakīm, bass háyda -ddáwa 3am biḍēyiʔni.*	ما تْواخِذْني حكيم، بسّ هَيْدا الدَّوا عم بيضايِقْني.
When will I be able to stop these injections?	*áymata biṣīr fíyi wáʔʔif háwdi -lʔíbar?*	أيْ متى بيصير فِيي وَقِّف هَوْدي الإبر؟
Excuse me, I made an appointment in advance but I still haven't seen the doctor.	*[sorry], ána ēxud máw3ad min ʔábil, bass bá3dni la-hállaʔ ma šífit ilḫakīm.*	سوْري، أنا آخُد مَوْعد مِن قبِل، بسّ بعْدْني لهلّق ما شِفِت الحكيم.

◇

What is bothering you/ hurting you?	*šū -lli zē3jak?* *šū -lli 3am ywájj3ak?*	شو اللي زاعْجك؟ شو اللي عم يْوَجْعك؟
The doctor regrets he has to reschedule your appointment for next week.	*-lḫakīm mitʔássif, bass báddu yitṭárr yʔájjil máw3adak la-lʔusbū3 iljēyi/ la-jím3it iljēyi.*	الحكيم مِتْأسّف بسّ بدّو يِتْطرّ يْأجِّل مَوْعدك للأُسْبوع الجايي/لجِمْعةْ الجايِة.

There aren't any openings before May 3rd.	*ma 3ínna mawā3īd ʔábil tlēti ayyār.*	ما عِنّا مَواعيد قبِل تْلاتِة أيّار.
The doctor had an emergency and apologizes that your appointment will be delayed for one hour.	*-lħakīm jad 3lē ħāli ţārʔa, w byitʔássaf ínnu raħ yʔáxxir máw3adak sē3a.*	الحكيم جد عْلَيْه حالِة طارْئة، وبْيِتْأسّف إنّو رح يْأخِّر مَوْعدك ساعة.
Unfortunately, the uric acid level is a bit height.	*li-lʔásaf, -l[ᶠacide urique] 3índak 3āli šwayy.*	لِلأسف، الأسيد أوريك عِنْدك عالي شْوَيّ.
We need to run a few tests before the operation.	*lēzim ná3mil kam fáħiş/taħlīl ʔabl il3amalíyyi.*	لازِم نعْمِل كم فحِص/ تحْليل قبْل العملية.

At the Pharmacy بِالصَّيْدليّة

There are so many صَيْدليّات *ṣaydaliyyēt* or فرْمشيّات *farmašiyyēt* **pharmacies** in Lebanon that the government has had to come up with a rule that pharmacies cannot be closer than 300 meters to each other. This means that you'll almost certainly be able to find a pharmacy when you need one. That said, pay attention to your local pharmacy's business hours, as these vary wildly. While most pharmacies close sometime in the evening, some are open 24/7. There are no pharmacy chains in Lebanon. Rather, they are individually owned establishments. To identify a pharmacy, look for either a green cross or a green crescent; this will depend on the area of Lebanon you're in and on whether the pharmacy is owned by a Christian or a Christian. When you explain your symptoms to the pharmacist, they will typically say something along the lines of سلامْتك *salēmtak* (lit. your well-being), عَ سلامِة *3a salēmi,* or فيك الشِّفا (انْشالله) *fīk iššífa (nšálla)* and again as you're paying or leaving. You can respond with الله يْسلْمك *álla ysállmak* (lit. May God keep you well).

DESCRIBING SYMPTOMS AND GETTING MEDICATION (1)

○ دُكْتوْرة، عِنْدي حرارة كْتير عالْيِة، ودِياريْه[1]، ومِعْدْتي زاعْجِتْني[2] مْن الصُّبْح.

◇ عَ سلامِة انْشالله! أكلِت شي معْقول يْكون ضرّك؟

○ صراحة أكلِت سالاد روس[3] فِيا توْن كان صرْلا يَوْمينْ معْمولِة.

◇ الأرْجح هَيْدا يَلّي سبّب التّسمُّم. رح أعْطيك[4] دَوا يْوَقِّف الدِّياريْه، وشي يْنزِّلّك الحرارة. جرِّب تاكُل إشْيا خفيفِة هاليَوْمينْ.

○ Doctor, I have a terrible fever, diarrhea, and my stomach has been upset since this morning.

◇ Speedy recovery! Did you eat something that made you sick?

○ To be honest, I ate some potato salad that had tuna in it and that was two days old.

◇ That's probably what caused the food poisoning. I'll give you an anti-diarrheal and a fever reducer. Try to eat light foods.

○ *[^{F}docteur]a, 3índi ɧarāra ktīr 3ályi, w [^{F}diarrhée][1], w mí3dti zē3ʝítni[2] mn iṣṣúbuɧ.*

◇ *3a salēmi, nšálla! akálit šī ma3ʔūl ykūn ḍárrak?*

○ *ṣarāɧa akálit [^{F}salade russe][3] fíya tōn kēn ṣárla yawmēn ma3mūli.*

◇ *-lʔárjaɧ háyda yálli sábbab ittasámmum. raɧ a3ṭīk[4] dáwa ywáʔʔif [^{F}diarrhée], w šī ynazzíllak ilɧarāra. járrib tēkul íšya xafīfi ha-lyawmēn.*

[1] = إسْهال *ishēl* / [2] = مْضايْقِتْني *mḍāyʔitni* / [3] = سلطة روسية *sálaṭa rūsíyyi* /

[4] أوصِفْلك *ūṣíflak* **I'll prescribe for you**

The pharmaceutical industry in Lebanon used to be a lot more lax, and people used to be able to buy all their medications before traveling abroad, as most things didn't require prescriptions–even antibiotics. However, stricter regulations have been introduced in recent years.

2

DESCRIBING SYMPTOMS AND GETTING MEDICATION (2)

o مرْحبا.

◇ مرْحبا أهْلا. كيف فِيي ساعْدك؟[1]

o بدّي دَوا لوَجع الرّاس عْمِلي معْروف.

◇ عِنْدك فِكْرة شو معْقول يْكون عم بيسبّبو؟

o ما بعْرِف. برْكي بدّي رشّح. والسّايْنسيس تبعي كْتير مْوجّعْني.

◇ عَ سلامِة انْشالله. أوْكيْ، خوْد پانادوْل عادي هلّق، وإذا بيّنوا عَوارِض أكْتر للرّشِح، بْتاخُد ساعِتا پانادوْل كوْلْد أنْد فْلو.

o Hello.

◇ Hello, welcome. How may I help you?

o I need some medicine for a headache, please.

◇ Do you have any idea what's causing the headache?

o I don't know. Maybe I'm coming down with a cold. And my sinuses are torturing me.

◇ I hope you get well soon. All right, you can take regular Panadol for now. If more cold symptoms appear, then you can switch to Panadol Cold & Flu.

o *márḫaba.*

◇ *márḫaba áhla. kīf fíyi sē3dak?*[1]

o *báddi dáwa la-wája3 irrās 3míli ma3rūf.*

◇ *3índak fíkra šū ma3ʔūl ykūn 3am bisábbibu?*

o *ma bá3rif. bárki báddi ráššiḫ. w is[sinuses] tába3i ktīr mwajjá3ni.*

◇ *3a salēmi nšálla. okē, xōd [Panadol] 3ādi hállaʔ, w íza báyyanu 3awāriḍ áktar la-rrášiḫ, btēxud sē3íta [Panadol Cold and Flu].*

[1] = أهْلينْ، كيف فِيي إخِدْمك؟ *ahlēn, kīf fíyi ixídmak?*

3

Describing symptoms and getting medication (3)

○ لَوْ سمحْتي،[1] عِنْدي سعْلِة كْتير قَوية. بدّي دَوا سعْلِة.

◇ سلامْتِك! أوْكيْ قدّيْ إلا السّعْلِة؟ وناشْفِة أَوْ حاسِّة إنّو في بلْغم؟

○ إلي مْن التّنينْ، يَعْني تْلات تِيّام[2]. وكْتير ناشْفِة.

◇ أوْكيْ، هَيْدا السّيرو خْصوصي للسّعْلِة النّاشْفِة. بيعالج السّعْلِة وبِذات الوَقِت بْيَعْمِل كِوْت[3] عَ زْلاعيمِك تما تِنْوِجْعي هالكم يوْم. ما تاخْديه عالرّيق.[4]

○ أوْكي، رح آكُل وإرْجع آخْدو دِغْري. مرْسي كْتير.

○ Excuse me. I have a terrible cough. I need some cough medicine.

◇ Hope you get well soon! Okay, how long have you had the cough, and is it dry or do you feel like there's mucus coming out?

○ I've had it since Monday. So, three days. It's very dry.

◇ Okay, this syrup is specifically for dry cough. It will help treat the cough while coating your throught so you don't hurt in the coming days. Don't take it on an empty stomach.

○ Okay, I'll eat then take it right away. Thanks a lot.

○ *law samáħti.[1] 3índi sá3li ktīr ʔawíyyi. báddi dáwa sá3li.*

◇ *salēmtik! okē ʔaddē íla -ssá3li? w nēšfi aw ħāssi ínnu fī bályam?*

○ *íli mn ittanēn, yá3ni tlēt tiyyēm[2]. w ktīr nēšfi.*

◇ *okē, háyda is[Fsirop] xṣūṣi la-ssá3li -nnēšfi. bi-3ālij issá3li w bi-zēt ilwáʔit byá3mil [coat][3] 3a zlē3īmik ta-má tinwíj3i ha-lkám yōm. ma tēxdī 3a-rrīʔ.[4]*

○ *okē, raħ ēkul w írja3 ēxdu díɣri. [Fmerci] ktīr.*

[1] = عفْواً *3áfwan* / [2] إيّام *iyyēm* is pronounced تِيّام *tiyyēm* after a number. / [3] = عازِل *3āzil* / [4] = ما تاخْدي عَ مِعْدِة فاضْيِة *ma tēxdi 3a mí3di fāḍyi*

FILLING A PRESCRIPTION (1)

o بدّي الأدْوِيِة عَ هَيْدي الرُّشيْتّة عْمِلي معْروف[1].

◇ يَلّا لحْظة وبْجِبْلك ياهُن.

(a few minutes later)

◇ كتبْتِلّك عالعِلب كيف تاخِدُن.

o أوْكيْ تمام! قدّيْ بدِّك مِنّي؟[2]

◇ كِلُّن سَوا مية وخمْسة وعِشْرين ألْف.

o بعْدْني شارِيْن هِنِّ ذاتُن شهْر الماضي وكانوا كْتير أرْخص. عَ كِلّ حال هَيْدي المصاري. مرْسي كْتير.

o I'd like to get the medicine on this prescription, please.

◇ Just a moment, and I'll get them for you.

(a few minutes later)

◇ I've written the dosage on each medicine.

o Okay, great! How much do I owe you?

◇ The total is 125,000 L.L.

o I just bought the same medications last month and it was much cheaper. Anyway, here's the money. Thank you!

o *báddi -lʔádwiyi 3a háydi -rrušētta, 3míli ma3rūf*[1].

◇ *yálla láħẓa w bjíblak yēhun.*

(a few minutes later)

◇ *katabtíllak 3a-l3ílab kīf tēxídun.*

o *okē tamēm! ʔaddē báddik mínni?*[2]

◇ *kíllun sáwa míyyi w xámsa w 3išrīn alf.*

o *bá3dni šēríyun hínni zētun šáhr ilmāḍi w kēnu ktīr árxaṣ. 3a kill ħāl háydi -lmaṣāri. [Fmerci] ktīr.*

[1] = إذا بِترْيدي *íza bitrīdi*

[2] = قدّيْ بِترْيدي؟ *ʔaddé bitrīdi?*

5

FILLING A PRESCRIPTION (2)

○ لَوْ سمحْتي، الحكيم وَصفْلي هَيْدا الدَّوا، بسّ منّي عم لاقي مِنّو.

◇ أيْه مظْبوط، سحبوه مْن السّوق مِش مِن زمان. بسّ فيك تاخُد هَيْدا مِتْلو، ذات التِّرْكيبِة.

○ أوْكي، كِلّ قدّيْ لازِم آخْدو؟ وكم حبِّة وكِلّ هالقُصص؟[1]

◇ خوْد حبْتيْن نُصّ ساعة قبْل التِّرْويقة والعشا.

○ Excuse me. The doctor has prescribed this medicine for me but I haven't been able to find it.

◇ It's been taken off the market, just recently, actually. But you can take this, its equivalent. It has the same composition.

○ All right. How often should I take it? And how many tablets, et cetera?

◇ Take two tablets half an hour before breakfast and dinner.

○ *law samáħti, -lħakīm waṣáfli háyda -ddáwa, bass mánni 3am lēʔi mínnu.*

◇ *ē, maẓbūṭ, saħabū mn issūʔ miš min zamēn. bass fīk tēxud háyda mítlu, zēt ittirkībi.*

○ *okē, kill ʔaddē lēzim ēxdu? w kam ħábbi w kill ha-lʔúṣaṣ?*[1]

◇ *xōd ħabbtēn nuṣṣ sē3a ʔabl ittirwīʔa w il3áša.*

[1] فيكي تِكِتْبيلي كيف آخْدو؟ *fīki tikitbīli kīf ēxdu?* **Can you write down the directions** (lit. how I take it)**?**

REFILLING A PRESCRIPTION

○ لَوْ سمحْتي، الحكيمِ وَصفْلي هَيْدي الإبْرةِ مرّة كِلّ تْلات تِيّامِ عَ شهِر.

◇ يَعْني بدِّك حدا يَعْمِلِّك ياها هلّق؟

○ لأ معْليْه، عِنْدي حدا بِالبيْت في يَعْمِلا. بسّ بدّي كْفايةِ يْقضّوني الفترْة اللي وَصفْلي ياها.

◇ أوْكيْ، حضّرْتلِّك سِرِنْجات[1] تْلاتةِ سنْتيمِترْ ودَوا الإبْرةِ بِالكمّية اللي إنْتي عايِزْتِيا.

○ مرْسي كْتير. وبدّي كمان قنينةْ سْبيرْتو وپاكيْه[2] قُطْن معُن پْليز.

○ Excuse me. My doctor has prescribed this injection for me, once every three days for a month.

◇ So, you want someone to administer it to you now?

○ No, that's fine. I have someone at home who can do it. I just need to buy enough to get me through the prescription period.

◇ All right, I have prepared for you 3-centimeter syringes and injection ampules in the quantity you will be needing.

○ Thank you very much. And a bottle of rubbing alcohol and a pack of cotton with that, please.

○ *law samáħti, -lħakīm waṣáfli háydi -lʔíbri márra kill tlēt tiyyēm 3a šáhir.*

◇ *yá3ni báddik ħáda ya3míllik yēha hálla??*

○ *laʔ ma3lē, 3índi ħáda bi-lbēt fī yá3mila. bass báddi kfēyi yʔaḍḍūni -lfátra -lli waṣáfli yēha.*

◇ *okē, ħaḍḍartíllik [^{F}seringue]-ēt[1] tlēti [^{F}centimètre] w dáwa -lʔíbri bi-lkammíyyi -lli ínti 3āyiztíya.*

○ *[^{F}merci] ktīr. w báddi kamēn ʔanīnit sbīrtu w [^{F}paquet][2] ʔúṭun má3un, [please].*

1 = إبْرة (إبر) *íbri (íbar)*

2 = كيس *kīs*

7

Making a purchase

○ إذا بِتْريدي بدّي فِرْشايةْ سْنان ناعْمِة، ومعْجون سْنان للسّْنان الحِسّاسِة.

◇ تِكْرم عَيْنِك. سْتعْمْلي هَيْدا المعْجون. كْتير مْنيح للسّْنان الحِسّاسِة.

○ أوْكي، فِيي آخُد الكْبير پْليز؟

◇ تْفضّلي،[1] وهَيْدي الفِرْشايِة مْنيحة. كِلُّن سَوا عشْرة دوْلار.

○ Excuse me. I wanted to buy a soft toothbrush and a toothpaste for sensitive teeth.

◇ My pleasure. You can use this toothpaste. It's really good for sensitive teeth.

○ Okay. Can I please get the large one?

◇ Here you go, ma'am. And this is a good toothbrush. That will be $10.

○ *íza bitrīdi, báddi firšēyit snēn nē3mi, w ma3jūn snēn la-ssnēn ilḫissēsi.*

◇ *tíkram 3áynik. stá3mli háyda -lma3jūn. ktīr mnīḫ la-ssnēn ilḫissēsi.*

○ *okē, fíyi ēxud likbīr, [please]?*

◇ *tfáḍḍali,*[1] *w háydi -lfiršēyi mnīḫa. kíllun sáwa 3ášra dólar.*

[1] ما تْواخْذينا. ما عِنّا مْقاس كْبير. *ma twēxzīna. ma 3ínna mʔēs kbīr.* **I applogize, but we don't have larger sizes.**

Like other businesses in Lebanon, pharmacies take both Lebanese lira and U.S. dollars. In recent years, some have also started taking debit and credit cards. However, this is still not very common, particularly in smaller towns; as such, it is always better to check before buying your medicine if the pharmacy does, in fact, take debit and credit cards.

○ لَوْ سمحِت، هاي. بعْدْني واصْلةِ عَ بَيْروت مِن جِمِعْتيْن، وعم ضلّْني صاخْنِة[1].

◇ أهْلا وسهْلا. ليْه بِرأْيِك هيْك عم بيصير؟[2]

○ الأرْجح غْيار الطّقِس، وبعْدْني منّي مِتْعوّْدِة عالأكِل. مِن هيْك بدّي آخُد كم شغْلِة، في حال سخِنْت[3] أكْتر، وما عاد فِيي إطْلع مْن البيْت.

◇ مسْألةْ وَقِت. بُكْرا بْتِتْعوّْدي إذا الله راد. قوليلي.

○ عايْزِة ميزان حرارة، تِلْزيق جرِح، سْبيرْتو، وشي دَوا للوَجع بِفْتِكِر. شو لازِم آخُد بعْد بِرأْيَك؟

◇ فينا نْزيد ميبو للحرِق، فْوْلْتارين جيْل لأَوْجاع العضل، پانادوْل للرّشِح، وسْتريْپْسيلْز لوَجع الزْلاعيم.

○ تمام. هلّق بيصير عِنْدي صيْدلية بِالبيْت!

◇ مية بِالمية. عَ كِلّ حال، عَ سلامِة. إذا بدِّك شي، هَيْدا رقِم الصَّيْدلية. حْكينا[4] ساعِةْ يَلّي بدِّك.

○ مرْسي كْتير. عِنْدْكُن حدا بْيَعْمِل طِعِم للرّشِح؟

◇ أيْه مدام، عِنّا. بسّ الأرْجح أحْسن تْنْطري تكِنْتي صِرْتي أحْسن.

○ اه أيْه معك حقّ. أوْكيْ بِرْجع بِهاليَوْمينْ إذا صِرْت أحْسن. مرْسي.

◇ تِكْرم عَيْنِك. كِلْنا تحْت أمْرِك.[5]

○ Excuse me, hi! I just arrived in Beirut a week ago, and I keep getting sick.

◇ Welcome! Why, in your opinion, is this happening?

○ Probably the change of climate, and I'm still not used to the food. That's why I need to pick up a few things to have on hand, in case I get sicker and can't leave the house.

◇ It's a matter of time. You'll get used to it, God willing. Go on then.

- ○ I needed a thermometer, bandages, antiseptic, and a pain killer, I guess. What else do you think I should take?
- ◇ We can add Mebo ointment for burns, Voltaren gel for muscle pain, Panadol for colds and flus, and Strepsils for a sore throat.
- ○ Excellent! Now I'll have a pharmacy with me at home.
- ◇ Exactly! Anyways, get well soon. And if you need anything, this is the pharmacy number. You can call us anytime.
- ○ Thank you so much. Also, do you guys administer flu vaccines?
- ◇ Yes, ma'am, we do, but it's probably best you wait till you get better before we do it.
- ○ Oh, yeah, you're right. Okay, I'll come back in the next few days if I feel better. Thank you!
- ◇ You're most welcome, ma'am. Always at your service!

- ○ *law samáḫit, [hi]. bá3dni wāṣli 3a bayrūt min jimi3tēn, w 3am ḍállni ṣāxni*[1].
- ◇ *áhla w sáhla. lē bi-ráʔyik hēk 3am biṣīr?*[2]
- ○ *-lʔárjaḫ ɣyār iṭṭáʔis, w bá3dni mánni mit3áwwdi 3a-lʔákil. min hēk báddi ēxud kam šáɣli, fī ḫāl saxánt*[3] *áktar, w ma 3ād fíyi íṭla3 mn ilbēt.*
- ◇ *másʔalit wáʔit. búkra btit3áwwdi, íza álla rād. ʔūlīli.*
- ○ *3āyzi mīzēn ḫarāra, tilzīʔ jíriḫ, sbīrtu, w šī dáwa la-lwája3 bíftikir. šū lēzim ēxud ba3d bi-ráʔyak?*
- ◇ *fīna nzīd [Mebo] la-lḫíriʔ, [Volaten] jēl la-awjē3 il3áḍal, [Panadol] la-rrášiḫ, w [Strepsils] la-wája3 lizzlē3īm.*
- ○ *tamēm. hállaʔ biṣīr 3índi ṣaydalíyyi bi-lbēt!*
- ◇ *míyyi bi-lmíyyi. 3a kill ḫāl, 3a salēmi. íza báddik šī, háyda ráʔim iṣṣaydalíyyi. ḫkīna*[4] *sē3it yálli báddik.*
- ○ *[Fmerci] ktīr. 3índkun ḫáda byá3mil ṭí3im la-rrášiḫ?*
- ◇ *ē, [Fmadame], 3ínna. bass ilʔárjaḫ áḫsan túnṭri ta-kínti ṣírti áḫsan.*
- ○ *āh ē, má3ak ḫaʔʔ. okē bírja3 bi-ha-lyawmēn íza ṣirt áḫsan. [Fmerci].*
- ◇ *tíkram 3áynik. kíllna taḫt ámrik.*[5]

[1] = مريضة *marīḍa*

[2] شو بْتِعْتِقْدي السّبب؟ *šū btí3tiʔdi -ssábab?* **What do you believe is the cause?**

[3] = مْرِضِت *mríḍit*

[4] = طْلُبينا *ṭlubīna* = اِتِّصْلي *ittíṣli*

[5] = أهْلا وسهْلا. أيّ خِدْمِة. *áhla w sáhla. ayya xídmi.*

Pharmacies are required by law to have at least one licensed pharmacist present at the pharmacy at all times. However, pharmacies don't always adhere to that law. Always check before asking for medical advice whether the person you're speaking to is, in fact, a pharmacist. Even though some pharmacist assistants in Lebanon have been doing their job for decades without an actual diploma and know almost as much as a licensed pharmacist, thanks to their experience, it is best to ensure that the pharmacist is the one answering your questions–especially given that even pharmacists are not always completely comfortable giving medical advice without a physician's recommendation.

In addition to filling prescriptions and selling over-the-counter medication, pharmacies also carry para pharmaceutical products, and, the bigger the pharmacy, the wider the selection. Further, pharmacies also offer services, such as injections, dressing wounds, and measuring blood pressure. Some pharmacies also go the extra mile and offer home visits to deliver these services right to a customer's home.

Vocabulary

Symptoms		
a cold	*(dōr) bard* *rášiɧ*	(دوْر) برْد رشِح
constipation	*ktēm (mí3di)* *kētmi mí3dtu* *[^{F}constipation]*	كْتام (مِعْدي) كاتْمِة مِعْدْتو كونْسْتيپاسْيوْن
cough	*sá3li* *qáɧɧa*	سعْلِة قحّة
diarrhea	*[^{F}diarrhée]* *shāl* *mēšyi mí3dtu*	دِياريْه سْهال ماشْيِة مِعْدْتو
flu	*[influenza]* *[^{F}grippe]*	إنْفْلُوِنْزا جْريپ
fever	*3āmil ɧarāra* *ţāl3a/3ālyi ɧarārtu*	عامِل حرارة طالْعة/عالْيِة حرارْتو
migraine	*[^{F}migraine]*	ميغْريْن
headache	*wája3 rās*	وَجع راس
pain	*wája3 (awjē3)*	وَجع (أوْجاع)
to vomit	*stáfraɣ (yistáfriɣ)* *rāja3 (yrāji3)*	سْتفْرغ (يِسْتِفْرِغ) راجع (يْراجِع)
upset stomach	*mí3di miš maẓbūţa* *mí3di maʔlūbi*	مِعْدِة مِش مظْبوطة مِعْدِة مقْلوبِة

(food) poisoning	*tasámmum*	تسمُّم

Medicine and Supplies

antibiotic	*[Fantibiotique]*	أنْتي بيوْتيك
adhesive bandage, Band-Aid	*[plaster]* *tilzīʔ jíriɧ*	پْلاسْتر تِلْزيق جِرِح
anti-diarrheal medicine	*dáwa lalʔishāl*	دَوا للسْهال
cotton	*ʔúṭun*	قُطِن
eye-drops	*ʔáṭra*	قطْرة
gauze, dressing	*šēš*	شاش
fever reducer	*dáwa ɧarāra*	دَوا حرارة.
medicine	*dáwa (ádwiyi)*	دَوا (أدْوِية)
ointment	*márham (marāhim)*	مرْهم (مراهِم)
painkiller	*musákkin* *dáwa la-lwája3*	مُسكِّن دَوا للوَجع
headache medicine	*dáwa la-wája3 irrās*	دَوا للوَجع الرّاس
pill	*ɧábbit dáwa*	حبِّةْ دَوا
rubbing alcohol, antiseptic	*sbīrtu*	سْبيرْتو
syringe	*[Fseringue]* *íbri*	سورِنْج إبْرِة
tablet	*ʔurṣ (ʔrāṣ)* *ɧábbi (ɧbūb)*	قُرْص (قْراص) حبِّة (حْبوب)

thermometer	*mīzēn (mawēzīn) ḥarāra*	ميزان (مَوازين) حرارة

Other Things You Can Buy at a Pharmacy

baby bottle	*bibrūni*	بِبْرونِة
baby pacifier	*tētīn*	تيْتين
shampoo for dry/ normal/oily hair	*[shampoo] la-ššá3r innēšif/il3ādi/ iddíhni/ḍidd ilqíšri*	شامْبو للشّعْر النّاشِف/ العادي/الدِّهْني
antidandruff shampoo	*[shampoo]*	شامْبو ضِدّ القِشْرِة
shaving blades	*šafrāt ḥlēʔa*	شفْرات حْلاقة
toothbrush	*firšēyit (farāši) snēn*	فِرْشايِةْ (فراشي) سْنان
toothpaste	*ma3jūn snēn*	معْجون سْنان
tube	*[ᶠtube]*	توب

Misc.

pharmacy	*ṣaydalíyyi farmašíyyi*	صَيْدلية فرْمشية
dose	*jír3a (jra3) [ᶠdose]*	جُرْعة (جُرع) دوْز
manufacture date	*tērīx ilʔintēj*	تاريخ الاِنْتاج
expiration date	*tērīx intihēʔ iṣṣalāḥíyyi [expiry date]*	تاريخ إنْتِهاء الصّلاحية إكْسْپَيْري دايْت
to measure blood pressure	*ʔēs (yʔīs) ḍáɣṭu zēn (yzīn) ḍáɣṭu*	قاس (يْقيس) ضغْطو زان (يْزين) ضغْطو

prescription	*rušētta* *wáşfit ḩakīm*	رُشيْتّة وَصْفِةْ حكيم
sick, ill	*sāxin* *marīḑ*	ساخِن مريض
to become ill	*míriḑ (yímraḑ)*	مِرِض (يمْرِض)
sinuses	*jyūb anfíyyi* *[sinuses]*	جْيوب أنفية سَيْنسِس
stitches	*ʔiţab*	قِطب
stomach	*mí3di (mí3ad)*	مِعْدِة (مِعد)
temperature	*dárajit ḩarāra*	درجِةْ حرارة
wound	*jirḩ*	جِرْح

Expressions

Can I weigh myself, please?	*fíyi zīn ḩāli, [please]?*	فِيي زين حالي پْليز؟
I need to measure my blood pressure.	*báddi zīn ḑáɣţi.*	بدّي زين ضغطي.
Can you read what medicine is written in this prescription?	*fīk tíʔra/tiʔrālī/tšífli šū -ddáwa -lli maḩţūţ bi-háydi -lwáşfi/ -rrušētta?*	فيك تِقْرا/تِقْرالي /تْشِفْلي شو الدَّوا اللي محْطوط بِهَيْدي الوَصْفِة/الرُّشيْتّة؟
I need to change the bandage on this wound.	*báddi ɣáyyir 3a-ljírḩ.*	بدّي غيرِّ عالجِرْح.
My stomach is upset.	*mí3dti miš maẓbūţa.*	مِعْدْتي مِش مظْبوطة.

	mí3dti maʔlūbi.	مِعْدْتي مقْلوبِة.
My head is going to explode.	*rāsi raɧ yinfíjir.*	راسي رح يِنْفِجِر.

◇

Speedy recovery!, Get well soon!	*salēmtak!* *3a salēmi (nšálla)!* *fīk iššífa!* *bi-ššífa!*	سلامْتك! عَ سلامِة (انْشالله)! فيك الشِّفا! بِالشِّفا!
But this [medicine] requires a stamped prescription.	*bass háyda -ddáwa báddu rušēttit/wáşfit ɧakīm.*	بسّ هَيْدا الدَّوا بدّو رْشيْتِّةْ/وَصْفِةْ حكيم.
You need to change the dressing on those stitches.	*lēzim tɣáyyir 3a-lʔíţab.*	لازِم تْغيرِّ عالقطِب .
Try going back to your doctor so he can prescribe another medicine.	*járrib trāji3 ilɧakīm bárki byūşiflak dáwa tēnī/ɣáyru.*	جرِّب تِرْجع عِنْد الحكيم برْكي بْيِوْصفْلك دَوا تاني/غيرْو.
This medicine has been discontinued.	*háyda -ddáwa miš 3am yíji/yijīna mínnu.* *háyda -ddáwa maʔţū3.*	هَيْدا الدَّوا مِش عم يِجي/يِجينا مِنّو. هَيْدا الدَّوا مقْطوع.

At the Gym بِالجيم

Gyms in Lebanon are referred to either by the English word جيم *[gym]* or the Arabic word نادي *nēdi,* which means **club**. Many women in Lebanon go to the gym just to use cardio machines and not to lift any weights because there's still the misconception that lifting weights will bulk them up. But this has been changing in recent years. And, yes, the stereotype about Lebanese women going to the gym with makeup on is true, to some extent! Unlike in other Arab countries, gyms in Lebanon are typically mixed;–men and women use the gym at their leisure during business hours. That said, there may still be classes for women only, such as belly dancing, as, especially in smaller cities and towns, it is still not acceptable for a man to take classes that are considered more feminine. Lebanon is relatively modest about nudity; you will rarely see someone completely naked in the locker room, so keep that in mind when you're changing, and use one of the private changing rooms.

Asking about gym membership

○ سوْري، حابّة إشْترِك بِالجيم، وبدّي آخُد فِكرة عن أسْعارْكُن.

◇ أهْلا وسهْلا دُمْوازيْل. الاِشْترِاك خمْسين دوْلار بِالشّهِر إذا بسّ عم تِسْتعْمْلي المكنات. خمْسة وتمْانين دوْلار إذا بدِّك كمان تاخْدي صْفوف. وفي خصِم إذا بْتاخْدي اِشْترِاك السِّتّ أُشْهُر.

○ اه أوْكي. وكيف ساعات[1] الجيم؟

◇ فاتْحين كِلّ يوْم[2] مْن السِّتّة الصُّبح لنُصّ ليْل.

○ اه عظيم! فِيي إتْفرّج شْوَيّ وشوف المكنات؟[3]

◇ أكيد! لْحقيني تفرْجيكي.[4]

○ I'd like to join the gym and wanted to get an idea about your membership prices.

◇ Welcome, miss. It's $50 a month, if you're only using the machines, and $85 if you also plan to take classes. There's a discount if you get a quarterly or six-month membership.

○ I see. What are the gym's hours?

◇ We're open every day from 6 a.m. to midnight.

○ That's great! Can I take a look around to see the equipment?

◇ For sure. Follow me. I'll show you around.

○ *[sorry], ḥābbi ištírik bi-l[gym], w báddi ēxud fíkra 3an as3ārkun.*

◇ *áhla w sáhla, [ᶠdemoiselle]. -lʔištirāk xamsīn dólar bi-ššáhir íza bass 3am tistá3mli -lmakanēt. xámsa w tmēnīn dólar íza báddik kamēn tēxdi ṣfūf. w fī xáṣim íza btēxdi ištirāk issítt úšhur.*

○ *āh okē. w kīf ṣē3āt[1] il[gym]?*

◇ *fētḥīn kill yōm[2] mn issítti -ṣṣúbuḥ la-nuṣṣ lēl.*

○ *āh 3aẓīm! fíyi itfárraj šwayy w šūf ilmakanēt?[3]*

◇ *akīd! lḥaʔīni ta-farjīki.[4]*

[1] = دَوام *dawēm* **business hours, workday**

[2] = كِلّ إيّام الأُسْبوع *kill iyyēm ilʔusbū3* **all days of the week**

[3] = اه تمام! فِيي أعْمِل لفِّة/برْمِة لآخُد فِكْرة عن المكنات؟ *āh tamēm! fíyi á3mil láffi/bármi la-ēxud fíkra 3an ilmakanēt?* (لفِّة/برْمِة *láffi/bármi* **tour**)

[4] = وَلَوْ طبْعاً! تعي معي أعْمِلّك برْمِة. *waláw ṭáb3an! tá3i má3i a3míllik bármi.*

2

Making a Fitness Plan with a Trainer

◇ شو أهْدافك[1] عالمظْبوط؟[2]

○ بدّي ظبِّط جِسْمي بِشكِل عامّ.

◇ كم يوْم بِالجِمْعة بدّك تعْمِل سْپوْر؟[3]

○ برْكي تْلات تِيّام[4] بالأوّل. فِيي إجي الأحد، التّلاتة، والخميس.

◇ كْتير مْنيح. رح أعْمِلّك پْلان[5] تْلات تِيّام بِالجِمْعة تتِحْرُق دْهون وتعْمِل عضل.

◇ What are your goals exactly?

○ I just want to get in better shape in general.

◇ How many days a week do you want to work out?

○ Maybe three to start with. I can come to the gym on Sundays, Tuesdays, and Thursdays.

◇ Perfect. I'll create a 3-day workout plan to burn fat and build muscle.

◇ *šū ahdēfak[1] 3a-lmazbūṭ?[2]*

○ *báddi zábbiṭ jísmi bi-šákil 3āmm.*

◇ *kam yōm bi-ljím3a báddak tá3mil [Fsport]?[3]*

○ *bárki tlēt tiyyēm[4] bi-lʔáwwal. fíyi íji -lʔáħad, -ttalēta, w ilxamīs.*

◇ *ktīr mnīħ. raħ a3míllak [plan][5] tlēt tiyyēm bi-ljím3a ta-tíħruʔ dhūn w tá3mil 3áḍal.*

1 = الغوْلْز تبعك *-l[goals] tába3ak*

2 شو سبب اِشْتِراكك بالنّادي؟ *šū sábab ištirākak bi-nnēdi?* **What is the reason for you joining the gym?**

3 = كم يوْم بِالجِمْعة بدّك تعْمِل رِياضة؟ *kam yōm bi-ljím3a báddak tá3mil riyāḍi?*

4 إيّام *iyyēm* is pronounced تِيّام *tiyyēm* after a number.

5 = برْنامِج *birnēmij* **program**

3

Waiting to use equipment

○ عم تِسْتعْمْلي هَيْدي المكنة؟

◇ أيْه بسّ رح خلِّص، عِنْدي بعْد ست واحد بسّ.

○ اه أوْكيْ. وَلا يْهِمِّك. خِدي وَقْتِك.

(waits a bit)

◇ أوْكيْ خلّصِت. كِلّا تحِت تصرُّفِك.

○ مرْسي كْتير. جْديدِة بِالجيم عِنّا؟

◇ أيْه بلّشِت جِمْعِةْ الماضْيِة[1]!

○ Are you using this machine?

◇ Ah, yes, but I'm almost done; I just have one more set left.

○ Ah, okay. No worries. Take your time.

(waits a bit)

◇ Okay, I'm done. It's all yours.

○ Thanks a lot! Are you new at the gym?

◇ Yes! I only started last week.

○ *3am tistá3mli háydi -lmákana?*

◇ *ē, bass raɧ xálliṣ, 3índi ba3d [set] wāɧad bass.*

○ *āh okē. wála yhímmik. xídi wáʔtik.*

(waits a bit)

◇ *okē xalláṣit. kílla táɧit taṣárrufik.*

○ *[ᶠmerci] ktīr. jdīdi bi-l[gym] 3ínna?*

◇ *ē, ballášit jím3it -lmāḍyi*[1]*!*

[1] = الأُسْبوع الماضي *-lʔusbū3 ilmāḍi*

4

Asking for Help with Equipment

○ سوْري بْتعْرِف كيف فِيي ظبِّط القعْدِة ع هَيْدي المكنة؟
◇ أكيد! لحْظة خلّيني فرْجيكي. بسّ بدِّك تْشيلي هَيْدا الپينْ، وتْزحْطي السّيت.
○ اه أوْكيْ! ما شِفْت الپينْ.[1] مرْسي!
◇ أهْلا وسهْلا، وَلَوْ.[2]

○ Excuse me, do you know how to adjust the seat on this machine?
◇ Sure! Wait and I'll show you. Look, You just have to pull out the pin underneath and slide the seat.
○ Ah, I see! I didn't see the pin. Thank you!
◇ Of course! Don't mention it.

○ *[sorry] btá3rif kīf fíyi ẓábbiṭ il?á3di 3a háydi -lmákana?*
◇ *akīd! láḫẓa xallīni farjīki. bass báddik tšīli háyda -l[pin], w tẓáḫḫṭi -s[seat].*
○ *āh okē! ma šift il[pin].*[1] *[^F merci]!*
◇ *áhla w sáhla, waláw.*[2]

[1] = ما نْتبهِت عالپِن *ma ntabáhit 3a-l[pin]* **I didn't notice the pin.**

[2] = تِكْرم عَيْنِك *tíkram 3áynik*

5

Working with a Trainer

◇ أوْكيْ مْنعْمِل تْلاتِة سيتْس كِلّ وِحْدِة عشْرة ريبْس. جاهْزِة؟
○ جاهْزِة!
◇ واحد، تْنيْن، تْلاتِة...
○ أوف، تْقيل عْلَيي شْوَيّ هَيْدا.
◇ أوْكيْ خلّينا نْجرِّب خمْسْتعْشر كيلو. كيف هَيْدا الوَزِن؟
○ أيْه هَيْدا أحْسن[1] شْوَيّ.

◇ Okay, we'll do three sets of ten reps. Ready?
○ Ready!
◇ One... two... three...
○ Oh, this is a bit heavy for me!
◇ Okay, let's try 15 kg instead. How is that weight?
○ Yes. That's a bit better.

◇ *okē mná3mil tlēti [sets] kill wíḫdi 3ášra [reps]. jēhzi?*
○ *jēhzi!*
◇ *wāḫad, tnēn, tlēti...*
○ *ūf, tʔīl 3láyi šwayy háyda.*
◇ *okē xallīna njárrib xamstá3šar kīlu. kīf háyda -lwázin?*
○ *ē, háyda áḫsan[1] šwayy.*

[1] أفضل *áfḍal*

6

Taking an Aerobics Class

◇ خلّينا نْبلِّش هَيْدا الإكْسرْسَيْس[1]. جاهِز؟

o أيْه معك.[2]

◇ واحد، تْنيْن، تْلاتِة، لفوْق. واحد، تْنيْن، تْلاتِة، لتحِت.

o سوْري، فيك تِرْجع تْعيد التِّمْرين بعْد مرّة عَ مهْلك؟[3]

◇ Let's start this exercise. Ready?

o Yes, I'm following you.

◇ One, two, three up... one two three down.

o Sorry! Can you repeat that movement again slowly?

◇ *xallīna nbálliš háyda -l?[exercise][1]. jēhiz?*

o *ē, má3ak.[2]*

◇ *wāɦad, tnēn, tlēti, la-fō?. wāɦad, tnēn, tlēti, la-táɦit.*

o *[sorry], fīk tírja3 t3īd ittimrīn ba3d márra 3a máhlak?[3]*

[1] = هَيْدا التِّمْرين *háyda -ttimrīn*

[2] جاهِز! *jēhiz!* **Ready!**

[3] كْتير عم تِمْشي بْسِرْعة. مُمْكِن تْخفِّف شْوَيّ؟ *ktīr 3am tímši b-sír3a. múmkin txáffif šwayy?* **You're going really fast. Can you slow down a bit?**

○ سوْري، حابّة إشْترِك بِالجيم[1].

◇ أهْلا وسهْلا دومْواذيْل. بِتْحِبّي اِشْتراِك سِنِة، سِتّ أُشْهُر، مَوْسمي، أَوْ شهْري؟

○ كِنْت عم فكّر جرِّب شهر بِالأوّل. بْيفْرُق السِّعر؟

◇ إذا عم تِدْفعي شهْري، بْيِطْلع خمْسة وسبْعين ألْف ليرة، يَلّي هِيِّ خمْسين دوْلار. بسّ إذا عم تِدْفعي سنَوي مثلاً، بِتْصير سبْع مية وخمْسين ألْف ليرة يَعْني خمْسميةْ دوْلار، بدل السِّتّ ميةْ دوْلار يَلّي هِيِّ تِسِعْميةْ ألْف.

○ اه أوْكيْ، وكيف ساعاتْكُن[2]؟

◇ مْنِفْتح أرْبْعة وعِشْرين ساعة بِالنّْهار، سبِع تِيّام[3] بِالجِمْعة.[4]

○ عِنْدْكُن شي ساعات بسّ للسِّتّات؟[5]

◇ لأ، سوْري ما عِنّا دُمْوازيْل. الجيم عِنّا ميكْس، ودايْماً فاتْحين لكِلّ المِمْبِرْز.[6]

○ دوْماج،[7] طيِّب عِنْدْكُن شي صْفوف بسّ للسِّتّات؟

◇ أيْه! عِنّا صفّ زومْبا للسِّتّات، وصفّ رقِص شرْقي، والباقي كِلّو مفْتوح للكلّ. عِنّا كمان زومْبا ميكْس. رقِص شرْقي ما عِنّا ميكْس.

○ اه أوْكيْ. طيِّب وپيرْسوْنل تْريْنرْز[8]، عِنْدْكُن؟

◇ فيكي تِطِلْبي پيرْسوْنل تْريْنر بِتْلاتين دوْلار بِالسّاعة، فوْق الاِشْتراِك الشّهْري. وبِغضّ النّظر عن كم ساعة بْتِطِلْبيه، المْدرِّب بْيَعْمِلّك پْلان للشّهِر كِلّو. والسّشنْز يَلّي بْتِطْلِبِيْنْ بيكون معِك تَيْفرْجيكي[9] كيف تَعْمْلي كِلّ شي.

○ أوْكي، عِنْدْكُن كمان خدمات سْپا؟

◇ لِلأسف لأ[10]، مِش بِهَيْدا الفرِع. عِنّا سْپا بِفرْع الحمْرا.

○ اه أوْكي، فِيي آخُد رقْمُن عْمِلي معْروف؟[11]

◇ أكيد! هَيْدا مِيْنو في عْليْه أرْقام كِلّ فْروعْنا[12]، والخدمات يَلّي كِلّ فِرع بيقدِّما.

○ أوْكي، رج دِقِّلُّن بِخْصوص خدمات السْپا. بسّ هلّق فِيي پْليز بلِّش بِاِشْترِاك شهْري[13]، وبعْدَيْن مِنْشوف؟

◇ أكيد! أهْلا وسهْلا فيكي. خلّيني جِبْلِك الفورْمْز[14] تْعبِّيُن.

○ Excuse me, I'd like to join the gym.

◇ Welcome, miss! Would you prefer an annual, six-month, seasonal or monthly membership?

○ I was thinking of just trying it out for a month. Does the price differ?

◇ If you're paying monthly, it's 75,000 L.L. a month, which is $50. But if you do yearly, for example, it's 750,000 L.L. or $500, instead of $600 (or 900,000 L.L.).

○ Hmmm... okay, and what are your hours?

◇ We're open 24 hours a day, 7 days a week.

○ Do you have ladies-only hours?

◇ Sorry, we do not, ma'am. It's a mixed gym, and we're open to all our members at all times.

○ That's unfortunate. Okay, do you have any ladies' only classes?

◇ Yes! We have one ladies' only zumba class, and one ladies' only belly dancing class. Otherwise, all of our classes are also mixed. We also have mixed Zumba classes, but no mixed belly dancing classes.

○ I see. What about personal trainers? Do you have any?

◇ You can get a personal trainer for $30 an hour, on top of the montly fee. Regardless of many hours you book them, the trainer will still come up with a monthly plan for you to follow. The sessions you book them, they will be with you and show you the way!

○ Okay, do you offer spa services as well?
◇ Unfortunately, not at this branch, ma'am. We do have a spa in our Hamra branch.
○ I see. May I have their number, please?
◇ Sure! Here's a list with the numbers of all of our branches, as well as the serves that they each offer.
○ Okay, I'll call them about spa services. For now, can I please start out with a one-month membership, and we'll go from there?
◇ Sure; we're glad to have you! Let me get you the forms to fill out.

○ *[sorry], ḫābbi ištírik bi-[gym]*[1].
◇ *áhla w sáhla, [ᶠdemoiselle]. bitḫíbbi ištirāk síni, sitt úšhur, máwsami, aw šáhri?*
○ *kínt 3am fákkir járrib šáhir bi-lʔáwwal. byífruʔ issí3ir?*
◇ *íza 3am tídfa3i šáhri, byíṭla3 xámsa w sab3īn alf līra, yálli híyyi xamsīn dólar. bass íza 3am tídfa3i sánawi masálan, bitṣīr sab3 míyyi w xamsīn alf līra yá3ni xamsmīt dólar, bádal issítt mīt dólar yálli híyyi tísi3mīt alf.*
○ *āh okē, w kīf sē3ātkun*[2]*?*
◇ *mníftaḫ árb3a w 3išrīn sē3a bi-nnhār, sábi3 tiyyēm*[3] *bi-ljím3a.*[4]
○ *3índkun šī sē3āt bass la-ssittēt?*[5]
◇ *laʔ, [sorry] ma 3ínna, [ᶠdemoiselle]. -l[gym] 3ínna [mix], w dēyman fētḫīn la-kíll il[members].*[6]
○ *[ᶠdommage].*[7] *ṭáyyib 3índkun šī ṣfūf bass la-ssittēt?*
◇ *ē! 3ínna ṣaff [Zumba] la-ssittēt, w ṣaff ráʔiṣ šárʔi, w ilbēʔi kíllu maftūḫ lá-lkill. 3ínna kamēn [Zumba] [mix]. ráʔiṣ šárʔi ma 3ínna [mix].*
○ *āh okē. ṭáyyib w [personal trainers]*[8]*, 3índkun?*
◇ *fīki tiṭílbi [personal trainer] bi-tlētīn dólar bi-ssē3a, fōʔ ilʔištirāk iššáhri. w bíɣaḍḍ innáẓar 3an kam sē3a btiṭilbī, limdárrib bya3míllik [plan] la-ššáhir kíllu. w is[sessions] yálli btiṭlibíyun bikūn má3ik ta-yfarjīki*[9] *kīf tá3mli kill šī.*
○ *okē, 3índkun kamēn xadamēt [spa]?*
◇ *li-lʔásaf laʔ*[10]*, miš bi-háyda -lfíri3. 3ínna [spa] bi-fír3 ilḫámra.*
○ *āh okē, fíyi ēxud ráʔmun, 3míli ma3rūf?*[11]
◇ *akīd! háyda [menu] fī 3lē arʔām kill frū3na*[12]*, w ilxadamēt yálli kill fíri3 biʔáddima.*

○ okē, raḫ di??íllun bi-xṣūṣ xadamēt is[spa]. bass hálla? fíyi [please] bálliš bi-ištirāk šáhri[13], w ba3dēn minšūf?
◇ akīd! áhla w sáhla fīki. xallīni jíblik il[forms][14] t3abbíyun.

[1] = بِالنّادي bi-nnēdi

[2] = دَواماتْكُن dawēmētkun

[3] إيّام iyyēm is pronounced تِيّام tiyyēm after a number.

[4] = فاتْحين أرْبْعة و عِشْرين عَ سبْعة fēthīn árb3a w 3išrīn 3a sáb3a

[5] = عِنْدْكُن دَوام بسّ للنِّسْوان؟ 3índkun dawēm bass la-nniswēn?

[6] = النّادي عِنّا مُخْتلط ومْنِسْتقْبِل كِلّ الأعْضاء -nnēdi 3ínna muxtálaṭ w mnistá?bil kill il?a3ḍā?.

[7] = لِلْأسف li-l?ásaf

[8] = مْدرِّب خاصّ mdárrib xāṣṣ

[9] = يْدِلِّك ydíllik

[10] = ما تْواخْذيني لأ ma twēxzīni, la?

[11] = فيكي تعْطيني نمِرْتُن إذا بْتْريدي؟ fīki ta3ṭīni nímritun, íza bitrīdi? **Can you give me their number, please?**

[12] طبْعاً. هَيْدي ليسْتة عْلَيا كِلّ نمِرْتُن. ṭáb3an. háydi līsta 3láya kill nímrun. **Of course. Here's a list with all of their numbers on it.**

[13] رح إتِّصِل فيُنْ إسْتعْلِم عن السْپا. رح إتْسجّل شهْري بِالوَقْت الحاضِر. raḫ ittíṣil fíyun istá3lim 3an is[spa]. raḫ itsájjal šáhri bi-lwá?t ilḫāḍir.

[14] = الاِسْتِمارة -l?istimāra

Vocabulary

gym, health club	[gym] nēdi	جيم نادي
fitness	layēʔa	لَياقة
member	3úḍu (a3ḍāʔ)	عُضو (أعْضاء)
membership	3uḍwíyyi	عُضْوية
to join a gym	ištárak (yištírik) bi-[gym]	اِشْترك (يِشْترِك) بِجيم
monthly (membership) fee	ištirāk šáhri	اِشْتِراك شهْري
personal trainer	mudárrib šáxṣi	مُدرِّب شخْصي
training session	ḫíṣṣit tidrīb	حِصّة تدْريب
workout	timrīn	تمْرينة
exercise	timrīn (tamārīn) tidrīb	تمْرين (تمارين) تدْريب
to exercise, work out	tdárrab (yitdárrab)	تْدرّب (يِتْدرّب)
to get in shape	ẓábbaṭ (yẓábbiṭ) jísmu	ظبّط (يْظبِّط) جِسْمو
to bulk up, put on muscle mass	rábba (yrábbi) 3aḍalāt	ربّى (يْربّي) عضلات
to be tired	tí3ib, yít3ab	تِعِب (يِتْعب)
gymnastics	[ᶠgymnastique]	جيمناسْتيك
to do push-ups	3ímil (yá3mil) [push-up]	عِمِل (يَعْمِل) پُش أپ
to do sit-ups, work one's abs	3ímil (yá3mil) mí3di	عِمِل (يَعْمِل) مِعْدِة
to jump rope	naṭṭ (ynuṭṭ) 3a-lḫábli	نطّ (يْنُطّ) عالحبْلِة

to do yoga	*3ímil (yá3mil) yōga*	عِمِل (يَعْمِل) يوْغا
to do aerobics	*3ímil (yá3mil) [aerobics]*	عِمِل (يَعْمِل) أيْروْبِكْس
to sweat	*3íriʔ (yí3raʔ)*	عِرِق (يِعْرق)
equipment, machines	*makanēt*	مكنات
to do cardio exercise	*3ímil (yá3mil) [cardio]*	عِمِل (يَعْمِل) كارْدِيو
to burn calories	*ɧáraʔ (yíɧruʔ) issi3rēt ilɧarēríyyi/ il[calories]*	حرق (يِحْرُق) السِّعْرات الحرارِيّة/ الكالوريز
cardio machine	*mákanit [cardio]*	مكنِةْ كارْدِيو
treadmill, running machine	*[treadmill]*	تْريْد ميل
to run	*rákaḑ (yírkuḑ)*	ركض (يِركُض)
elliptical machine	*[elliptical]*	إيليپْتيكال
(stationary) bicycle	*[ᶠbicyclette]*	بيسيكْليْت
weight lifting	*ráfi3 asqāl* *šáʔil awzēn*	رفع أَثْقال شقِل أَوْزان
weight machine	*jihēz (ájhizit) ɧadīd*	جِهاز (أجْهِزة) حديد
free weights	*awzēn ɧúrra*	أَوْزان حُرّة
dumbbell(s)	*[dumbbell]*	دامْبل
barbell	*bār ɧadīd*	بار حديد
(weight) bench	*máʔ3ad (maʔē3id)* *[bench]*	مقْعد (مقاعِد) بِنْش

a rep	*márra* *[rep]*	مرّة ريْپ
a set	*majmū3a* *[set]*	مجْموعة سيْت
to adjust the weight	*źábbaţ (yźábbiţ) ilwázin*	ظبّط (يْظبِّط) الوَزِن
to lift weights	*šēl (yšīl) ɧadīd*	شال (يْشيل) حديد
to spot (lit. help in lifting a weight)	*sē3ad (ysē3id) bi-ráf3 ilwázin*	ساعد (يْساعِد) بِرفْع الوَزِن
to lower	*názzal (ynázzil)*	نزّل (يْنزِّل)
to pull	*sáɧab (yísɧab)*	سحب (يِسْحب)
to push	*dáfaš (yídfuš)*	دفش (يِدْفُش)
thin, weak	*ḑ3īf*	ضْعيف
fat (adjective)	*nāşiɧ*	ناصِح
to gain weight, get fat	*níşiɧ (yínşaɧ)*	نِصِح (يِنْصح)
muscular	*m3áḑḑal*	مْعضّل
in shape	*jísmu ɧílu/mitnēsiʔ*	جِسْمو حِلو/مِتْناسِق
out of shape	*jísmu miš ɧílu/mitnēsiʔ*	جِسْمو مِش حِلو/مِتْناسِق
fat (noun)	*díhin (dhūn)*	دِهِن (دْهون)
muscle	*3áḑal*	عضل
abs; belly	*mí3di* *báţin*	مِعْدِة بطِن
arm	*zind (znūd)*	زِنْد (زنود)

back	*ḍáhir (ḍhūr)*	ضهِر (ضْهور)
chest	*ṣídir (ṣdūr, ṣdūra)*	صدِر(صْدور، صْدورة)
knee	*ríkbi (ríkab, rkēb)*	رِكْبِة (رِكب، رْكاب)
leg	*íjir (ijrēn)*	إجِر (إجْريْن)
shoulder	*kítif (ktēf)*	كِتِف (كْتاف)
wrist	*má3ṣam (ma3āṣim)*	معْصم (معاصِم)
locker	*[locker]*	لوكِر
locker room	*ūḍit taɣyīr ittyēb*	أوضِة تغْييرالتّياب
gym clothes, workout clothes	*tyēb il[gym]*	تْياب الجيم
to change one's clothes	*ɣáyyar (yɣáyyir) tyēbu*	غيّر (يْغيِّر) تْيابو
shower	*[shower]*	شاوِر
towel (for showering)	*mánšafi (manēšif)*	منْشفِة (مناشِف)
hair dryer	*[Fséchoir]*	سِشْوار
(bathroom) scale	*mīzēn (mawēzīn)*	ميزان (مَوازين)
to weigh oneself	*zēn (yzīn) ḫālu*	زان (يْزين) حالو
to lose weight	*ḍí3if (yíḍ3af)*	ضِعِف (يِضْعف)
to gain weight	*zēd (yzīd) wázin*	زاد (يْزيد) وَزِن
to go on a diet	*3ímil (yá3mil) [Frégime]*	عِمِل (يَعْمِل) ريْجيم
on a diet	*mēši 3a [Frégime]*	ماشي عَ ريجيم
to breathe in	*áxad (yēxud) náfas*	أخد (ياخْد) نفس
to breathe out	*ṭálla3 (yṭálli3) náfas*	طلّع (يْطلِّع) نفس

up	*fōʔ*	فوْق
down	*táħit*	تحِت
right	*yamīn*	يمَين
left	*šmēl*	شْمال
to jump	*naṭṭ (ynuṭṭ)*	نطّ (يْنُطّ)
to sit	*ʔá3ad (yíʔ3ud)*	قعد (يِقْعُد)
to stand	*wíʔif (yūʔaf)*	وِقِف (يوقف)
to squat	*3ímil (yá3mil) [squat]* *ʔárfaṣ (yʔárfiṣ)*	عِمِل (يَعْمِل) سْكْوات قرْفص (يْقرْفِص)

Expressions

Could you spot me?	*fīk tsē3ídni bi-ráf3 ilwázin?*	فيك تْساعِدْني بِرفْع الوَزِن؟
Where is the locker room?	*wēn ūḍt il[locker]?* *wēn il[locker room]?*	ويْن أوضْة اللّوْكر؟ ويْن اللّوْكر روم؟
Where is the toilet?	*wēn ilħammēm?*	ويْن الحمّام؟
My goal is to gain muscle.	*báddi rábbi 3aḍalāt.*	بدّي ربّي عضلات.
Is there a contract?	*fī 3áʔid?*	في عقِد؟
How much does it cost per training session?	*ʔaddē bitkállif ħíṣṣit ittadrīb?*	قدّيْ بِتْكلِّف حِصّة التدْريب؟
How much is a monthly membership at this gym?	*ʔaddē lʔištirāk iššáhri bi-l[gym]?*	قدّيْ الاِشْتراِك الشّهْري بِالجيم؟

I feel like I've gained a bit of weight.	*ђāsis ђāli zídit šwayy.*	حاسِس حالي زِدِت شْوَيّ.
I need to lose five kilos.	*báddi íḍ3af xámsi kīlu.*	بدّي إضْعف خمْسِة كيلو.
I try to exercise at least twice a week.	*bђāwil itdárrab 3ála -lʔaʔáll marrtēn b-ilʔusbū3.*	بْحاوِل إتْدرّب على الاقلّ مرْتين بِالأُسْبوع.
I want to lose weight.	*báddi íḍ3af.*	بدّي إضْعف.
I'd like to hire a personal trainer.	*báddi wáẓẓif mudárrib šáxṣi.*	بدّي وَظِّف مُدرِّب شخْصي.
I'm on a diet.	*ána 3āmil [ᶠrégime].*	أنا عامِل ريجيم.
Excuse me, how do you use this machine?	*[please], kīf bistá3mil ha-l[ᶠmachine]/ ha-lmákana?*	بْليز، كيف بِسْتعْمِل هالماشين/هالمكنة؟

◇

Adjust the weight before you get on the machine.	*ẓábbiṭ ilwázin ʔábil ma tíʔ3ud/tíṭla3 3a-lmákana.*	ظبِّط الوَزِن قبِل ما تِقْعُد/تِطْلع عالمكنة .
Do three sets of ten reps each.	*3mōl tlēti [sets], kill wāђad 3ášra [reps].*	عْمول تْلاتِة سيتْس، كِلّ واحد عشْرة ريبْس.
Rest for one minute between sets.	*rtēђ dʔīʔa bēn kill [set] w [set].*	رْتاح دْقيقة بينْ كِلّ سيْت وسيْت.
Lift the barbell over your head, then slowly lower it back down.	*rfē3 il[bar] fōʔ rāsak w názzlu 3a máhlak.*	رْفاع البار فوْق راسك ونزْلو ع مهْلك.

Don’t forget to breathe!	*ma tínsa titnáffas!*	ما تِنْسا تِتْنفّس.
Excuse me. Your outfit does not meet our dress code.	*law samáɧit, tyēbak miš ʐābʈīn ma3 ʔawē3id illíbis/id[dress code] tába3na.*	لَوْ سمحِت، تْيابك مِش ظابْطين مع قَواعِد اللِّبِس/الدّْريْس كوْد تبعْنا.

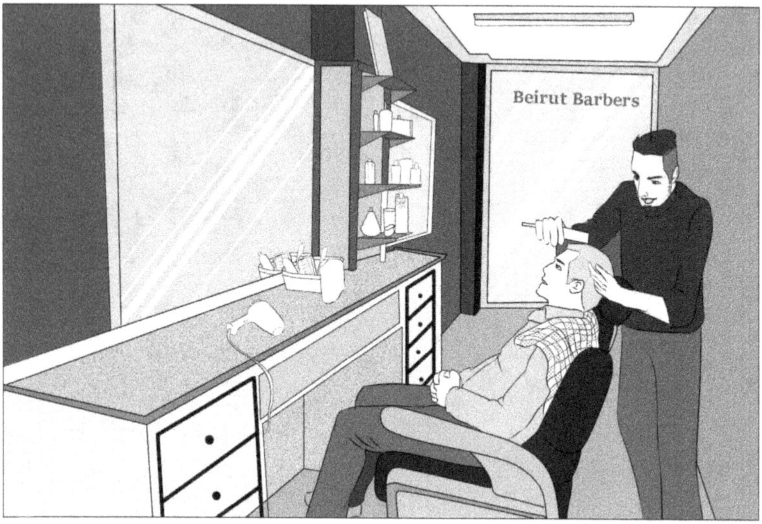

At a Barbershop عِنْد الحلّاق

Finding a barbershop is arguably as important as finding your nearest pharmacy, because you'll need it at least once, depending on how long you're staying in Lebanon. Luckily, Lebanese men share that appreciation of barbershops, so you won't have a difficulty to locate one, wherever you find yourself in Lebanon. Of course, these, like most things in life, will range from mediocre to very fancy. Fortunately, getting a haircut in Lebanon is relatively inexpensive–in expat areas it costs around $10, though it could be even cheaper in non-expat areas. As it becomes more and more acceptable for men to get services such as manicures, pedicures, and waxing, barbershops, especially in more upscale neighborhoods have been offering them. When your barber is done cutting your hair, he may tell you نعيماً *na3īman,* which roughly translates as **blessings**, but is essentially a formulaic greeting said to someone who has just gotten a haircut. If others notice that have a new hair cut, they'll also say this to you. You can respond with a simple thanks or say يِنْعم عْلَيْك *yín3am 3lēk*, which means **May God bless you**.

○ ليْش[1] هالقدّ في عجْقة[2]؟

◇ مْنِعْتِذِر إسْتاذ، بسّ لِأنّو نْهار جِمْعة والكِلّ بدّو يْقُصّ قبْل الويك أنْد.

○ طيِّب. أيّا ساعة لازِم إرْجع تتْكون فاضيلي وتْقُصِّلي[3]؟

◇ أحْسن تِرْجع العصِر، العجْقة بِتْكون خفِّت.

○ Why is it so crowded?

◇ Sorry about that, but it's Friday, and everyone is trying to get a haircut before the weekend!

○ So, when should I come to you for a haircut and you're free?

◇ You'd better come later in the afternoon. It'll be less crowded.

○ *lēš*[1] *ha-l?ádd fī 3áj?a*[2]*?*

◇ *mni3tízir istēz, bass li-ánnu nhār jím3a w ilkíll báddu y?uşş ?abl il[weekend].*

○ *ţáyyib. áyya sē3a lēzim írja3 ta-tkūn fāḑīli w t?uşşíli*[3]*?*

◇ *áɧsan tírja3 il3áşir, -l3áj?a bitkūn xáffit.*

[1] = ليْه *lē*

[2] = زحْمِة *záɧmi*

[3] تتْبلِّشْلي *ta-tballíšli* **so that you can start on me**

[4] وَلا يْهِمّك إسْتاذ مْنِمْرُقك هلّق، عِنّا حلّاقين كِفاية. *wála yhímmak istēz mnímru?ak hálla?, 3ínna ɧallē?īn kifēyi.* **Don't worry, sir. We can cut your hair now. We have enough barbers.**

2

SPECIFYING WHAT SERVICES YOU WOULD LIKE

◇ كيف فِيي إخِدْمك؟[1]

o بدّي قُصّ وإحْلُق وأعْمِل شْوَيّةْ سْوان لوِجّي.

◇ عِنّا كذا تْريتْمانْت للوِجّ. حابِب شي مْعينّ؟

o شي عالخفيف[2]، منْشفةْ ميّ سِخْنِة وماسْك مِن بعْد الحْلاقة.

◇ تحِت أمْرك![3]

◇ How can I help you?

o I'd like to have a haircut [and shave] and get some facial care.

◇ We have a full range of facial services. Anything in particular?

o Just something simple, like a hot towel and a nice mask after the shave.

◇ My pleasure!

◇ *kīf fíyi ixídmak?*[1]
o *báddi ʔuṣṣ w íḫluʔ w á3mil šwáyyit [*[F]*soin] la-wíjji.*
◇ *3ínna káza [treatment] la-lwíjj. ḫābib šī m3áyyan?*
o *šī 3a-lxafīf*[2]*, mánšafit mayy síxni w [mask] min ba3d liḫlēʔa.*
◇ *táḫit ámrak!*[3]

1 = أُمُرْني؟ *ʔmúrni?*

2 = شي بسيط *šī basīṭ*

3 = تِكْرم عَيْنك! *tíkram 3áynak!*

3

SPECIFYING HOW YOU WANT YOUR HAIR CUT

◇ بِتْحِبّ الجَوانِب تْكون أقْصر وِلّا كِلّو ذات الطّول[1]؟

○ بْتعْرِف شو؟ كْتير شوْب. قرّعو كِلّو[2].

◇ واللِحْيِة كمان؟

○ لأ خلّي اللِّحْيِة مِتِل منّا.

◇ Would you like the sides to be a bit shorter or all one length?

○ You know what, it's so hot. Shave it all off.

◇ What about the beard?

○ No, leave it as is.

◇ *bitḫíbb iljawēnib tkūn áʔṣar wílla kíllu zēt iṭṭūl*[1]*?*

○ *btá3rif šū? ktīr šōb. ʔárr3u kíllu*[2]*.*

◇ *w illíḫyi kamēn?*

○ *laʔ xálli -llíḫyi mítil mánna.*

[1] = نفْس الطّول *nafs iṭṭūl*

[2] عْمِلو عالزّيرو *3mílu 3a-zzīru*

[3] أيْ، شيلا. *ē, šīla.* **Yes, remove it.**

[4] = مِتِل ما هِيِّ *mítil ma híyyi* (See also note 4 on p. 48.)

4

A MOTHER BRINGS HER SMALL SON IN FOR A HAIRCUT.

◇ شو هَيْدا؟ شو صايِر[1] بِحالك؟

○ كان عم يِلْعب[2] بِالمْقصّ هالوِرِش.

◇ يَلّا ثَواني بسّ بْجِبْلو الطّبْلية يِقْعُد عْلَيا وبْظبِّطْلو ياه وَلا يْهِمّك.[3]

○ بسّ پْليز ما تعْمِلّو ياه عالزّيرو.[4]

◇ What's this? What happened to you?

○ This little guy was playing with scissors!

◇ Just a moment. I'll bring a booster for him to sit on, and I'll fix it for him. Don't worry.

○ But please don't make it a buzz cut.

◇ *šū háyda? šū ṣāyir*[1] *bi-ḫālak?*

○ *kēn 3am yíl3ab*[2] *bi-lim?áṣṣ ha-lwíriš.*

◇ *yálla sawēni bass bjíblu -ṭṭablíyyi yí?3ud 3láya w bẓabbíṭlu yēh, wála yhímmik.*[3]

○ *bass [please] ma ta3míllu yēh 3a-zzīru.*[4]

[1] = عامِل *3āmil* = مْساوي *msēwi*

[2] يِتْشَيْطن *yitšáyṭan* **misbehave, act naughty** (from شيْطان *šēṭān* **devil**)

[3] بسّ قاصِصُن شي طَويل وشي قصير. بدّي شوف شو فِيي أعْمِل تِطْلع القصّة مْنيحة. *bass ?āṣiṣun šī ṭawīl w šī ?aṣīr. báddi šūf šū fíyi á3mil ta-tíṭla3 il?áṣṣa mnīḫa.* **But he cut some of them long, some short. I'll see what I can do so that the haircut turns out good.**

[4] ما عِنْدي مِشْكْلِة تِحْلِقْلو عالزّيرو إذا هَيْدا أسْهل حلّ. *ma 3índi míškli tiḫlí?lu 3a-zzīru íza háyda áshal ḫall.* **I don't mind a buzz cut if it's the easiest solution.**

5

Getting your beard shaved

o مرْحبا، بدّي إحْلُق لِحْيِتي لَوْ سمحْت عالموس.

◇ مع إنّو لابْقِتْلك. بسّ عَ ذَوْقك.[1]

o بْتعْرِف؟ خلّينا نعْمِلا سكْسوكةِ أظْبط.

◇ أيْه بْتِطْلع حِلْوة.

o Hey! I'd like to get my beard shaved off with a razor.

◇ You look nice [with it], but as you wish.

o You know what? Let's make it a goatee. That would be better.

◇ That'll look nice.

o *márħaba, báddi íħluʔ líħyiti law samáħt 3a-lmūs.*

◇ *ma3 ínnu lēbʔítlak. bass 3a záwʔak.*[1]

o *btá3rif? xallīna ná3mila saksūki áẓbaṭ.*

◇ *ē, btíṭla3 ħílwi.*

[1] = مع إنّو رايْحِتْلك، بسّ مِتِل ما بدّك. *ma3 ínnu rāyħítlak, bass mítil ma báddak.*

6

PAYING FOR YOUR HAIRCUT

◇ نعيماً ريِّس.

o مرْسي! قدّيْ بِترْيد؟

◇ عشِرْتلاف ليرة لَوْ سمحِت[1].

o تْفضّل. يِسْلموا إيديْك!

◇ الله يْسلّمك![2]

◇ There you go, sir!

o Thank you! How much is the total?

◇ That's 10,000 L.L. please.

o Okay, here you are. Bless your hands!

◇ Bless you, too!

◇ *na3īman, ráyyis.*

o *[ᶠmerci]! ʔaddē bitrīd?*

◇ *3aširtalēf līra, law samáḫit*[1].

o *tfáḍḍal. yíslamu idēk!*

◇ *álla ysállmak!*[2]

[1] = إذا بِترْيد *íza bitrīd*

[2] = مْعوَّضين *m3áwwaḍīn* (from الله يْعوّض مِصْريّاتك *álla y3áwwaḍ miṣriyyētak* **may God compensate your money**)

○ يِسْعِد صباحك[1] إيلي.
◇ أهْلا خَواجة پوْل. ثَواني وبْكون معك.
○ خوْد وَقْتك صديقي.[2]

(a few minutes later)

◇ شو بِتْحِبّ نعْمِل ريِّس؟[3]
○ يا خيّي القُصّة وما فِيا[4] إنّو عِنْدي مُناسبِة وبدّي ياك تْظبِّطْني عَ ذَوْقك.
◇ مِن هالعينْ قبِل هالعينْ! بدّك تْقُصّو أَوْ بسّ تْظبِّط الطْراف؟
○ لأ بسّ تُظْبيط طْراف ويْكون كِلّو بمِسْتَوى بعضو.
◇ واللِحْيِة؟
○ إذا فيك تْرتِّبا تتْكون كِلّا ذات الطّول بلا ما تْقصِّر كْتير، بْكون ممْنونك.
◇ تمام، بِتْحِبّ حُطِّلّك شْوَيِّة أفْترْشايْف بسّ نْخلِّص؟
○ لأ دخيلك. ما بْحِبُّ وبْحِسّ ريحتُ قَوية. بسّ برْكي بسّ نْخلِّص منْحُطّ منْشفِة سِخْنِة وماسْك عَ ذَوْقك[5].
◇ مِن عينيّ. إجاني ماسْك جْديد بيجنّن.
○ أوْكيْ عظيم. مِنجرْبو، بسّ خلّينا نْقُصّ قبِل.
◇ بْتؤْمُر!

(barber finishes cutting)

○ يِسْلموا إيديْك يا إسْتاذ!
◇ نعيماً! عَ ذَوْقك؟
○ بيجنِّنوا! بسّ فيك تْقصِّر اللِّحْيِة نِتْفِة زْغيرِة هوْن؟ سوْري عم بزِعْجك!

◇ لا أبداً، ما في إزْعاج.

(barber finishes threading)

o تمام، إسْتاذ!

◇ الله يْخلّيلي ياك يا صديقي.

o ويْخلّيك يا ريِّس! قدّيْ بدّك منّي؟

◇ كِلُّن سَوا تْمانة وعِشْرين ألْف.

o أوْكي خيّ، تْفضّل.

◇ خلِّيا عْلَيْنا هالمرّة.[6]

o أكيد لأ، كِلّك ذوْق.

o Hello! Good morning, Elie!

◇ Good morning, Mr. Paul. I'll be right with you.

o Take your time, my friend.

(a few minutes later)

◇ What can I do for you, sir?

o Listen, brother, here's the thing: I have an important event, so I want you to pamper me.

◇ My pleasure! Are we going to cut it or just trim the sides?

o I just want to get my hair trimmed a bit and make it all even.

◇ What about the beard?

o If you could just even it up with the clippers without taking off too much, I'd be happy.

◇ All right. Would you like me to apply some aftershave afterwards?

o No, I beg you! I'm not a huge fan of their strong smells. Just a hot towel and a nice mask.

◇ My pleasure. There is this new mask I just got, and it's excellent.

o Okay, great, let's do it, but let's get the haircut done first.

◇ You're the boss!

(barber finishes cutting)

o Bless your hands, sir!

◇ There you are! Do you like it?

o It's great! Nice work! But can you trim the beard a bit more here? Sorry for the hassle.

◇ No, sir, it's nothing!

(barber finishes threading)

o Perfect!

◇ God bless you, my friend!

o You too, sir. How much do I owe you?

◇ All together, it's 28,000 L.L.

o Okay, bro, here you are.

◇ It's on the house this time!

o Absolutely not. You're too kind.

o *yís3id ṣabāḫak*[1] *[ᶠElie].*

◇ *áhla xawēja [Paul]. sawēni w bkūn má3ak.*

o *xūd wáʔtak ṣadīʔi.*[2]

(barber finishes cutting)

◇ *šū bitḫíbb ná3mil ráyyis?*[3]

o *ya xáyyi, -lʔúṣṣa w ma fíya*[4] *ínnu 3índi munēsabi w báddi yēk tẓabbíṭni 3a záwʔak.*

◇ *min ha-l3ēn ʔábil ha-l3ēn! báddak tʔúṣṣu aw bass tẓábbiṭ iṭṭrāf?*

o *laʔ bass tuẓbīṭ ṭrāf w ykūn kíllu bi-mústawa bá3ḍu.*

◇ *w illíḫyi?*

o *íza fīk trattíba ta-tkūn kílla zēt iṭṭūl bála ma tʔáṣṣir ktīr, bkūn mamnūnak.*

◇ *tamēm, bitḫíbb ḫuṭṭíllak šwáyyit [aftershave] bass nxálliṣ?*

o *laʔ daxīlak. ma bḫíbbun w bḫiss rīḫitun ʔawíyyi. bass bárki bass nxálliṣ minḫúṭṭ mánšafi síxni w [mask] 3a záwʔak*[5].

◇ *min 3īnáyyi. ijēni [mask] jdīd bijánnin.*

o *okē 3aẓīm. minjárrbu, bass xallīna nʔuṣṣ ʔábil.*

◇ *btúʔmur!*

(barber finishes threading)

o *tamēm, istēz!*

◇ *álla yxallīli yēk ya ṣadīʔi.*

○ *w yxallīk ya ráyyis! ʔaddē báddak mínni?*
◇ *kíllun sáwa tmēna w 3išrīn alf.*
○ *okē xáyyi, tfáḍḍal.*
◇ *xallíya 3láyna ha-lmárra.*[6]
○ *akīd laʔ, kíllak zōʔ.*

[1] = صباحو *ṣabāḫu*

[2] في كْتير نطْرة؟ لِأنّي مِسْتعْجِل. *fī ktīr náṭra? li-ánni mistá3jil.* **Is there a long wait? Because I'm in a hurry.**

[3] = أُمُرني. شو جايي عَ بالك تعْمِل الْيوم؟ *ʔmúrni. šū jēyi 3a bēlak tá3mil ilyōm?* **All right, what do you have in mind today?**

[4] **the story in a nutshell** lit. (the story and what's in it) Note: قُصّة *ʔúṣṣa* **story**; قصّة *ʔáṣṣa* **haircut**

[5] عَ ذَوْقك *3a záwʔak* (lit. up to your taste) implies that something will be done the way you want it. Sometimes, when a barber or hairdresser finishes, they'll ask عَ ذَوْقك؟ *3a záwʔak?* **Do you like it?** (lit. Is it up to your taste?)

[6] This expression is not meant to be taken literally. Your barber does expect you to pay for the haircut! This is just a set expression to show hospitality.

Vocabulary

barbershop	*[ᶠsalon] ɧlēʔa*	صالوْن حْلاقة
barber	*ɧallāʔ*	حلّاق
haircut; shave	*ʔáʂʂa, ɧlēʔa*	قصّة، حْلاقة.
to get a haircut; to cut (hair)	*ʔaʂʂ (yʔiʂʂ)*	قصّ (يْقِصّ)
to shave (one's head)	*ɧálaʔ (yíɧluʔ)*	حلق (يِحْلُق)
scissors	*mʔaʂʂ*	مْقصّ
straight razor	*mūs*	موس
blade, razor	*šáfra*	شفْرة
hair clippers	*mákanit ɧlēʔa*	مكنِة حْلاقة
comb	*mušʈ (mšāʈ)*	مُشْط
brush	*firšēyi (farāši)*	فِرْشايِة (فراشي)
mirror	*mrēyi*	مْرايِة
towel	*mánšafi (manēšif)*	منْشفِة (مناشِف)
mask	*[mask]*	ماسْك
cream	*[cream]*	كْريم
gel	*[gel]*	جِلّ
dye	*ʂábɣa*	صبْغة
shampoo	*[shampoo]*	شامْبو
hair	*šá3ir*	شعِر
face	*wijj (wjūh)*	وِجّ (وْجوه)
beard	*dáʔin (dʔūn)*	دقِن (دْقون)

mustache	*šērib (šwērib)*	شارِب (شْوارِب)
goatee, circle beard	*saksūki*	سكْسوكِة
"zero" cut, very short buzz cut	*zīro*	زيروْ
bangs	*ɣúrra*	غُرّة
front	*ʔiddēm*	قِدّام
top	*fōʔ*	فوْق
back	*ḍáhir (ḍhūr)*	ضهِر (ضْهور)
sides	*jawēnib*	جَوانِب
right side	*máylit ilyamīn*	مَيْلةْ اليَمين
left side	*máylit iššmēl*	مَيْلِةْ الشْمال
sideburns	*swēlif*	سْوالِف

Expressions

	○	
I'm going to the barber's.	*rāyiḫ 3ind ilḫallāʔ.*	رايح عِنْد الحلّاق.
I had my hair cut about a month ago.	*ʔaṣṣēt šá3ri min šáhir.*	قصّيْت شعْري مِن شهِر.
Give me a shave and haircut.	*ḫlíʔli w ʔíṣṣilli.*	حْلاقْلي وقِصْلي.
Please, wash my hair before cutting it.	*3mōl ma3rūf, ḫammímli šá3ri ʔábil ma tʔíṣṣu.*	عْموْل معْروف حمِّمْلي شعْري قبِل ما تْقِصّو.
Let's even up the hair.	*xallīna nʔíṣṣu kíllu 3a mústawa bá3ḍu.*	خلّينا نْقِصّو كِلّو عَ مْسْتَوى بعْضو.

Not too short.	*ma ykūn ktīr ʔaṣīr.*	ما يْكون كْتير قصير.
A little shorter, please.	*áʔṣar bi-šwáyy/ bi-nítfi ba3d.*	أقْصر بِشْوَيّ/بِنِتْفِة بعْد.
I just want you to take 2-3 centimeters off the top.	*bass báddi ʔiṣṣ tnēn tlēti [Fcentimètre] min fōʔ.*	بسّ بدّي قِصّ تْنين تْلاتِة سنْتيمِتْر مِن فوْق.
Let's use setting 3 on the hair clippers.	*ḫlíʔli 3a-ttlēti.*	حْلاقْلي عالتّْلاتِة.
Show me the back of my hair with a mirror.	*farjīni šá3ri min wára 3a-lmrēyi.*	فرْجيني شعْري مِن وَرا عالمْرايِة.
I want to have my beard shaved off.	*báddi íḫlu? ḍáʔni 3a-zzīru.*	بدّي إحْلُق دقْني عالزّيرو.
Can you fix my beard with some threading?	*fīk tẓabbíṭli dáʔni bi-lxēṭ?*	فيك تْظبِّطْلي دِقْني بِالخيْط؟
Shave my beard but leave the mustache.	*ḫlíʔli dáʔni, bass xallīli šwērbi.*	حْلاقْلي دقْني، بسّ خلّيلي شْوارْبي.

◇

[Are you here for] a shave, haircut, or both?	*ḫlēʔa, ʔaṣṣ, aw ittnēn?*	حْلاقة، قصّ، أَوْ التّْنين؟
Would you like to have your hair cut with hair clippers or with scissors and a comb?	*bitḫíbb ʔiṣṣillak bi-lmákana aw bi-lmʔáṣṣ w ilmúšuṭ?*	بْتِحِبّ قِصِّلّك بِالمكنة أَوْ بِالمْقصّ والمْشُط؟
Would you like me to cut it for you on setting 1 or 2?	*báddak ʔíṣṣillak 3a-lwāḫad aw 3a-ttnēn?*	بدّك قِصِّلّك عالواحد أَوْ عالتّْنين؟
Do you want sideburns?	*báddak swēlif?*	بدّك سْوالِف؟

How's that?	*šū ráʔyak?*	شو رأيَك؟
Would you like me to apply a facial mask?	*bitɦíbb a3míllak [mask] la-lwíjj/la-wíjjak?*	بِتْحِبّ أعْمِلّك ماسْك للوِجّ/لَوِجّك؟
Do you want a hot towel?	*báddak mánšafi síxni?*	بدّك منْشفِة سِخْنِة؟

At a Beauty Salon عِنْد الصّالوْن

A women's hairdresser is called كْوافور *[ᶠcoiffeur]* but also sometimes حلّاق *ḥallā?* barber. Interestingly, they are more likely to be men, which is not at all typical in other Arab countries. Beauty salons in Lebanon vary in size and range of services. Some only offer hair services, while others also have threading, waxing, massages, nail services, and the list goes on. A salon that offers only hair services is called صالوْن شعِر *[ᶠsalon] šá3ir* **hair salon**, whereas those that offer more services are simply called صالوْن *[ᶠsalon]* **salon.** Those that only offer nail services are colloquially called محلّ الضّفير *maḥáll iḍḍafīr* (lit. nails place), and صالوْن الضّفير *[ᶠsalon] iḍḍafīr* **nail salon.** Beauty salon services are, on average, cheaper than they are in the U.S. or Europe, and generally welcome walk-ins–although you may have to wait longer than if you had made an appointment. Only higher-end establishments (such as those found in major hotels) might have prices comparable to those in the U.S. or Europe and require that you make an appointment. In Lebanon, there is some status attached to which salon you go to. Salons are closed on Mondays. This has been the norm for as long as anyone can remember, and it's because they're open even on weekends and want to give their staff a day off.

Getting a haircut

o بدّي قُصّ الِطْراف بسّ عْموْل معْروف.[1]

◇ ما بدِّك قصّة جْديدِة؟

o لأ، بسّ الِطْراف. وبدّي كمان قُصّ غُرّة.[2]

◇ أكيد، تِكْرم عَيْنِك!

o I just wanted to get the tips trimmed.
◇ You don't want to try a new hair cut?
o No, just the tips, and I want to have bangs.
◇ Certainly! With pleasure!

o *báddi ʔuṣṣ liṭṭrāf bass, 3mōl ma3rūf*[1].
◇ *ma báddik ʔáṣṣa jdīdi?*
o *laʔ, bass liṭṭrāf. w báddi kamēn ʔuṣṣ ɣúrra.*[2]
◇ *akīd, tíkram 3áynik!*

[1] = إذا بِتْريد *íza bitrīd*

[2] فرْجيني مْن الكتوْلوْج شي موْديْل يِلْبقْلي. *farjīni mn il[Fcatalogue] šī [Fmodèle] yilbáʔli.* **Show me in the catalogue something that might suit me.**

2

Paying

○ كْتير حِلْوين[1] ، مرْسي[2]!

◇ القصّة كْتير لابْقِتْلِك[3]! نعيماً!

○ مرْسي كِلّك ذوْق! قدّيْه بدّك مِنّي؟

◇ عْمِلْنا قصّة كاريْه وغُرّة. فإذاً تْلاتين ألْف ليرة.

○ قدّيْ يَعْني بِالدّوْلار؟

◇ عِشْرين دوْلار.

○ Very nice! Thank you!
◇ This haircut looks incredible on you.
○ Merci! How much do I owe you then?
◇ We did a bob cut and bangs. That makes it 30,000 L.L.
○ How much is that in USD?
◇ That would be $20.

○ *ktīr ḫilwīn*[1]*, [[F]merci]*[2]*!*
◇ *-lʔáṣṣa ktīr lēbʔítlik*[3]*! na3īman!*
○ *[[F]merci] kíllak zōʔ! ʔaddē báddak mínni?*
◇ *3mílna ʔáṣṣa [[F]carré] w ɣúrra. fa-ízan tlētīn alf līra.*
○ *ʔaddē yá3ni bi-ddólar?*
◇ *3išrīn dólar.*

[1] عجبوني كْتير. *3ajabūni ktīr.* **I really like it!**

[2] = يِسْلمو إيديْك! *yíslamu idēk!*

[3] = رايْحِتْلِك *rāyḫítlik*

③

GETTING A NEW HAIRSTYLE

○ عَ بالي قُصّ كْتير قصير، وأعْمِل شي موْديْل جْديد.

◇ شو رأْيِك بِقصّة غرْسون مِتِل هَيْدي الصّورة، ومْنعْمِل هايْلايْتْس[1]!

○ لأ لأ مِش هالقدّ.[2] بسّ فينا نْجرِّب الصّورة اللي حدّا.

◇ هَيْدي كْتير حِلْوِة وبْتِلْبق عَ فوْرْم[3] وِجِّك.

○ Well, I want to get it cut really short and have a new hairstyle.

◇ How about we try a pixie cut like the one in this picture and add some highlights?

○ No, no, not to that extent, but we can try the picture next to it.

◇ That looks really nice and would suit your face shape.

○ *3a bēli ʔuṣṣ ktīr ʔaṣīr, w á3mil šī [ᶠmodèle] jdīd.*

◇ *šū ráʔyik bi-ʔáṣṣa [ᶠgarçon] mítil háydi -ṣṣūra, w mná3mil [highlights][1]!*

○ *laʔ laʔ miš ha-lʔádd[2]. bass fīna njárrib iṣṣūra -lli ḩádda.*

◇ *háydi ktīr ḩílwi w btílbaʔ 3a [form][3] wíjjik.*

[1] = خِصل *xíṣal* (lit. strands/locks of hair)

[2] لأ ، كْتير أوْڤر. *laʔ, ktīr [over].* **That's just too much.**

[3] = تِدْويرة *tidwīri*

Getting a Manicure and Pedicure

o كيفِك حبيبْتي؟ كيف كِلّ شي؟[1]

◇ أنا مْنيحة[2] مدام، مرْسي.[3]

o لَيْكي[4] بدّي أعْمِل مانيكور پيديكور.[5]

◇ أكيد تِكْرم عَيْنِك. يَلّا بسّ تجيب ميّ فاتْرة.

o How are you, dear? How's it going?

◇ I'm fine, ma'am. Thank you.

o Well, I'd like to get a manicure and a pedicure.

◇ Sure, with pleasure. Just a moment, and I'll bring some warm water.

o *kīfik ɧabībti? kīf kill šī?*[1]

◇ *ána mnīɧa*[2], *[Fmadame], [Fmerci].*[3]

o *láyki*[4] *báddi á3mil manikúr [Fpédicure].*[5]

◇ *akīd tíkram 3áynik. yálla bass ta-jīb mayy fētra.*

[1] شو أخْبارِك؟ *šū axbārik?* **What's new?**

[2] كِلّو تمام! *kíllu tamēm!* **Everything's great!**

[3] شو بِتْحِبّي تْساوي اليوْم؟ *šū bitɧíbbi tsēwi -lyōm?* **What would you like to have done today?**

[4] لَيْكي is a term used to address a woman and/or to get her attention. The closest equivalent in English would be **look** or **listen**. To a man, it's ليْك *lēk.*

[5] = حابّة أعْمِل ضفيري. *ɧābbi á3mil ɖafīri.* **I want to get my nails done.**

5

Getting a perm

○ بدّي أعْمِل هَيْدا المودْيْل بِشعْري.

◇ آه، بسّ هَيْدا المودْيْل بدّو پيرْم. في شي نوْع مْعيّن بِتْفضّليه؟

○ النّوْع اللي بْتِسْتعْمْلو كِلّ مرّة. بسّ پْليز نْتْبِه لأِنّو شعْري منّو كْتير عبي[1].

◇ ما تِعْطلي همّ أبداً. رح يِطْلع مِتِل الصّورة وأحْلى اِنشالله.

○ I want to get this hairstyle.

◇ Ah, but this will require us to use a perm. Is there a certain type you prefer using?

○ The one you use every time, but be careful because my hair isn't very thick/strong.

◇ Don't worry... it will come out just like in the picture, or even better, God willing.

○ *báddi á3mil háyda -l[^F^modèle] bi-šá3ri.*

◇ *ah, bass háyda -l[^F^modèle] báddu [perm]. fī šī nō3 m3áyyan bitfaḍḍlī?*

○ *-nnō3 -lli btistá3mlu kill márra. bass [please] ntíbih li-ánnu šá3ri mánnu ktīr 3ábi[1].*

◇ *ma tí3ṭali hamm ábadan. raḫ yíṭla3 mítil iṣṣūra w áḫla in-šálla.*

[1] = خفيف *xafīf* **thin**

6

Getting a Facial

- o بدّي أعْمِل فاشْيال إذا بِترْيدي.
- ◇ أكيد! بِتْحِبّي تعْمْلي الفاشْيال العادي يَلّي نُصّ ساعة؟ أَوْ فاشْيال الدّيپ كْلينْزينْغ؟
- o الفاشْيال العادي پْليز.
- ◇ بِتْحِبّي تعْمْلي شي شمِع أَوْ خيْط؟
- o لازِم أعْمِل حْواجْبي خيْط! صار بدّا[1]!

- o I'd like to have a facial, please.
- ◇ Sure, would you like the basic, 30-minute facial, or the deep-cleansing?
- o I'll just do the basic one today.
- ◇ Would you like to do any waxing or threading?
- o I have to get my eyebrows waxed! They need it!

- o *báddi á3mil [facial] íza bitrīdi.*
- ◇ *akīd! bitɧíbbi tá3mli -l[facial] il3ādi yálli nuṣṣ sē3a? aw [facial] id[deep cleansing]?*
- o *-l[facial] il3ādi, [please].*
- ◇ *bitɧíbbi tá3mli šī šámi3 aw xēṭ?*
- o *lēzim á3mil ɧwējbi xēṭ! ṣār bádda[1]!*

[1] صار بدّنا *ṣār bádda* (lit. started to want it) means 'it's about time!' or 'I've waited long enough!'

Extended Dialogue

◇ أهْلا وسهْلا مادام سارة.

○ مرْسي حبيبْتي، أهْلا فيكي.

◇ اليوْم منّا كْتير مشْغولين، بقى كِلْني تحِت تصرُّفِك![1]

○ عظيم.[2] مِن هيْك أنا قلِت بِجي بكّير.

◇ تحِت أمْرِك. شرّفْتي.

○ مرْسي حبيبْتي تِسْلمي. لَيْكي حابّة غيرّ اللّوْك وأعْمِل كم شغْلِة.

◇ أوْكيْ! بدْنا نْقُصّ؟

○ لأ بسّ نضِّف شْوَيّ الطِرْاف. بسّ عَ بالي كمان أعْمِل پيرْم وهايْلايْتْس.[3]

◇ في كذا درجِة للفْريزْيه[4]. حاطّة شي مْعينّ بِراسِك؟

○ أيْه، شوفي هَيْدي الصّورة. شِفْتا وحِبّيْتا[5] كْتير.

◇ أوْكيْ، يمْكِن ما تِطْلع ذات الشّي مِتِل الصّورة لِأنّو شعْرِك أعْبى مِن شعْرا.

○ معْليْه، مِنْجرِّب ومِنْشوف.

◇ شو كمان؟

○ بدّي كمان أعْمِل فاشْيال.

◇ بدِّك تعْمْلي شي واكْسينْغ[6] أَوْ خيْط؟

○ لأ مرْسي، بسّ بدّي مانيكير.

◇ بدِّك پيديكير كمان؟

○ لأ مرْسي. خلّينا نعْمِل هَوْدي هلّق، ومْنرْجع مِنْشوف.

◇ تِكْرم عَيْنِك.

(after the hairdresser has finished)

- ○ رَوْعة! بْتعْرْفي، لوْن الهايْلايْتْس يَلّي نصحْتيني في كْتير أحْلى مْن اللّوْن اللي أنا كِنِت مْنِقّايِتو.
- ◇ قِلْتِلِّك، هَيْدا أحْلى مع لوْن شعْرِك وبشِرْتِك.
- ○ مرْسي كْتير حبيبْتي. قدّيْ بدِّك مِنّي؟[7]
- ◇ كِلُّن سَوا[8] مية وعِشْرين ألْف.
- ○ تْفضّلي حبيبْتي.

- ◇ Welcome, Mrs. Sarah.
- ○ Thank you, dear.
- ◇ Today, we aren't that busy, so I will be all yours and do what you want.
- ○ Wonderful! That's why I thought of coming early today.
- ◇ I'm at your service. We're thrilled that you're here.
- ○ Thank you, dear. Look, I'd like to have a new look, and get a few things done.
- ◇ Okay, are we cutting your hair?
- ○ No, we'll just trim the tips, but I want to get a curly perm and apply some highlights.
- ◇ There are so many levels of curly. Do you have a particular thing in mind?
- ○ Yes, look at this picture. I saw it, and I really like it.
- ◇ Okay, we will try to get as close to the picture as possible, but it might not come out exactly the same because your hair is thicker than her hair.
- ○ It's okay. Let's see!
- ◇ And what else?
- ○ I also want to get a facial.
- ◇ Would you like a threading or a wax?
- ○ No thanks, but I also want to get a manicure.
- ◇ Would you like a pedicure, too?

o No, let's get these done first and then we'll see.
◇ With pleasure.

(after the hairdresser has finished)

o Very nice! You know what? The shade of highlights that you suggested is really much better than the color I'd chosen.
◇ I told you this one would match your hair and skin tones better.
o Thanks a lot, dear! How much is the total then?
◇ All together it's 120,000 L.L.
o Here you are, dear.

◇ *áhla w sáhla, [Fmadame] [Sarah].*
o *[Fmerci] ђabībti, áhla fīki.*
◇ *-lyōm mánna ktīr mašɣūlīn, báʔa kíllni táђit taṣárrufik![1]*
o *3aẓīm.[2] min hēk ána ʔílit bíji bakkīr.*
◇ *táђit ámrik. šarráfti.*
o *[Fmerci] ђabībti, tislámi. láyki ђābbi ɣáyyir il[look] w á3mil kam šáɣli.*
◇ *okē! báddna nʔuṣṣ?*
o *laʔ, bass náḍḍif šwayy liṭrāf. bass 3a bēli kamēn á3mil [perm] w [highlights][3].*
◇ *fī káza dáraji la-l[Ffrisé][4]. ђāṭṭa šī m3áyyan bi-rāsik?*
o *ē, šūfi háydi -ṣṣūra. šífta w ђabbáyta[5] ktīr.*
◇ *okē, yímkin ma tíṭla3 zēt iššī mítil iṣṣūra li-ánnu šá3rik á3ba min šá3ra.*
o *ma3lē, minjárrib w minšūf.*
◇ *šū kamēn?*
o *báddi kamēn á3mil [facial].*
◇ *báddik tá3mli šī [waxing][6] aw xēṭ?*
o *laʔ [Fmerci], bass báddi manikúr.*
◇ *báddik [Fpédicure] kamēn?*
o *laʔ [Fmerci]. xallīna ná3mil háwdi hállaʔ, w mnírja3 minšūf.*
◇ *tíkram 3áynik.*

(after the hairdresser has finished)

o *ráw3a! btá3rfi, lōn il[highlights] yálli naṣaђtīni fī ktīr áђla mn illōn -lli ána kínit mneʔʔēyitu.*
◇ *ʔiltíllik, háyda áђla ma3 lōn šá3rik w báširtik.*

- ○ *[^F merci] ktīr ɦabībti. ʔaddē báddik mínni?*[7]
- ◇ *kíllun sáwa*[8] *míyyi w 3išrīn alf.*
- ○ *tfáḍḍali ɦabībti.*

[1] اليوْم كْتير عاجْقة عْلَيْنا، و ما عِنْدِك مَوْعد. في نطْرة. عِنْدِك مِشْكْلة؟ *-lyōm ktīr 3ājʔa 3láyna, w ma 3índik máw3ad. fī náṭra. 3índik míškli?* **We are super busy today, and you don't have an appoinment. Do you mind waiting?** (lit. There's a wait. Is that a problem?)

[2] = تمام *tamēm*

[3] = خِصل *xíṣal* (lit. strands/locks of hair)

[4] = مْجعّد *mjá33ad*

[5] = عجبِتْني *3ajabítni*

[6] = شمِع *šámi3*

[7] = قدّيْ بِترْيدي؟ *ʔaddē bitrīdi?*

[8] = بْيِطْلعوا *byíṭla3u*

Vocabulary

beauty salon	*[^F salon]*	صالوْن
hairdresser	*[^F coiffeur]*	كْوافور
to cut	*ʔáṭṭa3 (yʔáṭṭi3)*	قطّع (يْقطِّع)
haircut	*ʔáṣṣa*	قصّة
bob cut	*[^F carré]*	كاريْه
pixie cut	*[^F garçon]*	جارْسوْن
highlights	*[highlights]* *xíṣal*	هايْلايْتْس خِصل
hair	*šá3ir*	شعِر

type of hair (thickness, etc.)	*nō3 šá3ir*	نوْع شعِر
curly	*[ᶠfrisé]* *[curly]* *mjá33ad*	فْريزيْه كيرْلي مْجعّد
perm	*[perm]* *[ᶠfrisé]*	پيرْم فْريزيْه
straight	*[ᶠlisse]*	ليس
straightening iron	*[baby] [ᶠlisse]* *[ᶠfer]*	بيْبى ليس فيرْ
hair dryer	*[ᶠséchoir]*	سِشْوار
layered	*[ᶠdégradé]*	ديْجْراديْه
bangs	*ɣúrra*	غُرّة
bun	*ká3ki*	كعْكِة
ponytail	*[ᶠqueue de cheval]*	كو دو شوڤال
part	*fíriʔ*	فِرِق
face	*wijj (wjūh)*	وِجّ (وْجوه)
steam facial	*[facial] buxār*	فايْشال بُخار
cleansing	*tanḍīf*	تنْضيف
threading	*xēṭ*	خيْط
pedicure	*[ᶠpédicure]*	پيديكير
manicure	*manikūr*	مانيكير

Expressions

I want to have the tips trimmed.	*báddi ʔiṣṣ iṭṭrāf.* *báddi á3mil [trimming] la-ṭṭrāf.*	بدّي قِصّ الطّراف. بدّي أعْمِل تْريمينْغ للطّراف .
I want to have bangs.	*báddi ʔiṣṣ ɣúrra.*	بدّي قِصّ غُرّة.
I want to use the straightening iron.	*báddi á3mil [Ffer].* *báddi á3mil [baby] [lisse].*	بدّي أعْمِل فير. بدّي أعْمِل بيْبى ليس.
(showing a photo) Can you do this haircut?	*fīk ta3mílli háydi -lʔáṣṣa?*	فيك تعْمِلّي هَيْدي القصّة؟
I want to do threading for my whole face.	*báddi á3mil xēṭ la-wíjji kíllu.*	بدّي أعْمِل خيْط لَوِجّي كِلّو.
I want to have my face waxed.	*báddi á3mil šámi3 la-wíjji.*	بدّي أعْمِل شمِع لوِجّي.
I'd like my hair washed and blow-dried.	*báddi ɦámmim šá3ri w á3mil [Fséchoir].*	بدّي حمِّم شعْري وأعْمِل سِشْوار.
Do you have dye in this color?	*3índak ṣábɣa háyda -llōn?*	عِنْدك صبْغة هَيْدا اللّوْن؟
What colors of highlights do you have?	*áyya lōn [highlights] 3índak?*	أيّا لوْن هايْلايْتْس عِنْدك؟

www.ingramcontent.com/pod-product-compliance
Lightning Source LLC
Chambersburg PA
CBHW052054110526
44591CB00013B/2206
* 9 7 8 1 9 4 9 6 5 0 0 6 8 *